AF413645

^{THE}

Fiber Formula

THE Fiber Formula

Eat your way to better health through the power of fiber

RHIANNON LAMBERT

Contents

Fiber: the missing piece

After more than a decade in nutrition and running a clinic, I've watched our food landscape change dramatically. At the same time, health continues to decline in Western nations. My research into ultra-processed foods made one thing very clear: we're missing a vital component in our modern diets, and that's fiber.

In the UK, 96 per cent of us aren't getting enough of this vital nutrient, managing only 16–18g of the recommended 30g per day. In the US, fewer than one in ten Americans meets their country's recommendations. Amid endless health trends, we're consistently missing one of the simplest, most powerful foundations of our health.

I call this problem the "fiber gap," and I understand why the gap exists. Fiber, gut health, and bowel habits don't feel "sexy" compared with protein and muscle gain. But the focus on protein, or any other nutrient in isolation, distracts us from the bigger picture. No single nutrient is a magic bullet to optimum health, well-being, and long-lasting youthfulness. Good health is—and always has been—about balance.

We've also become obsessed with the "quick fix," papering over issues rather than addressing root causes. We increasingly find it hard to make the time to cook from scratch. Through my work, I've tried to stem the tide on these issues, but it's obvious we need to go further. Eating more fiber is a simple, accessible way to do just that.

The Hadza peoples of Tanzania, one of the last indigenous hunter-gatherer groups, consume around 100g to 150g of fiber a day through a diet of wild plants, tubers, berries, baobab, and other foraged foods. They are eating five to ten times more fiber than the average Westerner. Without so-called diet gurus and endless diet apps, the Hadza live in a way that supports nutritional balance and health. As a result, these people have highly diverse gut microbiomes and low rates of chronic disease.

This book was born out of frustration with the Western food environment—the noise, fad diets, wellness trends, and health-halo marketing that confuse more than they help. We deserve better. We deserve to understand what's happening to our health and to have realistic strategies for increasing our fiber intake. *The Fiber Formula* arms you with the tools to achieve your 30:30:30 (30g of fiber a day, 30 different plants a week, and roughly 30 chews per bite) for better digestion and, ultimately, improved longevity.

Happily, I'm not alone in my mission. In 2025, a campaign in the UK launched with the sole purpose of increasing our consumption of beans, recognizing them as an affordable, readily available, and practical way to increase the nation's fiber intake. Through this initiative, the aim is to double our bean consumption by 2028—it is a sign that fiber-rich foods are finally receiving the attention they deserve.

This book is your first step to joining us on the journey, effecting change that will help protect your good health not only now, but far into the future.

What is

Fiber isn't just one thing: it's a whole family of complex carbohydrates—including soluble and insoluble fiber, resistant starches, beta-glucans, and pectins. Each type plays a unique role in supporting gut bacteria, stabilizing blood sugar, and keeping us fuller for longer—all crucial to long-term health.

Modern life gives us extraordinary food choice, but that abundance can be confusing. Ultra-processed foods often crowd out fiber-rich ingredients, making it easy to miss out on the very nutrients that nourish us. In fact, about 96 percent of people fall short of the daily recommended intake of fiber.

Rather than simply suggesting a return to how our ancestors ate, this chapter focuses first on understanding what fiber is and how it works inside the body, then looks at how to make the most of the foods available today so that we can choose smarter combinations of grains, pulses and legumes, fruits, and vegetables—and close the "fiber gap."

fiber?

What is fiber?

People are often surprised to learn that fiber is, in fact, a special type of carbohydrate. It is special because it's found only in plant-based foods, by which we mean not just fruits and vegetables, but whole grains, legumes, nuts, and seeds too. Unlike other carbohydrates, though, fiber isn't digested in the small intestine. Instead, it travels largely intact into the large intestine (your colon), where it plays a vital role in keeping your gut—and the rest of your body—healthy.

There are two main types of fiber: soluble and insoluble. Soluble fiber dissolves in water to form a gel-like substance and can help lower cholesterol and steady blood-sugar levels—you can find out more about these functions on pages 39 and 41, respectively. Insoluble fiber adds bulk to your stool and helps food pass more quickly through your digestive system. This not only keeps your bowel movements healthy, it also has myriad other benefits, including supporting your immune system, improving sleep quality, and boosting mood.

Types of fiber

All fibers actually contain a mixture of both "soluble" and "insoluble" fiber. Throughout this book I'll refer not just to these simplified terms, but to the properties of fiber, such as how fermentable or viscous it is. These are the characteristics that truly shape how fiber behaves in the body.

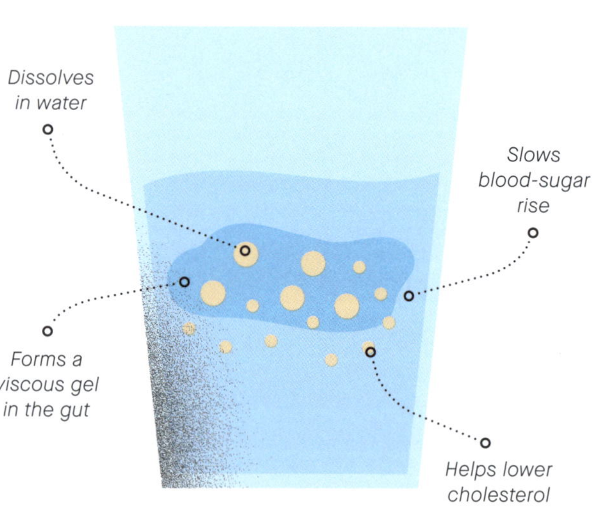

Soluble Fiber

Insoluble Fiber

What can fiber help us fight?

Studies show that diets high in fiber, especially fiber derived from whole grains such as brown rice, whole-grain (whole-wheat) bread, oats, barley, and quinoa, are linked with a lower risk of several major diseases. These include:

- Heart disease, including angina and heart attack
- Stroke
- Type-2 diabetes
- High blood pressure
- Colorectal cancer

SCFAs and other fiber benefits

In the past, fiber has been an overlooked nutrient, simply because the body can't digest it. But we now know that it is essential not only for good digestion, but also for other aspects of health. Once in the colon, fiber becomes food for our gut bacteria. Collectively, these bacteria along with other microorganisms are known as the gut microbiome. Through a process of fermentation, the gut microbes break down the fiber we eat, producing compounds called short-chain fatty acids (SCFAs). SCFAs—butyrate, acetate, and propionate among them—are incredibly important for overall health: they nourish the cells lining the colon, reduce inflammation, support our immune system, and lower the risk of diseases such as colorectal cancer. Butyrate may be linked to improved sleep quality. These fatty acids are called "short chain" because they are made up of short chains of carbon molecules (see panel, right), which helps to make them particularly water-soluble—and that means that the body is able to use them quickly and efficiently as a source of energy.

A high-fiber diet can also help with healthy weight management. That's because fiber not only slows down digestion (helping us feel fuller for longer), but also influences the hormones that control blood sugar (reducing spikes in blood sugar after eating, staving off the urge for a sugary snack) and regulate appetite.

How can plant-based nutrition boost fiber?

As we've just learned, fiber is found only in plant foods. It stands to reason, then, that a plant-based diet, varied, interesting, and fiber-dense as it must be, will help you improve your fiber intake.

What does an SCFA look like?

Short-chain fatty acids (SCFAs) are the outcome of fiber breakdown in the gut. But why are they called "short chain"? All fatty acids are major carbon fuel sources made of carbon, hydrogen, and oxygen. Each has a small acidic "head" and a long carbon–hydrogen "tail" that defines its structure. The number of carbon atoms in the chain determines the label: short, medium, or long.

Short-chain fatty acids (SCFAs)

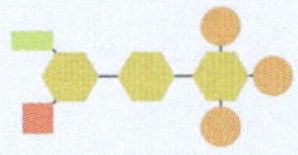

Produced when gut bacteria ferment dietary fiber, SCFAs have fewer than 6 carbon atoms—typically 2 to 6. Examples include acetate (C; 2 carbon atoms), propionate (C3), and butyrate (C4). SCFAs are one of the key benefits of eating dietary fiber. They provide energy to the cells lining the gut, help regulate metabolism, support heart health, reduce inflammation in the body, and help maintain healthy immunity. They are vital to our overall well-being.

Medium-chain fatty acids (MCFAs)

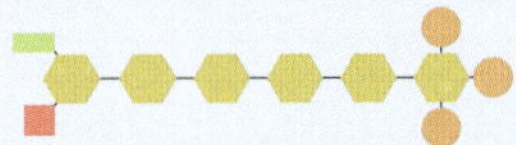

MCFAs have between 6 and 12 carbon atoms. They are found in foods such as coconut oil, palm kernel oil, and some dairy products. Unlike SCFAs, MCFAs are mostly absorbed quickly in the digestive system and used for energy. While they can be beneficial, especially for quick energy, they don't have the same wide-ranging health effects as SCFAs.

Long-chain fatty acids (LCFAs)

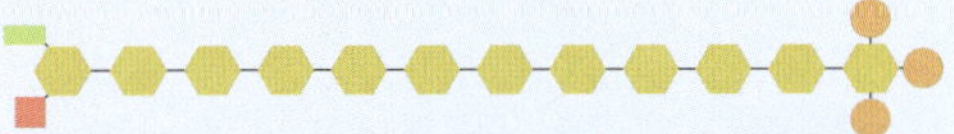

LCFAs have 13 or more carbon atoms. They are found in foods such as red meat, fatty fish (salmon, mackerel), nuts, seeds, avocados, and vegetable oils. They are important sources of energy, and contain essential fats like omega-3 and omega-6, but they don't reduce inflammation, nourish gut cells, or support the immune system to directly support gut health in the way of SCFAs.

Recent studies have reinforced the understanding that plant-based diets rich in dietary fiber and phytochemicals (natural plant compounds) are crucial for supporting gut health in ways more significant than simply keeping our bowel movements healthy. For a start, consuming a variety of plant foods increases the diversity and abundance of beneficial gut bacteria. These "friendly" bacteria—such as *Bifidobacterium* and *Lactobacillus*—help reduce inflammation, support immunity, and improve metabolic and cardiovascular health.

Phytochemicals (from the Greek *phyton,* meaning "plant")—such as the polyphenol compounds that are especially abundant in foods like spinach, broccoli, tomatoes, grapes, and dark berries such as blueberries—act as prebiotics that not only nourish these beneficial microbes, but also inhibit harmful ones. Some phytochemicals, such as resveratrol (found in grapes, raspberries, and peanuts), also have antioxidant and anti-inflammatory effects. These properties may provide further protection against conditions such as cardiovascular disease, neurodegenerative disorders, obesity, and cancer.

Fiber in the carbohydrate family

Carbohydrates fall into two broad categories: simple and complex. **Simple carbs** (or "simple sugars") are made up of just one or two sugar molecules and include foods such as white bread, refined sugar, and fruit juice.

Variety is the spice of life

A large study published in *Nature* in 2025 found that vegans, vegetarians, and omnivores each have distinct gut microbiome "signatures." Vegans tend to have more bacteria that produce SCFAs. Importantly, omnivores who ate a wide variety of plant foods showed many of the same beneficial microbes found in vegan diets. In other words, the label you give your diet matters less than the quality and diversity of the plants you eat. Aiming for around 30 different plants each week (page 62) can help feed a broad variety of microbes, making the gut more resilient and balanced.

They release quickly into the bloodstream as a fast energy source. While this can help before exercise, or for a quick burst of energy, it may also cause blood-sugar levels to rise and fall too quickly, leaving you feeling tired or hungry. **Complex carbohydrates** are so called because they contain chains of sugar molecules that are released more slowly into the bloodstream. They are subdivided into starches and fiber. Our gut metabolizes starches for use in the body, while fiber travels through the gut intact to be fermented by friendly bacteria and converted to SCFAs.

Simple and complex carbs

Whole, unprocessed foods are, generally, more complex in structure, often meaning they contain more fiber.

Brown rice

A complex carbohydrate, brown rice provides fiber and sustained energy.

Potato

Potatoes can be complex or simple carbohydrates, depending on how they are prepared and cooked (page 67).

White bread

White bread is processed and therefore a low-fiber, simple carbohydrate.

Whole-grain bread

Made using, literally, whole grains, whole-grain bread is a complex carb.

White pasta

White pasta loses the fiber during the refining process.

Resistant starch—a form of fiber

Named for its ability to "resist" digestion in the small intestine, resistant starch ferments in the large intestine, acting as a form of fiber—and so producing SCFAs. The fermented compounds help to nourish gut bacteria, reduce inflammation, and support metabolic health, including improved insulin sensitivity (page 51). There are several types of resistant starch (we label them RS1 to RS5), which are found in foods such as oats and legumes, as well as cooked and cooled potatoes, rice, and pasta. Green bananas are one of the richest natural sources of resistant starch; while uncooked oats (as in overnight oats) contain more resistant starch than cooked oatmeal. Including these foods in our diet can therefore enhance both fiber intake and gut health.

Fiber's time to shine

Despite all the benefits to digestion of a fiber-rich diet, most people still aren't eating enough of this superhero nutrient. Health programs all over the world agree that adults should aim for a daily fiber intake of 25–30g—but in many countries average intake is far lower (page 18). That's why experts now recommend that we make an effort to include more whole-plant foods in our meals every day. A key takeaway from all these drives for more fiber in our diets is that variety matters. Different plant foods contain different types of fiber and different phytochemicals. Eating a wide range of plant-based foods ensures you're feeding diverse strains of gut bacteria, encouraging microbial diversity, which is closely linked to improved digestive and immune health, and potentially even mental health (see page 37).

Fiber travels through the gut to be fermented by friendly bacteria and converted to short-chain fatty acids.

The benefits of resistant starch

Resistant starch, which is easily incorporated into a healthy diet, acts on the body in key positive ways.

Cool, then reheat = better for blood sugar

When starchy foods—like **pasta**, **rice**, or **potatoes**—are cooked, cooled, and even reheated, their starch structure changes, increasing resistant starch. This means that the foods release glucose more slowly into the bloodstream, helping with blood-sugar control.

Prebiotic action

Prebiotics are the whole foods that the beneficial bacteria in our gut need in order to thrive (page 28). In the large intestine, resistant starch acts as a prebiotic, boosting gut health and producing SCFAs.

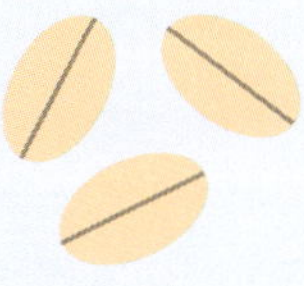

Metabolic health-booster

Research shows that resistant starch can improve insulin sensitivity and may reduce appetite, making it a helpful tool for managing weight and Type-2 diabetes (pages 40 and 50).

Naturally gluten-free

Many foods naturally high in resistant starch (such as beans, lentils, rice, and potatoes) are also naturally gluten-free, making them accessible for those with celiac disease or gluten sensitivity.

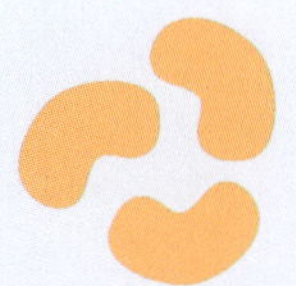

The history of fiber intake

It's remarkable that, despite having greater access to fresh and diverse produce than ever before in the Western world, fiber intake has significantly declined. In the early 20th century, the average daily fiber intake in Western diets was estimated to be between 30g and 50g, largely owing to a diet based on unrefined grains, root vegetables, pulses, and seasonal produce.

Much of the population relied on home-cooked meals using affordable, plant-based ingredients. Even during periods of wartime rationing, people consumed substantial amounts of whole foods, which consequentially supported higher fiber intake. Today, though, the amount of fiber in our diets has fallen dramatically. This timeline tracks global changes over the decades since the 1920s.

Fiber intake over time

1920s

UK
Post-World War I, fiber intake was high, estimated at 35–50g per day thanks to homemade, seasonal meals using locally grown whole grains, root vegetables, pulses, and fresh produce. Bread was minimally refined; processed foods were scarce. Diets were frugal but rich in plant-based staples.

US
As in the UK, fiber intake was relatively high (30–40g per day). Rural families, especially, relied on local produce: fiber-rich staples (beans, corn, and root vegetables) were the heart of meals.

Mainland Europe
Fiber intake was around 30–45g per day. Fiber-rich staples such as rye, barley, beans, and root vegetables were central to daily diets, especially in rural areas.

1930s

UK
Post-war, diets remained modest, but fiber intake stayed high: oats, legumes, cabbage, and skin-on potatoes were staples. Economic hardship in the Great Depression limited access to luxuries, preserving a whole-food, fiber-rich diet for many.

US
During the Great Depression, most families cooked at home, relying on staples like beans, corn, oats, and potatoes with skins, as well as seasonal fruits and vegetables. Fiber intake dipped only slightly below early 20th-century levels.

Mainland Europe
Meals continued to feature whole grains, legumes, root vegetables, and cabbage, often grown locally or in home gardens. Fiber intakes remained substantial.

1940s

UK
World War II made a significant impact. Rationing included whole-grain bread, potatoes, vegetables, and dried legumes. Government campaigns like "Dig for Victory" encouraged homegrown produce. This was a time of unexpectedly balanced and fiber-friendly nutrition.

US
Rationing and food conservation boosted fiber-rich staples, while "Victory Gardens" supplied additional fresh produce. Despite economic and logistical challenges, many Americans maintained plant-based, fiber-containing diets.

Mainland Europe
Government and local initiatives encouraged self-sufficiency, supporting a likely fiber intake of about 25–40g daily.

1950s

UK
Rationing ended in 1954. The British diet began to diversify, but home cooking remained the norm. Even so, fiber intake likely declined to about 30g per day.

US
Post-war economic boom brought more processed and convenience foods. Refined white bread, canned foods, and sugary snacks began to displace fiber-rich staples. Intake likely fell to around 20–30g fiber per day, though seasonal foods, in rural areas especially, remained high.

Mainland Europe
Food industrialization accelerated. White bread and refined cereals increased. Fiber intake remained moderate thanks to local gardens and home-cooked meals, but a downward trend had begun.

1960s

UK
A cultural and dietary shift from supermarkets, frozen foods, and TV dinners; intake of legumes and whole grains fell. Diets of refined carbs rose, and fiber levels likely dropped slightly below 30g, as eating patterns leaned in to convenience.

US
Convenience foods, sliced bread, breakfast cereals, and canned goods continued to replace whole grains and legumes. Many adults likely consumed around 18–25g fiber daily. Even so, homegrown foods still added to fiber intakes.

Mainland Europe
Urbanization and supermarket culture brought more refined, sugary, and packaged foods. Total fiber fell to around 20–30g daily in many places.

1970s

UK
Fiber intake fell to 25–30g per day, owing to industrialized foods (breakfast cereals, white bread, etc.). Meat consumption rose. In working-class homes especially, home cooking and vegetables remained the norm.

US
Average intakes are thought to have been around 15–20g per day—another dip. Health-focused families or those preserving traditional cooking habits consumed higher levels.

Mainland Europe
Industrialized food production and supermarket shopping meant refined bread, white rice, and packaged foods increasingly replaced higher fiber foods, lowering intake to about 15–25g per day. General awareness of dietary fiber was still limited.

Fiber and the environment

The Planetary Health Diet, outlined in the EAT-Lancet Report (published in October 2025), presents a model for how we can eat to protect both the health of humans and the planet. Centered around vegetables, fruits, whole grains, legumes, nuts, and seeds, it encourages a shift toward plant-rich meals while limiting red and processed meats, free and added sugars, and excess salt. Small, flexible amounts of dairy, fish, poultry, and eggs can be included where needed, but the emphasis remains on plants as the foundation of every plate. This model is not only sustainable for the planet as it's projected to halve food-system emissions by 2050, but is also grounded in evidence-based research that supports our well-being. The Lancet Commission estimates that global adherence to this diet could prevent up to 15 million premature deaths each year and substantially reduce rates of chronic disease. It is no coincidence that fiber sits at the heart of this model, whereby foods highest in fiber are often the very ones that provide our body with essential nutrients for long-term health and help protect the planet through lower environmental impact.

1980s

UK
Branded convenience foods, and low-fat, high-sugar, and fast food rose. Consumption of white bread peaked. Messaging began to promote fiber for digestive health, but average intake lowered to about 22–25g daily.

US
Fast-food culture and ready meals became established. Fiber intake remained low, around 15–18g per day, as white bread, refined cereals, and processed snacks dominated. Nutrition education was limited: few made an effort to increase fiber intake.

Mainland Europe
Fiber intake declined, often given as 15–20g per day. Rural and Mediterranean regions retained slightly higher intakes through homegrown vegetables, legumes, and whole grains.

1990s

UK
Average UK fiber intake fell below 20g per day, as processed foods became dominant. Advertising heavily influenced diet, as did "grab-and-go" and ready meals. Despite growing evidence for fiber's health benefits, trends declined into the early 2000s.

US
Growing awareness of diet-related chronic disease gave fiber some attention, yet intake remained at 15–17g per day. Whole-grain bread, cereal, and fruit intake increased modestly, but processed foods dominated.

Mainland Europe
Early whole-grain campaigns began. Fiber intake in urban areas was still low (15–20g per day), but Mediterranean regions maintained slightly higher levels owing to cultural norms.

Modern times

The modern Western diet contains far more refined carbohydrates, ultra-processed foods, and added sugars than ever before, while intakes of whole grains, legumes, and fibrous vegetables have sharply decreased. The current average intake of fiber in the UK, US, and mainland European countries sits well below the WHO's recommended 30g (page 18). This shift reflects broader changes in food production, industrial milling practices, and eating habits, all of which have contributed to a significant reduction in dietary fiber and, consequently, poorer gut-health outcomes across the whole of the Western world.

The map on pages 18–19 breaks down the global averages of the modern-day world.

Why are we eating less fiber?

Despite decades of nutrition advice, many people still don't eat enough fiber. Several key factors are driving this global fiber gap.

Processed and ultra-processed foods
Most modern diets are heavy in low-fiber, packaged foods.

Shifting eating patterns
We've moved away from traditional, plant-rich meals toward more meat, dairy, and refined carbohydrates.

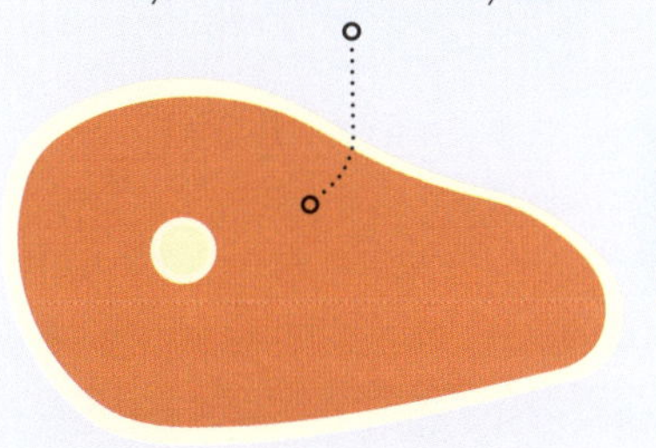

Lack of awareness
Many people don't realize how important fiber is or which foods contain it.

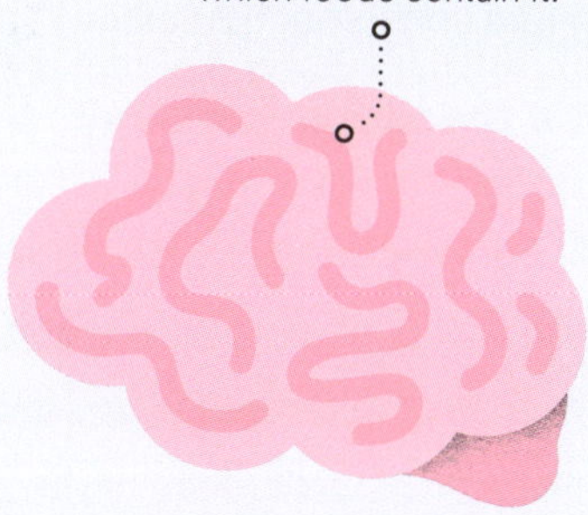

Convenience and cost
Foods like pulses, legumes, nuts, and whole grains are often seen as harder to prepare or more expensive.

Marketing and advertising
Highly processed, low-fiber foods are aggressively marketed, especially to children.

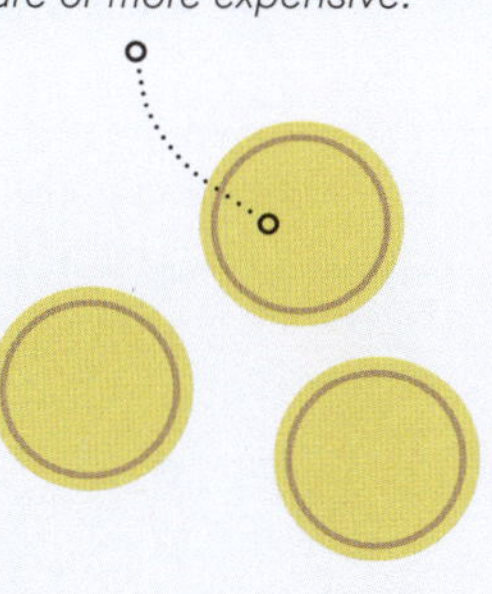

Busy lifestyles
Time-poor consumers often choose quick, pre-packaged options that are low in fiber.

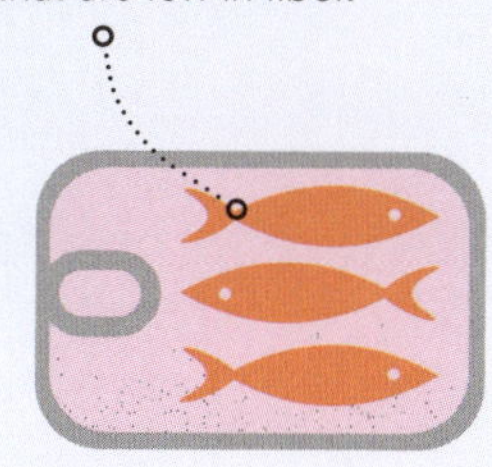

How much fiber are we consuming today?

Improving fiber intake globally could prevent millions of chronic disease cases and enhance quality of life worldwide. Success stories from Denmark and other Nordic countries and Ghana, highlight the power of coordinated public health strategies, food industry reformulation, policy measures, and consumer education.

So, what's the global picture?

This map gives a sense of population fiber intake across the world. The gram figures represent the average adult daily intake in each of the featured countries, while the percentages (where data is readily available—unfortunately in some territories it is not) reveal the proportion of the adult population meeting the WHO's recommended 30g of fiber per day. Finally, I've indicated the main fiber sources in each country.

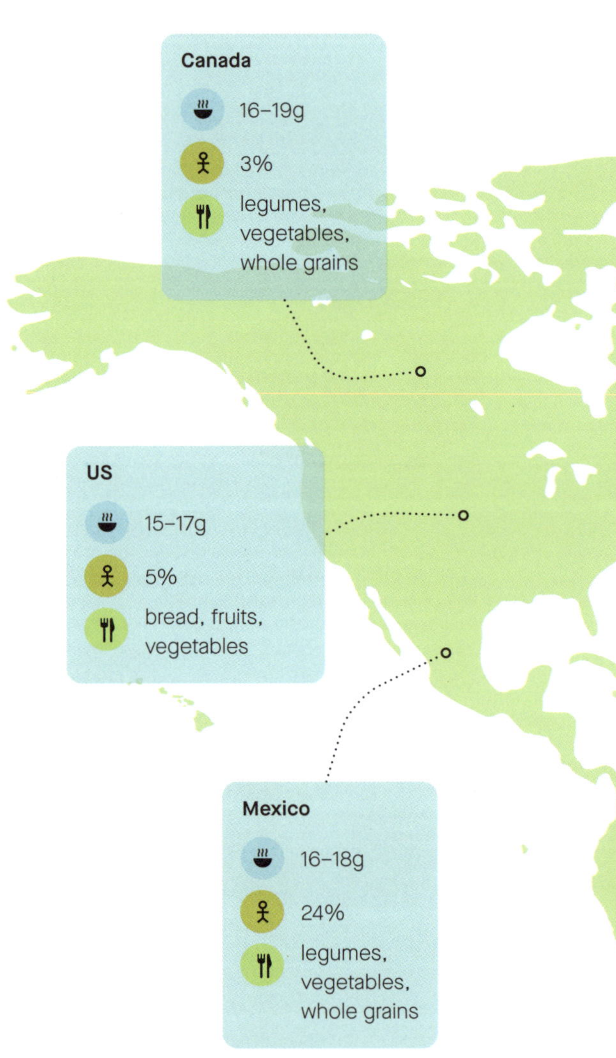

Key to symbols

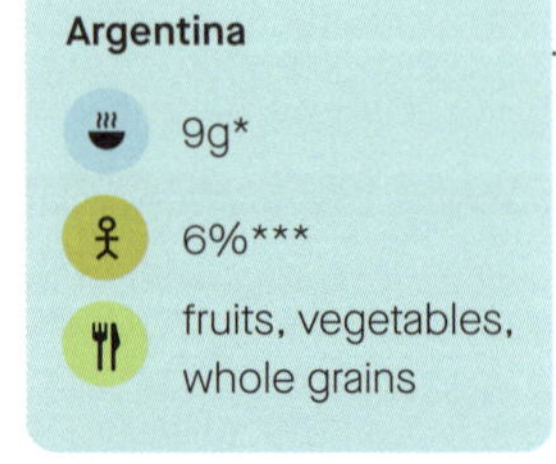

Average adult daily intake

Percentage of the adult population meeting 30g target

Main food sources

*No age-range is given for this data

**Based on recommendations for whole-grain consumption

***Based on recommended amounts of fruit and vegetables

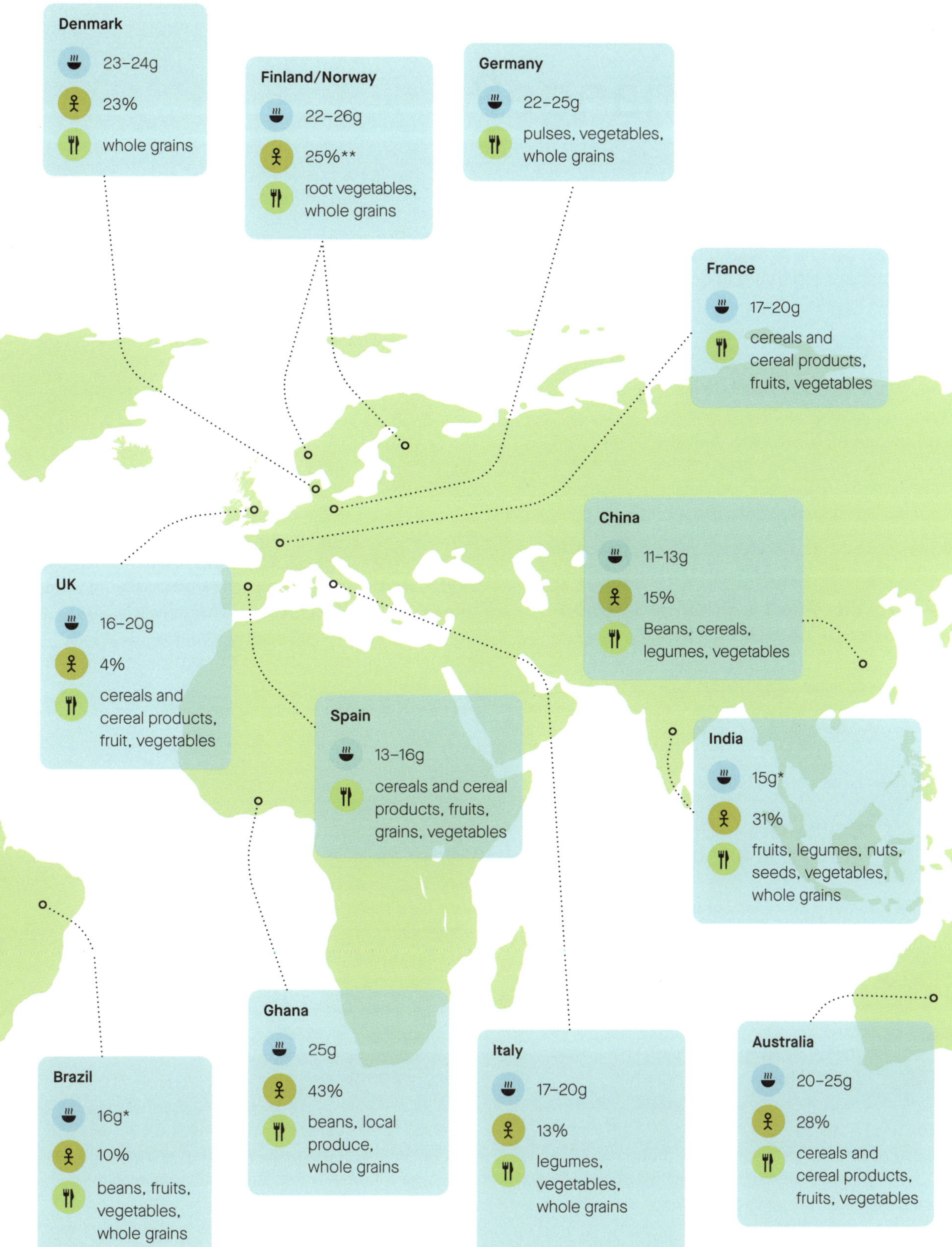

Denmark
23–24g
23%
whole grains

Finland/Norway
22–26g
25%**
root vegetables, whole grains

Germany
22–25g
pulses, vegetables, whole grains

France
17–20g
cereals and cereal products, fruits, vegetables

China
11–13g
15%
Beans, cereals, legumes, vegetables

UK
16–20g
4%
cereals and cereal products, fruit, vegetables

Spain
13–16g
cereals and cereal products, fruits, grains, vegetables

India
15g*
31%
fruits, legumes, nuts, seeds, vegetables, whole grains

Brazil
16g*
10%
beans, fruits, vegetables, whole grains

Ghana
25g
43%
beans, local produce, whole grains

Italy
17–20g
13%
legumes, vegetables, whole grains

Australia
20–25g
28%
cereals and cereal products, fruits, vegetables

How are nations making positive change?

The good news is that while intakes all over the world are generally lower than they should be, many nations are trying to do something about it.

 **1 Denmark—Danish Whole Grain Partnership (DWGP)**

A long-running collaboration between government, NGOs, and industry, launched in 2008. It successfully increased average whole grain intake from 36g to 82g per day by 2019—now the highest in Europe.

 **2 UK—Food & Drink Federation (FDF) Action on Fiber**

Industry-led initiative partnering brands and retailers to launch high-fiber lines. By 2023, it had delivered about 1.5 billion additional servings of fiber into UK diets.

 **3 EU (general)—School Meal Fiber Standards & Labeling**

More than 15 EU countries enforce minimum fiber standards in school meals (generally 10g of fiber per 1,000 calories). EU regulations also standardize nutrition labelling and claims (pages 70–71).

 **4 Australia**

The Health Star Rating System (since 2014) nudges manufacturers toward higher-fiber products via front-of-package labeling. The National Obesity Strategy (launched in 2022) integrates nutrition standards supporting fiber intake.

 **5 France**

The voluntary Nutri-Score label scores foods on fiber and other nutrients (page 70). The PNNS (Public Dietary Guidance) promotes pulses, legumes, whole grains, fruits, and vegetables. A proposed national strategy on food-nutrition-climate could strengthen fiber promotion.

 **6 US**

The Dietary Guidelines for Americans (2020–2025) highlight pulses, legumes, whole grains, nuts, and vegetables. The Food & Drug Administration's (FDA) 2024 "Healthy" Label Update includes fiber thresholds. A Front-of-Package Nutrition Label Proposal (2025) aims to clarify fiber content. The Healthy, Hunger-Free Kids Act (2010) mandates fiber-rich school meals, with standards maintained beyond the Act's expiration date.

 **7 Japan**

The 2025 Dietary Reference Intakes raised fiber targets to 20–22g per day for men and at least 18g for women—although, that's still below WHO recommendations. The Japanese Food Guide Spinning Top emphasizes grains, vegetables, and beans; and also seaweed, which is a significant source of fiber.

 **8 Spain**

The 2025 Royal Decree on School Meals mandates daily fruit and vegetables (≥45% seasonal/local, ≥5% organic), weekly fish, and vegetarian/vegan options, and it bans sugary drinks. Indirectly, then, it is supporting increased fiber intake in school lunches.

Is sex a factor?

Looking more closely at UK figures specifically reveals an apparent anomaly between men and women when it comes to fiber intake. In those over age 65, only 1% of women but 8–9% of men hit the target. Is that statistic as meaningful as it seems? Probably not, particularly when we take into account the relevance of age.

Different energy requirements

Men generally eat more calories than women because of higher energy needs. As fiber is tied to food volume, a higher food intake means men are more likely to reach higher absolute fiber amounts, even if their diets aren't especially fiber rich.

Portion sizes and food choice

Men often consume larger portions of starchy foods like bread, cereals, rice, and potatoes—all key fiber contributors. Women, particularly older women, may eat smaller portions or lighter meals, reducing fiber-intake opportunities.

Different dietary patterns

Surveys show women are more likely to avoid bread, potatoes, or carbohydrate-rich foods (sometimes owing to diet culture or weight-control signaling), which are major fiber sources in the UK diet. This avoidance can unintentionally lower fiber intake.

Appetite and physiological changes

Appetite tends to decline with age, especially in older women, and reduced food intake means less chance of meeting fiber targets. Men, on average, may sustain higher intake levels into older age.

So the gender gap isn't because men are necessarily choosing more fiber-rich foods, but rather that their overall greater calorie intake and different dietary patterns make it easier to eat more fiber. Nonetheless, the fact remains that both sexes in the UK—at over 65, but also throughout life—are consuming far below the recommended 30g of fiber per day. However, simple daily changes—switching to whole-grain bread, adding beans to meals, or snacking on fruit—can close the fiber gap and support lifelong health.

Simple daily changes—switching to whole-grain bread, adding beans to meals, or snacking on fruit—can close the fiber gap and support lifelong health.

How have UPFs affected fiber intake?

Ultra-processed foods (UPFs) have become a dominant part of modern diets in many countries, often making up over half of the daily calories we consume. These foods, ranging from packaged snacks and ready meals to sugary drinks and instant noodles, are typically made from refined ingredients that have been stripped of their natural fiber. As a result, diets high in UPFs tend to be low in fiber and other essential nutrients. Even when fiber is added back into processed products in isolated forms (such as inulin or oat fiber), it may not provide the same benefits as fiber from whole foods. Over time, a dietary pattern that loads up on UPFs can increase the risk of digestive issues, weight gain, and chronic disease.

There's no doubt that UPFs have become an issue for our diets, but it's important to approach that issue with empathy and nuance. For many people, UPFs are not simply a matter of poor choice, they are often the most accessible, affordable, and time-efficient options available. Factors like income, food education, cultural background, and limited access to fresh produce all play a significant role in shaping eating habits. The widespread marketing of UPFs, especially to children and low-income communities, further complicates the picture. Addressing the fiber gap, therefore, isn't just about urging people to "eat better"; it also means tackling systemic problems, improving food education, and making healthy, fiber-rich foods more accessible and appealing for everyone, regardless of circumstance.

To close the global fiber gap, we need more than just nutritional guidelines—we need systemic change. That includes public-health policies that support better food education, transparent labeling, reformulation of processed products, and subsidies that make fiber-rich foods more affordable. School-meal programs, community initiatives, and urban food-access projects also play a vital role. Encouraging a return to whole, minimally processed plant foods is important, but we must do so with empathy, recognizing that for change to be lasting, it must be made possible and practical for all.

Levels of fiber in processed foods

The Nova framework, developed in Brazil in 2009, categorizes foods into four groups, from un- (or minimally) processed to ultra-processed. Understanding fiber distribution across these groups highlights how processing can influence diet quality.

1. No or little processing
Whole or almost-whole foods, with no added ingredients. With skin, these foods provide good levels of fiber.

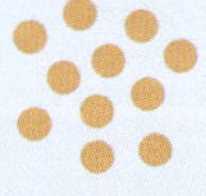

2. Processed cooking ingredients
Foods to cook and season our food (salt, vegetable oils, sugar, vinegar, and so on). They provide no fiber.

3. Processed foods
Group 1 foods with added Group 2; or minimally processed (like canned beans). May contain good levels of fiber.

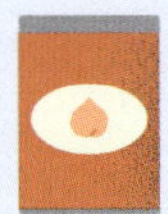

4. Ultra-processed foods
Additive-packed, industrial. Often low in fiber. Exceptions, such as high-fiber cereal, still have many additives.

Making choices

There are very few individuals or families in the world for whom choice—in whatever form and for whatever reason—is genuinely straightforward. When it comes to choosing between foods on a weekly shopping budget, it can be helpful to know whether high-fiber processed foods or low-fiber whole foods are the better option, enabling you to make informed decisions to buy not just the best value for the money but the best "health value" for the money.

What's better? High-fiber processed or low-fiber whole foods?

You should aim to consume more *minimally processed*, *high-fiber* foods, but if you're choosing between high-fiber ultra-processed foods (such as fortified bars, high-fiber cereals, and fiber-added yogurts) and low-fiber minimally processed foods (such as white rice, peeled potatoes, and white bread), the high-fiber option often wins out in terms of gut health and satiety—*but only to a point*. The tables below offer the best way to think about the options.

Can I trust the label?

A popular low-calorie snack bar often praised for its fiber content is a clear example of a well-marketed UPF. While it contains 5g of fiber per bar, it also comes with a long list of ingredients: wheat flour, oligofructose, vegetable fats (palm, shea), sugar, fructose, fat-reduced cocoa powder (8%), humectant (glycerol), water, wheat fiber, egg white powder, raising agents (diphosphates, sodium bicarbonate), salt, flavorings, thickeners (locust bean gum, xanthan gum), emulsifiers (soy lecithin), whole milk powder, and antioxidant (tocopherol-rich extract). It's a perfect example of how fiber can be engineered into a product that is otherwise far removed from a whole food.

High-fiber ultra-processed foods

High-fiber UPFs (such as fortified bars, high-fiber cereals, and fiber-added yogurts) contain fiber, but also many additives.

Pros	Cons
• Convenient	• Often contain added sugar, salt, emulsifiers, and preservatives
• Can boost fiber intake quickly (especially if fortified)	• May lack *diverse* types of fiber (such as resistant starch, inulin, pectins)
• May help close the fiber gap for people who eat very few plant foods	• May promote overconsumption owing to being engineered for taste

** High-fiber UPFs can supplement an otherwise whole-food-rich diet, but not replace it.**

Low-fiber minimally processed foods

Low-fiber, less-processed foods (such as white rice, peeled potatoes, and white bread) are more "natural."

Pros	Cons
• Typically free from additives and closer to how foods occur in nature	• Don't provide good amounts of fuel for a proliferation of healthy gut microbes
• Easy to digest and tolerated by people with sensitive guts or during illness	• Can cause blood-sugar spikes and won't keep you full as long
	• Miss the opportunity to improve diversity in the microbiome

** Low-fiber minimally processed foods are fine in moderation, alongside higher-fiber whole foods.**

Why does my gut need fiber?

When we talk about "gut health," we often mean the trillions of microbes, bacteria, fungi, and viruses that live in our large intestine. Clinically, though, the term actually refers to the well-being of the entire gastrointestinal tract, from mouth to rectum. The gut does more than digest food. It plays a vital role in immune defense, energy production, hormone balance, mood regulation, and nutrient synthesis. Fiber is central to all of this, as it feeds our gut microbes and supports the production of the short-chain fatty acids (SCFAs) that keep the gut lining strong. Feeding the gut fiber is key to feeling and functioning well.

Gut health is increasingly recognized as a core indicator of overall health, yet studies suggest it has deteriorated across much of the industrialized world. Compared with previous generations, today we tend to have less diverse gut microbiomes, a trend linked to processed diets, high use of antibiotics, reduced exposure to environmental microbes—and, significantly, low fiber intake. The typical Western-style diet, high in refined carbohydrates, fats, sweeteners, and additives, can deplete beneficial bacteria and reduce production of the SCFAs that help regulate inflammation and immunity.

Evidence now links microbial shifts to rising rates of non-communicable diseases such as obesity, Type-2 diabetes, heart disease, inflammatory bowel disease (IBD), and depression and anxiety. One global study found that countries with the highest intake of minimally processed plant foods had more resilient and diverse microbiomes and notably lower rates of chronic disease.

More microbes, more balance

A diet rich in plant-based whole foods high in fiber, polyphenols, and prebiotics supports the growth of beneficial microbes. These microbes ferment fiber to produce metabolites like SCFAs, which nourish colon cells, strengthen the gut barrier, and regulate the immune and hormonal pathways that influence appetite, mood, sleep, and energy levels. In contrast, ultra-processed foods, hydrogenated fats, emulsifiers, artificial sweeteners, and additives can disrupt microbial balance and weaken gut function.

Top 5 gut benefits of a high-fiber diet

Gut microbiome modulation

Fiber is fermented by gut bacteria to produce short-chain fatty acids (SCFAs). These help maintain the strength of the gut lining, reduce inflammation, regulate lipid and glucose metabolism, and may protect against colorectal cancer and metabolic disorders.

Cholesterol reduction and heart health

Soluble fiber binds bile acids in the intestine, which are then excreted. The liver uses cholesterol to make more bile, lowering circulating LDL ("bad") cholesterol levels. This contributes to a reduced risk of cardiovascular disease.

Blood-glucose regulation

Soluble fiber forms a gel in the gut that slows the absorption of glucose, reducing postprandial blood-sugar spikes. This can lower the risk of Type-2 diabetes.

Anti-inflammatory effects

High-fiber diets are linked to lower systemic inflammation, as measured by markers such as C-reactive protein. Chronic inflammation underpins many diseases, including heart disease, diabetes, and some cancers.

Weight management

Fiber increases satiety because it slows gastric emptying and adds bulk to meals. This can lower overall calorie intake, helping prevent obesity, a risk factor for multiple diseases.

A feedback loop

Eating the right amounts of fiber is only one part of the puzzle. We also need to ensure that the gut is at optimal health to make *the best use of* the fiber our diet provides. It's a kind of fiber–gut feedback loop. Give the gut what it needs but also make sure that the gut can make the best of what it has. So, how do we do this?

Regular exercise and adequate hydration further support healthy digestion and gut integrity, but minimizing stress levels is one of the most important ways to ensure the gut is in good working order.

The Gut–Brain axis

Stress doesn't just affect your mind. Acute stress (sudden stress in response to a specific trigger) takes only minutes to disrupt microbial diversity and weaken the tight junctions in the intestinal lining. This increases gut permeability (so-called "leaky gut"), in which, harmful bacteria and toxins, say, can cross the intestinal barrier into the bloodstream, causing inflammation in the body. Chronic (long-lasting) stress drives sustained changes in the microbiome, hampers barrier function, and shifts immune responses. This can contribute to gut–brain disorders and conditions such as irritable bowel syndrome (IBS; page 34) and post-traumatic stress symptoms, and can worsen IBD symptoms.

Emerging evidence highlights SCFAs as key messengers in the gut–brain axis, signaling to affect mood, cognition, and neurological function. Their production depends heavily on SCFA-producing microbes that thrive on fiber-rich diets, emphasizing (once again) that promoting microbial diversity through varied plant intake is fundamental to supporting both gut and brain health. Research reveals fascinating mechanisms: stress hormones, like cortisol, reduce SCFA production, impair gut and blood-brain barriers, and alter the gut's microbial composition. There are even sex-specific responses: women may experience more pronounced microbiome shifts under acute stress than men. And, new evidence links the gut microbiome to brain function via neural circuits that connect the gut to the amygdala (which helps regulate emotions, stress, and memory) and hippocampus (crucial for learning and forming memories).

Gut–Brain communication

The microbes in your gut produce chemicals, such as SCFAs and neurotransmitters, which influence your immune and endocrine (hormonal) systems. Likewise, your thoughts and emotions can affect digestion and gut function.

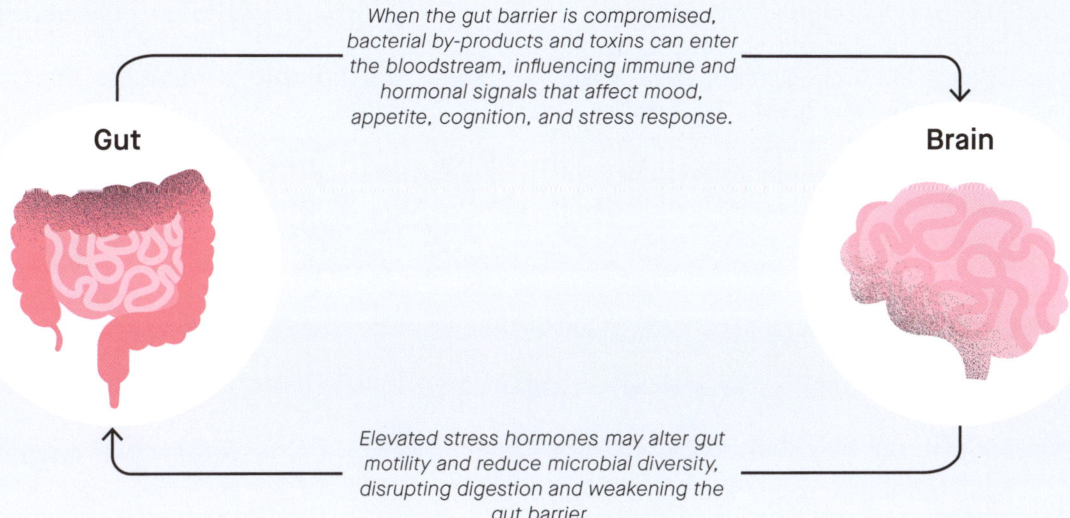

What does my stool tell me about my fiber intake?

Having regular, healthy bowel movements is a key—although often overlooked—marker of digestive health. A healthy stool is typically soft but well-formed, passed without straining, and occurs regularly. While frequency varies from person to person, anything between three times a day to three times a week can be considered normal, as long as it's consistent.

Fiber plays a central role in maintaining this balance: *soluble fiber* helps soften stools by holding onto water, while *insoluble fiber* adds bulk and supports regular movement through the gut (page 38). For some, simply "eating more fiber" doesn't seem to help with gut or bowel problems, and may even make things feel worse. This tells us that both types of fiber are essential for healthy bowel habits.

Not all fiber is equal. A diet overloaded with insoluble fiber, like raw wheat bran, can sometimes irritate the gut lining or worsen bloating, especially in those with a sensitive digestive system. Individuals with conditions such as irritable bowel syndrome (IBS) or celiac disease may find that certain fibers trigger discomfort, while their body is better able to tolerate others. In short, how your body responds to fiber depends on a range of factors. Hydration is also important: fiber needs water to work properly (page 73). Things don't stop there—there are other influences like stress (page 27), gut motility, and hormonal fluctuations, which can all impact how your gut functions and how it processes fiber. Your toileting habits and your stools' appearance are good indicators as to what is going on inside you when it comes to your gut.

Getting the right fiber for your gut

Now that we know that not all fiber works the same way and some types may suit you better than others, what sources are available and which work best when? Among the most researched interventions are psyllium husk, wheat bran, and kiwi fruit, each with its own benefits and quirks.

Psyllium husk (soluble fiber)

 Constipation-predominant IBS (IBS-C)

 Gently eases stool passage through the gut; well-tolerated for many gut types

 Risk of choking and blockages if too much is consumed

Wheat bran (insoluble fiber)

 Sluggish bowels (speeds up transit time)

 Often too coarse for those with a sensitive gut or IBS (can lead to bloating/discomfort)

Kiwi fruit (soluble + insoluble fiber)

 Sluggish bowels (speeds up transit time; also contains digestive enzyme actinidin)

 Provides a whole-food approach with added benefit of other natural enzymes

Psyllium husk for healthy stools

A type of soluble fiber derived from the husks of the *Plantago ovata* seed, psyllium husk, when mixed with water, forms a gel-like substance that helps soften stools and increase regularity. What makes psyllium unique is its versatility: it's one of the few fibers effective for both constipation and diarrhea. It also has prebiotic properties, helping feed beneficial gut bacteria and support overall microbiome health. The research around psyllium is strong, particularly for relieving symptoms of constipation-predominant IBS (IBS-C) and improving overall stool consistency. However, it's crucial to take psyllium with plenty of water: without enough fluid, it can lead to blockages rather than relief. It's also wise to introduce it gradually to avoid bloating, and to space it out by a couple of hours from any medications, as it can interfere with their absorption.

What does a healthy stool look like?

To help us better understand what's happening in our gut, the Bristol Stool Chart (see panel, right) offers a visual guide. It's important to remember that a *normal* stool appearance for you may not be normal for someone else. That said, stool types 3 and 4 are considered the ideal: they're soft, formed, and easy to pass without straining. Types 1 and 2 often suggest constipation: typically linked to not getting enough fiber, fluids, or exercise. These stools are hard, lumpy, and uncomfortable to pass. Types 5 to 7 can indicate that you have eaten too much fiber too quickly, a sensitivity to certain fiber types, or an imbalance in gut health. At this end of the scale, stools become loose, mushy, or diarrhea-like.

Fiber and hydration work together to keep digestion running smoothly. Without enough fluid, fiber can lead to hard, dry stools; sudden increases in fiber, especially without adequate water, may cause bloating. Rather than aiming for perfection every day, it's more useful to watch overall patterns: occasional variations in stool consistency are normal, but persistent trends toward either extreme may indicate that your fiber intake, fluid levels, or gut health need attention. If you have ongoing concerns about your bowel habits, a doctor or registered dietitian can provide personalized guidance.

Bristol Stool Scale

The Bristol Stool Scale is a visual guide for identifying the health of your poop. Gradually increasing fiber, alongside drinking plenty of water, can help bring stool consistency toward the ideal type 3–4 range.

Type 1

Small, hard, separate lumps; difficult, often painful to pass.

Type 2

Lumpy, sausage-shaped; firm, dry; uncomfortable to pass.

Type 3

Sausage-shaped with surface cracks; firm but passes easily.

Type 4

Smooth, soft, sausage- or snake-like; easy to pass.

Type 5

Soft blobs with clear-cut edges; passes easily but can lack shape.

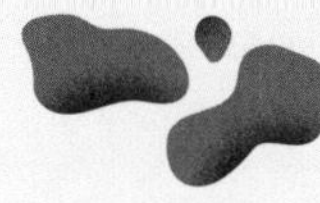

Type 6

Fluffy pieces with ragged edges; mushy consistency.

Type 7

Watery, entirely liquid stool—diarrhea.

What's the difference between prebiotics and probiotics?

Prebiotics are specific types of fiber found in certain plant-based foods. They "feed" the good bacteria in your gut, helping it—and myriad other physiological processes—function optimally. Probiotics are live bacteria that are found in fermented foods. While these are not found in fiber foods themselves, they are important to support your microbiome for optimal gut health so that your body can make the most of the fiber—and other nutrients—you eat.

Why do I need prebiotics?

Unlike most nutrients, prebiotic fibers are resistant to digestion. They pass through the stomach and small intestine without being broken down, and eventually reach the colon intact. Here, they become food for millions of beneficial bacteria.

As these beneficial bacteria "feed" on the prebiotics (through a process of fermentation), they produce helpful compounds like short-chain fatty acids (SCFAs), which, as we saw on page 11, have anti-inflammatory and gut-healing effects that are good for your entire health and well-being.

Not all the fiber you eat is prebiotic—only certain types of fiber feed good bacteria and help them grow. Among those types are foods containing compounds such as inulin, pectin, and fructooligosaccharides. You can find these in fruits such as apples, dates, prunes and bananas; vegetables such as asparagus, leeks, onions, chicory, and garlic; and whole foods and pulses, such as wheat bran, nuts, and beans. Resistant starch (page 15) is another source. Eating a variety of prebiotic foods helps maintain a diverse and healthy gut microbiome, which in turn supports digestion, immunity, and even mental well-being.

What are probiotics?

Unlike prebiotics, which feed your existing gut bacteria, probiotics add new strains of beneficial bacteria directly into your digestive system. These microbes help balance the gut microbiome and support a healthy immune response. In the UK, US, and the EU, the word "probiotic" is classified as an unauthorized health claim and can't be used on food labels or packaging to imply a health benefit. Instead, you might see phrases such as "contains live cultures" or "fermented with live bacteria." While shopping, check the labels of fermented foods (below and opposite) for specific strains, like *Lactobacillus acidophilus* or *Bifidobacterium lactis*, which are good, active probiotic sources.

Probiotics—the four Ks

One way to remember some of the most popular groups of probiotic foods is to think of the four Ks. Adding some or all of these to your diet, along with other probiotic-rich foods such as yogurt, miso, tempeh, and certain aged cheeses, will support your gut microbiome.

1. Kefir
A tangy, fermented milk drink

2. Kombucha
A slightly fizzy fermented tea

3. Kimchi
Spicy fermented Korean vegetables

4. Sauerkraut
Fermented cabbage

What are fermented foods?

Fermented foods like the four Ks (opposite, below) are among the best sources of probiotics. We now know far more about them than ever before. During fermentation, natural bacteria and yeasts break down the sugars and fibers within plant-based foods, softening their cell walls and making certain nutrients more bioavailable. This process also produces beneficial compounds known as postbiotics, sometimes called "zombie bacteria," which remain active even after the microbes have become inactive. These by-products may continue to support immune and gut health, much like how a vaccine made from inactivated microbes can still train the immune system to respond to it. In other words, even though the bacteria are no longer alive, their components can still have powerful health-promoting effects.

A 2025 study of more than 6,000 adults found that increasing fermented-food intake by just three portions per day for three weeks led to notable improvements in well-being (one portion is about 1 tablespoon of miso or half a cup of kimchi). Around half of participants reported a significant improvement in mood (47%), energy levels (56%), and hunger control (52%), and four in ten reported signs of reduced bloating (42%). The effects were especially pronounced among participants who were living with obesity. The findings suggest that even short-term increases in fermented-food intake can lead to meaningful benefits for gut comfort and day-to-day well-being. What does this tell us? The gut responds quickly to positive dietary changes!

Eat a diet rich in prebiotic fibers and probiotic foods to support a thriving, balanced gut microbiome.

What are healthy-gut supplements and are they worth taking?

Probiotics are widely available in many forms. Synbiotics are supplements or foods that combine both prebiotics and probiotics. These aim to improve the survival of probiotics in the gut by feeding them the prebiotic fibers they need to thrive. However, healthy individuals really don't need to supplement, as food sources are enough. Getting your probiotics from food is usually more reliable, more affordable, and safer (supplements are expensive and often unregulated). Many probiotic-rich foods, like the four Ks (see box, opposite) can be made easily and cheaply at home.

Prebiotics
Prebiotics come from certain types of fiber-containing foods and "feed" the beneficial bacteria already in the gut.

+

Probiotics
Probiotics exist in certain foods (usually aged or fermented foods) and add beneficial bacteria to your gut.

=

Synbiotics
Synbiotics are the combination of prebiotics and probiotics in synthetic (manufactured) supplement form.

Do I have to choose between fiber and protein?

The short answer to this question is no—there is absolutely no scientific or metabolic need to choose between fiber and protein. In fact, it's important that we reframe our thinking, unpacking decades of high-protein, low-fiber narrative to bring fiber back into our diets in a healthy, sustainable way—while still getting enough protein for optimum health, too.

Is protein essential?

In the body, protein supports growth, cell repair, hormone balance, enzyme production, and immunity. Country-by-country recommendations suggest that adults need around 0.75g protein per kilogram of body weight daily—about 53g of protein each day for a 130lb (60kg) woman and 55g each day for a 165lb (75kg) man.

You need only look at the list of foods in the box (right) to see that, whatever your dietary preference, it's relatively easy to hit around 50g of protein a day. That means that most of us consume more protein than the body needs to function well. Indeed, in my work at the Rhitrition clinic, I have yet to see a true case of protein deficiency (whereas I frequently see fiber deficiency). In the context of Western diets, it's worth questioning, therefore, how useful extra protein really is and why we talk so much about protein when looking at nutrition.

In modern times, protein has become entwined with strength, youth, beauty ideals, and wellness marketing. Yes, protein matters and needs increase with age (women benefit from maintaining intake through menopause and beyond; page 48). But any cultural fixation on "high-protein everything" runs the risk of leaving fiber—the nutrient that protects against heart disease, diabetes, and colon disorders, and even supports healthy weight management—forgotten. In fact, the better way to think of things is to look at how fiber and protein work together for optimum health, and even to focus on foods that can provide both, so that the body is getting everything it needs, in balance.

The main actions of protein on the body

While there is much focus on protein as a means to build muscle in a health-and-fitness sense, its actions on the body are far more physiologically varied and significant than any focus on aesthetic ideal might suggest.

Growth and maintenance Protein provides the body with structural "building blocks" to grow new tissue and maintain healthy muscles, bones, and organs throughout life.

Enzyme production Enzymes, which are mostly proteins, catalyze countless biochemical reactions inside and outside cells, facilitating processes like digestion and energy production.

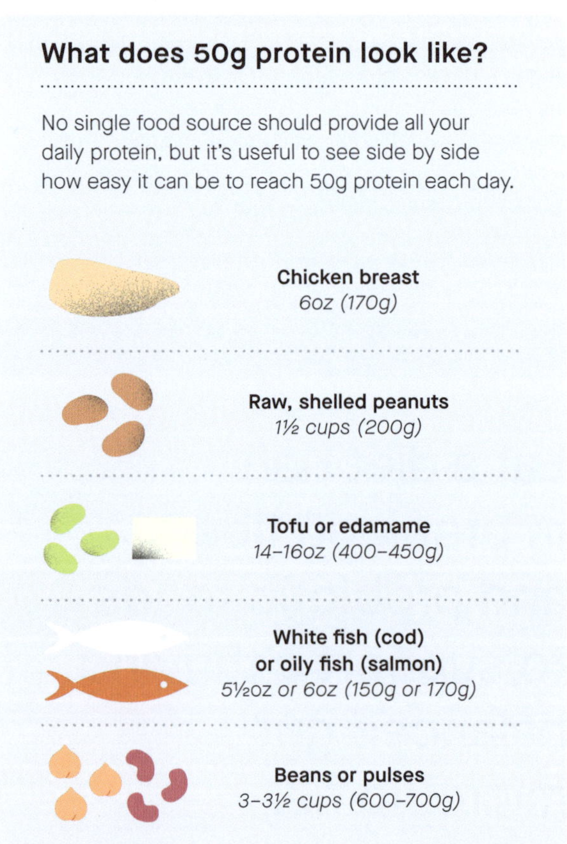

What does 50g protein look like?

No single food source should provide all your daily protein, but it's useful to see side by side how easy it can be to reach 50g protein each day.

Hormone production Many hormones, such as insulin and growth hormone, are proteins or polypeptides that act as chemical messengers for the brain to regulate various bodily functions.

Structure provision Proteins like collagen, elastin, and keratin contribute to the structural integrity of tissues such as skin, hair, nails, bones, and cartilage.

Immune support Protein is essential for producing antibodies, which fight infections and bolster the immune system.

Fluid balance Proteins like albumin help maintain the body's fluid balance, preventing swelling (edema).

Nutrient transportation and storage Some proteins move substances like oxygen (hemoglobin), glucose, cholesterol, vitamins, and minerals throughout the bloodstream and within cells. Others provide storage—for example, the protein ferritin stores iron.

Challenging the narrative

While most of us already meet our daily protein needs for all these physiological benefits, many still fall short on fiber. In order to challenge the narrative that we need to increase protein to optimize strength, weight maintenance, and timeless aging, it's worth taking each of these in turn to consider where fiber fits into those ideals, too. The specific circumstances of each of these outcomes highlight protein–fiber interactions, but taking steps to get the right balance of fiber and protein in our diet, no matter the goal, is an approach that can benefit everyone, not just when the aim is an aesthetic one.

The better way... is to look at how fiber and protein work together for optimum health, and even to focus on foods that can provide both.

The consumerism effect

The protein health obsession isn't new. In the 1960s and '70s bodybuilding appeared on the scene, messaging that we need to be eating enough protein to fulfill shape, size, and muscle goals. In the '80s, popular bodybuilder figures like Arnold Schwarzenegger appeared in marketing that endorsed protein powders. Today, a protein shake is accepted as a normal supplement—among the public as well as for athletes. This popularity has proved huge commercially: the market for high-protein products in the US is estimated at $114 billion, and is projected to grow annually until at least 2028. Today, social-media platforms drive the high-protein trend to phenomenal levels—with record surges for products like protein bars. These days we even see high-protein cereals and high-protein chocolate bars—all of which have been driven by consumer demand.

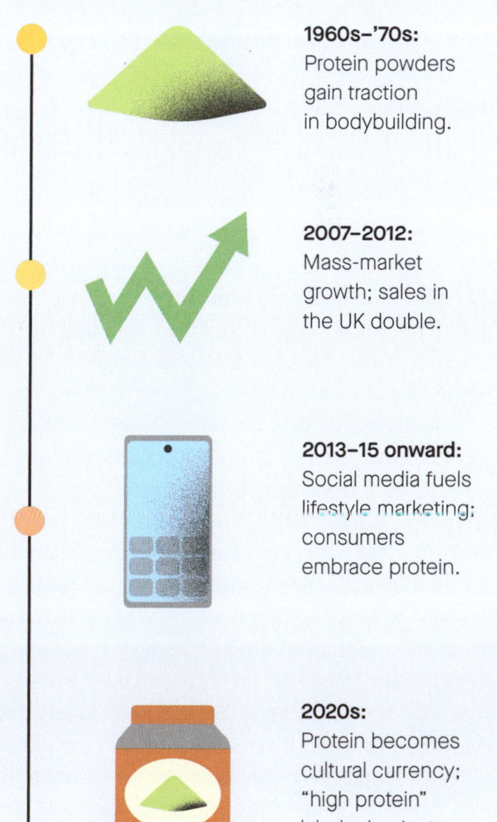

Building strength

Building strength depends not just on protein intake but also resistance exercise and, importantly, overall diet quality. Plant proteins like beans, lentils, and soy can make good inroads for—and even meet—your daily protein needs (remember: 53g of protein each day for women and 55g each day for men) while boosting fiber.

Achieving a healthy weight

For those tackling overweight or obesity, protein can certainly support satiety. However, its reputation as a metabolism-boosting nutrient is overstated and inaccurate—high-protein diets (below, right) are a red herring. Sustainable weight loss still depends on energy balance. In this case, it's better to look to fiber. Fiber plays an even greater role in appetite regulation, slowing digestion, and nurturing the gut microbiome, all of which support healthy body weight. Importantly, for anyone looking to achieve a healthy weight, carbohydrate foods are not the enemy. Whole-grain bread, brown rice, oats, and legumes are not only good carbohydrate sources but also contain both protein and fiber, delivering balanced energy that helps manage hunger and stabilize blood sugar.

Easing menopause

During menopause, protein becomes increasingly important in the female diet to help counteract age-related muscle loss (known medically as sarcopenia). Protein supports the maintenance of lean body mass, which can decline as a result of hormonal changes. Higher protein intake may also help manage postmenopausal body weight by enhancing satiety and supporting metabolism. Additionally, protein contributes to bone health, which is especially important as estrogen levels fall and the risk of osteoporosis (a condition adversely affecting bone density) rises.

But what does this mean in practice? For postmenopausal women, while recommended daily levels (around 0.75g per kilogram of body weight pre-menopause) can maintain lean mass, optimal protein intake of around 1–1.6g per kilogram of body weight per day is associated with better muscle function, increased strength, and improved physical capacity and resilience. Consistent protein consumption across meals (for example, eating about 20–25g of protein per main meal) supports metabolic balance and helps manage body composition during hormonal transitions.

In the SPOON trial (2025), 84 postmenopausal women were, for 18 months, randomly assigned to one of two groups: one received a whey protein supplement providing 40g of protein per day, while the other received a placebo. Researchers measured circulating branched-chain amino acids (BCAAs) and markers of insulin sensitivity. Although the protein group had significantly higher BCAA levels, they showed no improvement in insulin sensitivity or menopausal symptoms compared with the placebo group. This suggests that simply increasing protein intake isn't enough to improve metabolic health after menopause: it's the overall quality, balance, and context of the diet that matter most, including fiber-rich, plant-based foods that support gut health and metabolism.

Choosing protein-fiber power foods

We need protein but we already get enough of it. Fiber is the nutrient missing from our plates. Rather than asking "Do I need more protein?," a more useful question is: "Am I getting enough fiber, and where can I swap animal proteins for plant proteins to boost both?" That's because when you choose beans, lentils, whole grains, nuts, seeds, and soy, you naturally cover your protein needs while also increasing fiber intake. And that's where the real health gains lie, from supporting your microbiome to reduce your risk of chronic disease.

In short, then, by leaning into plant proteins and whole carbohydrate sources, you get the best of both worlds: all the protein you need, plus the fiber and nutrients that protect your heart, gut, and long-term health. As with so much about diet and well-being: balance always wins over excess.

High-protein diets

Popular among athletes and dieters, high-protein diets often focus on meat, eggs, and dairy, leaving little room for fiber-rich plant foods and meaning that fiber intake in these adult groups can fall well below recommended levels. This can result in hard, dry stools (Bristol Types 1–2; page 27) leading to constipation, and reduced microbial diversity, especially in low-carb or bodybuilding-style meal plans.

Protein + Fiber power foods

Here are a top 10 of protein + fiber foods. If you can increase these in your diet, you are giving your body good amounts of protein without sacrificing fiber.

Almonds
(1oz/30g)

Protein **6g**
Fiber **4g**

Lentils
(5½oz/150g)

Protein **12g**
Fiber **10g**

Butter (lima) beans, cooked
(5½oz/150g)

Protein **10g**
Fiber **9g**

Oats, dry
(1¾oz/40g)

Protein **5g**
Fiber **4g**

Chia seeds
(1oz/25g)

Protein **4g**
Fiber **9g**

Quinoa
(6½oz/185g)

Protein **8g**
Fiber **5g**

Chickpeas, cooked
(5½oz/150g)

Protein **11g**
Fiber **9g**

Tofu, firm
(5½oz/150g)

Protein **15g**
Fiber **2g**

Edamame, shelled
(3½oz/100g)

Protein **11g**
Fiber **5g**

Tempeh
(3½oz/100g)

Protein **11g**
Fiber **9g**

Can I eat fiber if I have IBS?

Irritable bowel syndrome (IBS) is a common condition that affects how the gut works. Symptoms vary but often include bloating, abdominal pain, gas, constipation, diarrhea, or a mixture of all. Because fiber directly affects how food moves through the gut, it can play a role in either easing or worsening symptoms.

IBS is a chronic functional gut disorder affecting approximately 10–15% of the population in the UK, around 12% in the US, and 8–12% across mainland Europe. Although its symptoms are physical and can be debilitating, the precise cause remains uncertain. IBS may have a hereditary component, and can occur when food moves either too quickly or too slowly through the gut, or when there is heightened sensitivity in the intestinal lining. Stress is also known to exacerbate symptoms, supporting evidence that IBS may stem partly from disrupted communication between the brain and gut, the so-called Gut–Brain axis (page 25).

What we do know is that IBS does not present in the same way for everyone, and fiber can have different effects depending on dominant symptoms. Eating too little fiber can make constipation and discomfort worse. On the other hand, eating too much fiber, or the wrong

type, can trigger bloating, excess gas, and loose stools. This is why fiber can feel confusing if you have IBS— what may trigger symptoms in one person may not trigger symptoms in another.

In IBS with constipation and bloating, increasing soluble fibers such as psyllium, chia seeds, flaxseeds, and oats may help soften stools, support regularity, and reduce discomfort. In contrast, for those with IBS with diarrhea, too much fiber or certain types (for example, wheat bran or high-FODMAP sources; opposite) can worsen loose stools and urgency. This highlights why there is no single "IBS-friendly" fiber. What to eat and what to avoid depend on both the type of fiber and the individual's symptom patterns. A dietitian can help navigate that path specifically for you.

What are FODMAPs?

As we already know, fiber is not a single nutrient and the effect it has on the body depends on how it behaves in the gut. Gut bacteria can quickly break down readily fermentable fibers such as inulin and fructooligosaccharides (FOS), often added to snack bars, yogurts, and cereals. This rapid fermentation produces gas, which can worsen bloating and pain in sensitive people. Some fibers, like psyllium husk (page 27), dissolve in water to form a gel and are only moderately fermented. They can soften hard stools, ease constipation, and improve overall IBS symptoms with less bloating. Insoluble fibers (for example, wheat bran) add bulk and speed up transit. Some people with IBS tolerate them well, but others find that they irritate the gut if introduced too quickly.

Some fibers also fall under the category of FODMAPs—short-chain carbohydrates that are easily fermented in the gut and can trigger symptoms like bloating, pain, and diarrhea in some people with IBS. Many high-FODMAP foods are also naturally high in fiber. For example, beans, lentils, onions, and certain fruits provide excellent fiber, but for those with IBS can be harder to tolerate. This is where the overlap between FODMAPs and fiber can become confusing—foods that are normally encouraged for gut health may worsen symptoms in sensitive individuals.

There is no single "IBS-friendly" fiber. What to eat and what to avoid depend on both the type of fiber and the individual's symptom patterns.

Adopting a low-FODMAP diet

The low-FODMAP diet is one strategy sometimes used to manage IBS. It involves temporarily reducing high-FODMAP foods before reintroducing them step by step to identify personal triggers. Importantly, this is not a diet to follow long term nor to attempt without support. Cutting out many high-FODMAP foods on your own can unnecessarily reduce fiber intake and restrict the diet more than is helpful. For this reason, the low-FODMAP diet should be carried out only with support from a registered dietitian, who can ensure your fiber intake remains balanced, help you reduce and then reintroduce foods carefully and sustainably, and avoid unnecessary long-term dietary restriction. Not everyone with IBS needs a low-FODMAP diet, but when used correctly, it can be a useful tool for finding out which fiber-rich foods you tolerate best so that you have the best chance of being able to eat a well-rounded, balanced diet that minimizes your IBS symptoms.

Top 5 tips for an IBS-friendly, fiber-rich diet

1. Increase your fiber intake gradually
Sudden jumps in fiber often worsen bloating.

2. Hydrate well
Fiber needs water to work effectively.

3. Choose soluble, moderately fermentable fibers
Oats, chia seeds, flaxseeds, and psyllium are often well tolerated.

4. Be cautious with "added fiber" foods
Products that contain added fiber such as inulin or FOS may cause extra gas and bloating.

5. Remember: it's personal
What flares symptoms in one person may be fine for another—be prepared for trial and error.

FODMAP foods

These are examples of low, medium, and high FODMAP foods. Talk to a dietitian before going on any kind of restrictive diet.

Low	Medium	High
Arugula	Avocado	Apples
Blueberries	Brazil nuts	Asparagus
Carrots	Broccoli	Blackberries
Cucumber	Brussels sprouts	Cauliflower
Grapes	Butternut squash	Dates
Green beans	Cannellini (navy) beans	Garlic
Kale	Celery	Honey
Kiwi	Eggplant	Leeks (bulb and white part)
Oranges	Nectarines	Legumes
Parsnip	Pineapple	Mangoes
Pineapple	Ricotta	Mushrooms
Potatoes	Raspberries	Onions
Quinoa	Sweet corn	Pears
Strawberries	Sweet potatoes	Pulses
Tomatoes	Zucchini	Watermelon

Can fiber help reduce rates of colon cancer?

One thing I've seen time and again is how low fiber intake seems quietly to contribute to serious health issues, particularly colorectal cancer. This type of cancer has been rising alarmingly over recent years, especially among younger adults in many Western countries. Despite the advances we've made in screening and treatment, colon cancer remains one of the most common and serious cancers of all.

In the UK, colorectal cancer is the third most diagnosed cancer and the second leading cause of cancer death. Screening programs have helped stabilize rates among older adults, but there seems to be a trend toward more cases among younger people. Hugely concerning, it is clearly linked to lifestyle factors like low-fiber intake, poor diet, and less physical activity. In the US and in Germany, similar trends are emerging. Even in Italy, where the traditional Mediterranean diet is rich in fiber, modern shifts toward ultra-processed foods are changing the picture. On the other side of the coin, colorectal cancer rates are notably lower in certain parts of Africa and South Asia—regions where traditional, high-fiber diets have long prevailed.

The common thread is the same: diets low in fiber, high in processed foods, and increasingly sedentary lifestyles lead to higher cancer rates for certain kinds of cancer. While multiple factors influence cancer incidence, consistent evidence suggests that fiber-rich diets could be a powerful component of prevention strategies. In Western countries, we all need to prioritize fiber as a vital, nourishing part of our everyday lives.

Throughout my work, I've met many people who felt overwhelmed by the confusing health messages out there. It's easy to feel like prevention is complicated or out of reach, but it's really about the small, consistent steps we take every day. Adding fiber is one of those simple, loving acts we can do for ourselves. Together, by understanding and embracing this, we can help turn these troubling trends around, one meal at a time.

Fiber and different types of cancer

Higher fiber intake is strongly linked to lower colorectal cancer risk and may benefit the prevention of other cancers.

Cancer type	Evidence strength	How might fiber be helping?
Colorectal	Strong	By improving digestion and gut health to reduce risk.
Breast	Moderate	By helping reduce estrogen levels to reduce risk.
Stomach	Moderate	By lowering glycemic load to reduce risk.
Endometrial	Moderate	By helping to regulate hormones to reduce risk.
Pancreatic	Limited	By potentially offering a protective role to reduce risk.
Lung	Limited	Through links with overall healthier diet patterns.

Can fiber improve my mood?

We've long known that what we eat shapes how we feel physically, but scientists are now uncovering just how much it might influence how we think and feel too. On page 25 we learned about the Gut–Brain axis, a busy two-way system that plays a crucial role in our overall well-being.

Fiber is one of the main dietary contributors in the conversation between our gut and our brain. Short-chain fatty acids (SCFAs; page 11) don't just keep the gut lining healthy, they may also help regulate inflammation and support the production of serotonin. Often called the "feel-good" hormone, serotonin helps regulate mood, sleep, and even appetite. Remarkably, even though serotonin's effects are experienced in the brain, about 90% of it is produced in the gut! By fueling the bacteria that influence serotonin production, and therefore the gut–brain connection, fiber could be one way our diet supports our mental well-being.

Fiber may also reduce inflammation through a healthier gut environment by balancing its pH and keeping the gut barrier strong. This can mean fewer inflammatory compounds are able to circulate through the body: inflammation has been tied to both low mood and poor sleep quality. Studies show that people eating the lowest amount of fiber tend to sleep worst and report more symptoms of depression and anxiety, while those eating more fiber report the opposite.

Cognitive health, fiber, and aging

Preliminary research into the connections between fiber and brain health in older adults is especially intriguing. A recent analysis of US data found that people over age 60 who consumed more fiber performed better on certain tests of thinking speed and mental processing, with benefits leveling off at around 34g of fiber per day. Although not every area of memory improved, the study has highlighted that meeting fiber recommendations could be one simple step to help protect the brain as we age. Another compelling study in adults over age 60 found that a simple prebiotic supplement designed to feed gut bacteria (page 29) not only reshaped the gut microbiome but also led to measurable improvements in cognitive performance. Together, these findings suggest that supporting the gut with fiber and prebiotics could become an accessible way to help maintain brain health as we get older—although we need much more research before we can say for sure.

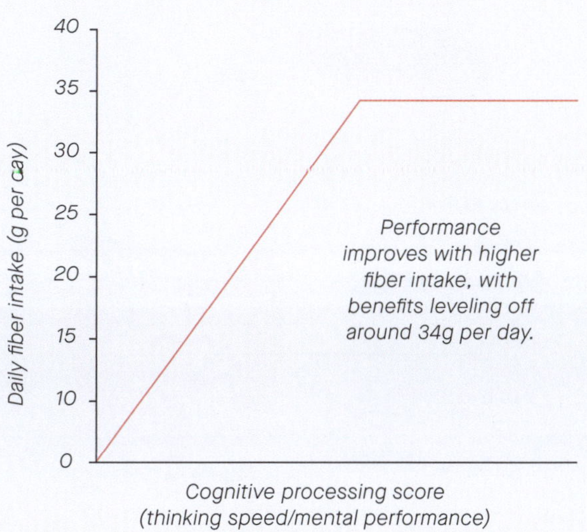

How does fiber impact my heart health?

The search for everyday dietary habits that can protect cardiovascular health has never been more crucial. Fiber continues to stand out as one of the simplest yet most effective tools we have to help keep our heart and circulation in top condition.

What's the scale of the problem?

Heart and circulatory diseases are the leading cause of death worldwide, responsible for almost one in three deaths, amounting to around 20 million deaths each year. In the UK alone it's estimated that one in 12 people is living with a heart or circulatory condition. In Germany, statistics from 2019 show that around 1.1 million inpatient hospitalizations and 174,000 rehabilitations were related to atherosclerotic cardiovascular disease diagnoses. The picture is no less startling on the other side of the Atlantic: in the US approximately 695,000 people die from heart disease each year (about one in every five deaths). Additionally, about 805,000 Americans have a heart attack annually. Of these heart attacks, 605,000 are first-time occurrences, while 200,000 are in individuals who have previously experienced a heart attack.

Fiber's effects on circulating cholesterol

Soluble fiber binds to bile acids in the small intestine, preventing them from being reabsorbed into the bloodstream. As a result, the liver draws on circulating cholesterol to produce more bile acids, which helps lower levels of LDL ("bad") cholesterol in the blood. In diets low in soluble fiber, more bile acids are reabsorbed and cholesterol is recycled rather than excreted. Regular intake of soluble fibers such as beta-glucan (oats, barley) and psyllium husk may significantly reduce LDL cholesterol concentrations and support heart health.

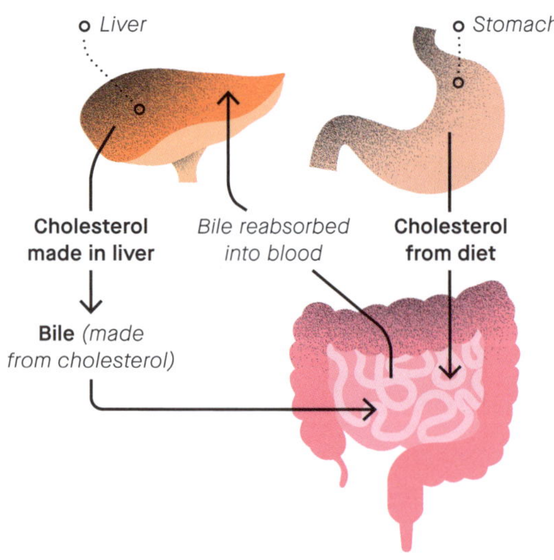

Most bile is reabsorbed, so cholesterol is reused and remains in circulation.

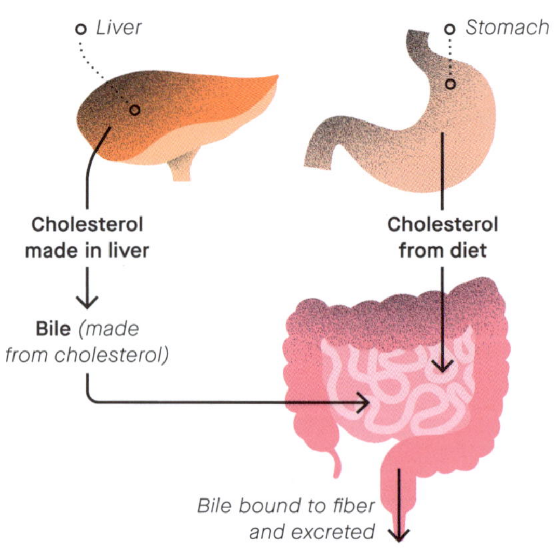

By binding to bile, soluble fiber ensures more LDL (bad) cholesterol is excreted.

Decades of research have consistently linked higher fiber intake with a lower risk of cardiovascular disease, coronary heart disease, stroke, and Type-2 diabetes. Large-scale analyses show that those who consume the most fiber have up to a 30% lower risk of developing heart disease compared to those who eat the least. Furthermore, just 5g extra fiber each day can reduce blood pressure, cholesterol, and markers of inflammation—all of which impact heart health.

Why is fiber so good for the heart?

Fiber's heart benefits are thought to stem from several different mechanisms.

Lowering cholesterol

Cholesterol is a fatty, wax-like substance that the body needs in small amounts for making hormones, building cells, making bile acids (which help us digest fats from food), and other functions. However, too much of the wrong kind, known as low-density lipoprotein (LDL) cholesterol, can lead to a deposit build-up in the artery walls. Over time, these deposits, called plaques, can narrow or block arteries, raising the risk of heart attacks and strokes. Soluble fibers, though, found in foods like oats, barley, beans, and some fruits, form a gel in the gut that binds to bile acids. Normally, once they've done their job, bile acids are reabsorbed and recycled in the body, but when fiber locks onto them, they're carried out and excreted instead. This sets off a chain reaction: the liver pulls cholesterol out of the bloodstream to make new bile acids. Some of that is LDL cholesterol, therefore lowering blood levels and reducing the risk of plaque build-up (see diagram, opposite).

Maintaining healthy weight

Fiber slows digestion and helps you feel fuller for longer, which reduces the likelihood of overeating. Maintaining a healthy weight in turn lowers blood pressure and improves blood-sugar control—two key risk factors for heart disease.

Making short-chain fatty acids

Prebiotic fibers (page 28) trigger an effect that produces short-chain fatty acids (SCFAs) in the gut. These enter the bloodstream and have wide-reaching effects, from helping lower inflammation to helping moderate blood-sugar and cholesterol levels (page 11).

Contributing to the bigger picture

High-fiber diets rarely exist in isolation—by definition they are rich in fruits, vegetables, legumes, whole grains, nuts, and seeds. These foods provide not just fiber, but a wide array of vitamins, minerals, antioxidants, and plant compounds that also protect the heart. In other words, fiber may partly serve as a marker of an overall diet that supports cardiovascular health.

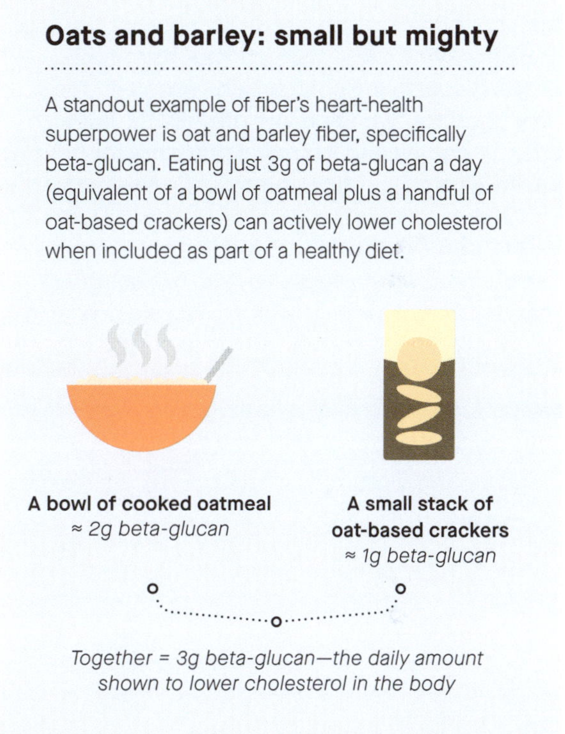

Just 5g extra fiber each day can reduce blood pressure, cholesterol, and markers of inflammation—all of which impact heart health.

Can fiber help me manage my weight?

Weight management is so much more complex than counting calories. Whether you want to lose or gain weight, fiber plays an important role. That's because many fiber-rich foods are not only good for digestion and gut health, but also provide energy and essential nutrients, optimizing health whatever your weight-management goals.

What is a "healthy" weight?

There is no straightforward answer to this question—"healthy" weight needs to look at your genetics (some people are naturally smaller and lighter or taller and heavier) and your overall health to determine what is healthy *for you*. If, though, you are underweight due to stress, illness, or low appetite, and if as a result you are fatigued, nutrient deficient, immunocompromised, or suffering hormonal imbalance or other signs of ill health, a gradual increase in weight (about 0.5–1kg per week) may help, especially paired with light activity to build muscle mass. If you are overweight or obese, a careful, sustained weight-loss program that optimizes nutrient intake and is paired with exercise can help you lose weight safely and sustainably. (Note that, if you're struggling with gaining or losing weight, seek support from a doctor or registered dietitian.)

Why fiber works for weight gain

Carbohydrates are the body's main source of energy, and, as we know, fiber is a type of carbohydrate found in plant foods. The misconception that "carbohydrates cause unhealthy weight gain" has led many people to cut them out unnecessarily. In reality, whole-grain and fiber-rich carbohydrate foods provide both energy (needed for weight gain) and fiber (needed for gut health and nutrient absorption). This makes them ideal for underweight individuals trying to eat more without sacrificing the nutritional quality of their diet by relying on ultra-processed options.

Weight-gain superfoods

Practical foods to include in a fiber-rich, but balanced healthy weight-gain diet, include:

Carbohydrate sources

Whole-grain starchy carbs such as brown rice, oats, and potatoes.

High-quality protein foods

Protein-rich foods including beans, lentils, dairy, eggs, fish, and meat.

Energy-dense plant foods

Energy-dense fiber sources like nuts, seeds, and avocados.

Dairy foods

Smoothies, yogurts, and milk-based puddings made with whole ingredients.

Why fiber works for weight loss

In the UK alone there are an average of 136,000 monthly searches for "how can I lose weight fast." In 2021, a study found that 45% of people globally are actively trying to lose weight at any one time. The figure increased to 60% of people in Chile, and more than 50% in Spain, Peru, Saudi Arabia, Singapore, and the US. Clearly weight is a growing concern all over the world: research published by *The Lancet* suggests that more than one billion people worldwide are living with obesity. This comprises roughly 880 million adults and 159 million children.

Fiber-rich whole foods are fundamental to sustainable weight loss: research published in 2025 provides compelling evidence that they can represent a practical and effective strategy within a minimally processed dietary pattern. In a well-controlled UK-based trial, adults with overweight or obesity followed two distinct eight-week diets: one based on minimally processed foods and the other on ultra-processed foods (UPFs). Both diets were nutritionally matched, and aligned with national dietary guidelines. However, participants lost significantly more weight on the minimally processed diet—it is likely that fiber played a contributing role in this outcome. Minimally processed meals tend to be naturally higher in dietary fiber, which supports appetite regulation through greater satiety, slower digestion, and reduced energy intake over time. These findings highlight the importance of food *form and structure*, not just nutrient content, and suggest that fiber-rich, whole foods may support weight-loss efforts more effectively than their ultra-processed counterparts.

Carbohydrate choice matters

It's not the carbohydrates themselves that drive weight changes—it's the quality of those carbohydrates. Fiber-rich foods like whole grains, fruit, beans, and vegetables provide energy for weight gain while also supporting digestion, stable blood sugar, and long-term health. In contrast, refined and ultra-processed carbohydrates (such as white bread, cookies, and sugary cereals) give quick calories but little else. By choosing whole, fiber-containing carbohydrates, you can optimize both your calorie intake and the nutritional value of your diet. Put simply, carbohydrates—including fiber-rich carbohydrates—complement each other when it comes to healthy weight gain or healthy weight loss.

Feeling full

One of fiber's most valuable traits is its ability to increase satiety (feeling full) by adding bulk, slowing digestion, and giving sustained energy release. Hand in hand with protein (which triggers fullness hormones; page 30), fiber is a weight-stabilizing hero. Plant-based proteins, such as beans, lentils, and quinoa, naturally combine both fiber and protein, delivering the double benefit in one package (animal proteins contain little to no fiber).

Regulating blood sugar

Fiber can level out blood-sugar spikes and crashes, which are often responsible for mid-morning and afternoon cravings and slumps. By slowing digestion, a high-fiber diet releases glucose into the bloodstream gradually and steadily, so we are more likely to resist the urge to snack, particularly on sugary foods. (On the other hand, ultra-processed foods hijack our brain's dopamine system to give a rapid hit of pleasure, followed by a crash that drives us to go back for more.)

Healthy bacteria (again)

As we know, prebiotic dietary fiber feeds beneficial bacteria, and in turn produces short-chain fatty acids (SCFAs). While the relationship between SCFAs and body weight is still being clarified, some evidence suggests that specific changes in gut bacteria and their fermentation activity may support a healthier weight. Studies in obese patients have found microbiome imbalance with an overgrowth of harmful bacteria.

How might resistant starch help with weight loss?

Resistant starch (page 15) bypasses digestion, and may offer two potential benefits for weight management. First, because the small intestine does not absorb some of the starch, the energy (number of calories) in the food is slightly lowered compared with the same food without resistant starch. Second, once resistant starch reaches the colon, gut bacteria ferment it to produce SCFAs. These may increase feelings of fullness, improve the body's response to insulin, and support overall metabolic health. However, much of the research on resistant starch and weight control is rodent-based. Although there appear to be consistent benefits for satiety, fat metabolism, and body composition in rodents, evidence in humans is mixed. A few small trials suggest possible reductions in appetite or body weight; many others show little or no effect. It's a case of watch this space.

How do weight-loss drugs change my nutritional needs?

Over the past few years, weight-loss injections have made headlines around the world. Once prescribed almost exclusively for people with Type-2 diabetes, drugs such as Ozempic®, Wegovy®, and Mounjaro® are now being used far more widely for weight management.

Demand has surged, with prescriptions rising sharply in the UK and US, fueled in part by social media and celebrity endorsements. For many, these medicines seem to offer a quick solution to weight loss and undoubtedly save lives, but they also raise important questions about long-term nutrition and health.

What is GLP-1 and how does it work?

At the heart of these treatments is glucagon-like peptide-1 (GLP-1), a hormone naturally released from the gut after eating. GLP-1 helps regulate appetite by slowing gastric emptying, moderating post-meal blood glucose, and signaling to the brain that we have consumed enough food. Medications such as semaglutide (sold as Ozempic or Wegovy) and tirzepatide (sold as Mounjaro, which also mimics another gut hormone, called GIP) act on the same GLP-1 receptors in the gut, pancreas, and brain, but remain active much longer than the body's own GLP-1.

How do weight-loss injections work?

Weight-loss injections provide extra GLP-1—a hormone that the body naturally releases after we eat and which regulates appetite. GLP-1 medications have longer-lasting effects in the body, thus reducing cravings for food over a longer period of time and suppressing our need to eat.

Suppressing appetite

While originally developed to improve blood-sugar control in Type-2 diabetes, these medications' strong appetite-suppressing effects also drive significant weight loss. People often describe a sudden quieting of "food noise" (the constant urge to eat), alongside satisfaction with much smaller meals. But this reduced appetite brings challenges as well as benefits. Because the medications reduce appetite and slow digestion, one of the nutrients most at risk of being reduced in the diet is fiber, along with protein and essential vitamins and minerals. Fiber is especially vulnerable when portion sizes shrink or when meals become more protein-centered, yet we know it is crucial for digestion, appetite regulation, and long-term metabolic health.

Slowing the gut

GLP-1 medicines slow the rate at which food leaves the stomach. This effect can help with blood-sugar control and satiety, but it increases the risk of digestive side effects, such as nausea, bloating, or constipation. Fiber becomes particularly important here. As we know, insoluble fiber adds bulk to stool and keeps bowel movements regular (page 26), while soluble fiber, such as beta-glucan (found in oats and barley) and pectin (in apples, pears, and berries) helps normalize digestion and stabilize blood glucose. People who cut back on meal size but fail to include these fibers may notice sluggish digestion or irregular stools.

Getting the fiber fix

For those using GLP-1 medications, it is clear that there is increased risk of key nutrient deficiencies—this applies to micronutrients such as iron and calcium, but also to fiber. The lack of nutritional diversity and fiber also leads to poor gut health. The focus for anyone taking GLP-1s should be on nutrient density and variety in smaller portions. Prioritizing fiber-rich foods within smaller, regular meals helps support gut health, maintain satiety, and ensure that reduced calorie intake does not come at the expense of long-term well-being. In the context of the use of these medications, fiber is not just a background nutrient, it is central to good digestive function and to good health beyond weight loss. Fiber-rich plant foods provide both nourishment and digestive support without large food volumes.

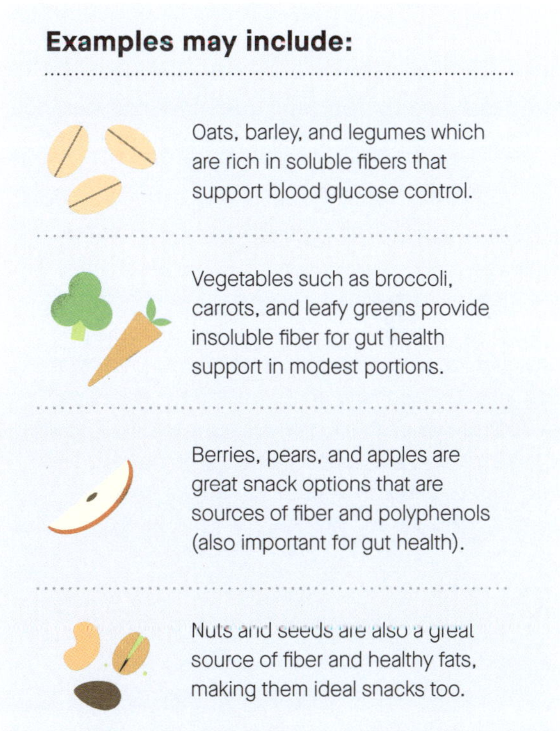

Examples may include:

Oats, barley, and legumes which are rich in soluble fibers that support blood glucose control.

Vegetables such as broccoli, carrots, and leafy greens provide insoluble fiber for gut health support in modest portions.

Berries, pears, and apples are great snack options that are sources of fiber and polyphenols (also important for gut health).

Nuts and seeds are also a great source of fiber and healthy fats, making them ideal snacks too.

Fiber is especially vulnerable when portion sizes shrink or when meals become more protein-centered.

How does fiber affect my athletic performance?

During exercise, blood is directed away from the gastrointestinal (GI) tract and toward the working muscles. This is a normal physiological response that ensures oxygen and nutrients are delivered where they're needed most—primarily to the limbs and peripheral tissues. However, this shift in blood flow means there's less oxygen—along with fewer other resources—available for digestion. So, if you eat a fiber-rich meal too close to a sports session, your gut will struggle to manage the digestive load. As a consequence, you may experience symptoms such as bloating, abdominal discomfort, cramping, urgency, or even diarrhea (particularly common in endurance athletes where GI distress is already prevalent).

You might think, given all this, that fiber shouldn't therefore feature at all in an athlete's diet, but that would be a huge misconception. Fiber is essential for athletes just as it is for everyone else because it supports regular bowel function, helps stabilize blood-glucose levels, and contributes to long-term cardiovascular and metabolic health. Nonetheless, to optimize your athletic performance and your fiber intake, there is one important thing you need to take into account: exactly when you eat your fiber.

Not "if" or "how," but "when"

As a general rule, athletes should eat high-fiber meals at least 3–4 hours before prolonged or intense activity. This allows enough time for digestion and minimizes the risk of gut discomfort during exercise.

In the 60–90 minutes before endurance training or racing, the focus should shift to "simple sugars." These are carbohydrates that contain very little fiber and are quickly absorbed into the body to provide a rapid release of energy. They include foods such as white bread, sweets, sports drinks, and low-fiber cereal bars.

You may be surprised to hear me encouraging simple sugars. But this is where the nuance comes in. These foods are ultra-processed, low in fiber, and offer very few nutrients overall—but in the context of endurance sports nutrition (such as running training and racing), they have a place. When used appropriately, they can provide fast, accessible energy without placing unnecessary strain on the digestive system.

For those regularly experiencing gut issues during endurance fitness sessions, adjusting fiber intake around exercise can be a simple and effective change. Over time, it's also possible to train the gut to tolerate slightly higher amounts of fiber or carbohydrates closer to exercise, but do this gradually—and ideally with the support of a sports nutritionist who can guide you through the transition safely and effectively.

Should I eat fiber to fuel a race?

For endurance or racing athletes, fiber plays an important but often misunderstood role. While fiber is essential for long-term health, including digestive function and metabolic regulation, it's one nutrient you may want to avoid too close to a competition. Fiber's ability to slow down digestion is one of its many benefits to the general population, but this effect can become problematic when the goal is quick energy release for exercise.

> Athletes should eat high-fiber meals at least 3–4 hours before prolonged or intense activity.

Timing your sports nutrition

If you're an athlete, eat fiber strategically—away from training windows and around rest days to ensure optimum nutritional benefit without compromising performance. Immediately before a race or workout, foods made up of simple sugars will give you the energy you need with minimal bloating or discomfort.

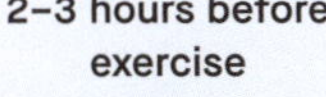

2–3 hours before exercise

Aim to begin exercise well-hydrated. Fluid needs depend on body size, sweat rate, and training conditions.

Eat a balanced meal that includes slower-releasing carbohydrates (page 12) for sustained energy and moderate amounts of fiber. If you're prone to gastrointestinal discomfort during exercise, choose lower-fiber options (page 23), reserving higher-fiber foods for after training or on rest days.

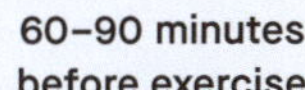

60–90 minutes before exercise

Sports drinks provide quick-release carbohydrates and hydration to support energy needed for exercise.

Choose low-fiber, quick-release carbohydrate foods (page 23). These foods and drinks are easy to digest and low in fiber, reducing some risk of bloating or discomfort during training.

Can fiber help relieve symptoms of menopause?

All women born with ovaries will experience menopause. Despite that certainty, the term itself was coined only in 1821—by French physician Charles de Gardanne. Then, it wasn't until the mid-20th century that scientists began to study hormonal changes more closely—with the discovery of estrogen and the introduction of hormone replacement therapy (HRT), especially.

Large-scale research, like the Women's Health Initiative (WHI) launched in the 1990s, revealed potential risks associated with HRT, which led to a decline in prescriptions and stalled progress in menopause research for over a decade. Only in the past 10–15 years has menopause gained more serious attention. Although there is no evidence-based "menopause diet," emerging research suggests that what we eat may influence how we experience this natural transition.

Phytoestrogens and the Mediterranean diet

Diets rich in whole plant foods have consistently been linked with reduced menopause symptoms. A key area of interest is the role of phytoestrogens. These are naturally occurring plant compounds that can mimic the effect of estrogen in the body. In particular, adherence to the Mediterranean diet—which includes abundant pulses, legumes, whole grains, extra virgin olive oil, fruit, and vegetables—has been associated with better health outcomes after menopause, such as improved bone density, lower cholesterol, and reduced inflammation. A 2022 study found that women with obesity who followed a Mediterranean diet experienced fewer and less severe menopausal symptoms overall. Specifically, higher legume intake was associated with reduced physical symptoms, and extra virgin olive oil appeared to ease psychological symptoms.

Populations with higher intakes of these foods often report fewer vasomotor symptoms (those linked to the relaxation and contraction of the blood vessels, like hot flashes and night sweats). Notably, consuming two servings of soy per day may offer symptom relief. This is especially true for women who produce equol, a compound derived from the metabolism of soy isoflavones by specific intestinal bacteria. Only about 30–50% of all adults have the right gut microbes to produce equol, which may enhance the beneficial effects of soy on menopausal symptoms.

A recent cross-sectional study in Australia involving over 200 peri- and postmenopausal women found that adherence to a Mediterranean-style diet was associated with improved physical functioning, general health, and joint/muscle comfort, although it was not directly linked to symptom severity. Similarly, a systematic review of interventional studies concluded that the Mediterranean diet can help reduce blood pressure, body weight, and cholesterol levels among postmenopausal women.

While findings overall are mixed, and cultural, genetic, and lifestyle differences may also play a role, they do appear to support the growing consensus that a plant-forward, whole food–rich dietary approach, particularly one based on Mediterranean principles, may offer significant benefits during menopause, especially when rich in fiber and phytoestrogens. Diet is not a cure-all, but making fiber- and plant-focused changes can support overall health during menopause.

Soybeans for menopause

A 2025 analysis of a low-fat vegan diet with added daily soybeans showed significant reductions in the frequency and severity of hot flashes, alongside improved plant-based dietary index scores. Soybeans provide a unique mix of high-quality plant protein, soluble fiber, and isoflavones (which act as mild phytoestrogens in the body). Isoflavones can help support bone and heart health; while soy fiber can contribute to better digestion and cholesterol management, and its protein supports muscle mass as estrogen levels decline (page 32).

Fiber, gut health, and hormonal balance

Good gut health is essential not only for our overall well-being, but also for supporting hormonal (particularly estrogen) balance. In one large study of 17,000 menopausal women, those with higher intakes of fiber from fruits and vegetables, along with soy, experienced a 19% reduction in hot flashes compared to the control group. Similarly, findings from the UK Women's Cohort Study, which involved over 900 women, indicated that a gut-friendly diet rich in prebiotic fiber may help delay the onset of natural menopause.

While more robust research is needed in this area, current evidence supports the benefits of a predominantly plant-based, fiber-rich diet as a sensible and safe nutritional strategy during menopause transition. If you're experiencing troublesome symptoms, it's always advisable to speak with a health care professional for a personalized plan.

Those with higher intakes of fiber from fruits and vegetables, along with soy, experienced a 19% reduction in hot flashes.

Top 10 fiber-rich phytoestrogen foods

Many fiber-rich foods are also top-notch sources of phytoestrogen. Among them are:

1. Soybeans (and their products, including tempeh, tofu, miso, and edamame)

2. Flaxseeds

3. Sesame seeds

4. Lentils

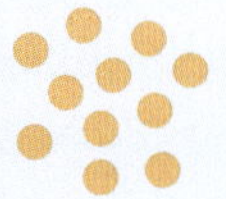

5. Chickpeas

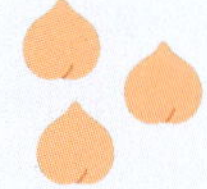

6. Chia seeds

7. Rye

8. Barley

9. Oats

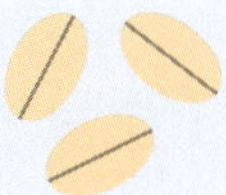

10. Nuts (especially cashews, pistachios, and almonds)

Can fiber make me look and feel younger?

From collagen powders claiming to smooth wrinkles, to omega-3s touted for skin elasticity, and vitamins A and C praised for repair and radiance, the search for the nutritional fountain of youth grows ever wider. Aging well is big business. But, beyond the hype, what does science actually tell us about the relationship between diet and aging? Two main markers—skin health and bone health—are good ways to see whether eating more fiber can help us look and feel younger.

Examining the science

The skin's microbiome (the "skin flora") consists of about 1,000 diverse microorganisms that primarily inhabit the outer layers of the epidermis and the upper portions of hair follicles. This complex community is critical in maintaining skin health by providing a barrier against harmful pathogens and by modulating the immune system. A balanced microbiome helps protect the skin and supports its structural and functional integrity.

While some research has explored the link between individual micronutrient deficiencies and skin function, there is limited clinical evidence to support any notion that specific foods or dietary patterns lead to optimal skin health. However, populations with higher intakes of plant-based foods have been found to experience less photoaging (skin damage caused by persistent sun exposure) compared with those consuming a typical Western diet rich in red and processed meats, full-fat dairy, refined carbohydrates, and sugary drinks.

The Gut–Skin axis

On pages 24–25 we introduced the idea of the Gut–Brain axis—well, there is a Gut–Skin axis, too. Emerging research suggests that Western-style diets may disrupt the gut microbiome, which can lead to systemic inflammation in the body. This includes compromising skin quality—manifested as reduced elasticity and firmness, and uneven pigmentation. In contrast, plant-based diets, rich in fiber, polyphenols, and antioxidants, have been shown to support a diverse gut microbiome and may positively affect skin appearance and function.

Fiber and the skin

One observational study found that for every 5g increase in daily fiber intake, patients undergoing immunotherapy for melanoma (cancer of the skin) experienced a 30% lower risk of disease progression or death. This could suggest that fiber may enhance treatment outcomes through immune modulation and by reinforcing the links between the Gut–Skin axis and immunity. Supporting this notion, animal research has shown that the process of gut microbes fermenting dietary fiber to produce short-chain fatty acids (SCFAs; page 11) enhances skin-barrier function (such as improving the activity of keratinocytes, cells in the skin's dermis, which form part of the immune system), and reduces allergic skin inflammation. It stands to reason, then, that there is potential for fiber to play a protective role in maintaining skin integrity.

Additionally, data from the Nurses' Health Study (conducted in the US looking at data over a 22-year period from 1984 to 2016 and published in 2025), linked higher midlife intake of fiber and high-quality carbohydrates with up to a 37% increased likelihood of healthy aging—further suggesting that fiber intake may influence skin-cell aging and resilience over time.

While direct research on fiber specifically impacting skin-age markers remains limited, mounting evidence supports its role in improving skin-related health through immune support, enhanced skin-barrier integrity, and systemic aging pathways. These findings point toward fiber as a subtle but powerful ally in maintaining skin vitality as we age.

Fiber and the bones

As we get older our bones become more brittle, our joints more stiff, and the ligaments that hold everything together more loose. But there is plenty we can do to preserve the integrity of our bones and joints into old age. In fact, some studies suggest that dietary fiber may play a protective role in joint health. As we already know short-chain fatty acids (SCFAs), which are the direct result of the fermentation of fiber in the gut (page 11), have anti-inflammatory properties that can help reduce systemic inflammation—a key factor in age-related joint degeneration. One large cohort study found that individuals with higher fiber intake had a significantly lower risk of developing symptomatic knee osteoarthritis. Finally, as we know, fiber plays a significant role in weight management (page 40). Reducing the strain on weight-bearing joints may help regulate immune responses implicated in autoimmune conditions such as rheumatoid arthritis.

Data from the Nurses' Health Study... linked higher midlife intake of fiber and high-quality carbohydrates with up to a 37% increased likelihood of healthy aging.

Keeping your chromosomes young

An exciting recent research analysis of more than 5,600 adults in the US showed that, for every 10g increase in fiber per 1,000 calories, telomeres (the protein caps at the ends of chromosomes) were on average 83 base pairs longer. As each year of chronological age equates to about 15½ fewer base pairs, this means that biological aging slowed by around five years. The study controlled for variables including smoking, body mass index, alcohol use, and physical activity, suggesting a meaningful link between more fiber and preserved cellular youth.

1. Young and healthy

Telomeres are long and protective, safeguarding chromosomes from damage and keeping cells youthful.

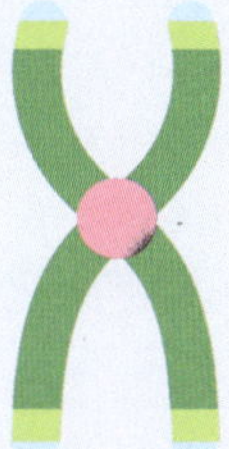

2. Early adulthood

Each cell division shortens the telomeres slightly, a natural part of aging. But axtioxidants and a high-fiber diet help slow the process.

3. Midlife

Shorter telomeres make DNA more vulnerable, increasing oxidative stress and reducing the cell's ability to repair itself.

4. Older age

Critically short telomeres trigger cell aging and dysfunction, contributing to inflammation, slower regeneration, and age-related disease.

Can fiber manage my diabetes?

An estimated 537 million adults worldwide are currently living with diabetes. Around 90–95% of these cases are of Type-2 diabetes, which is often linked to diet and lifestyle. In other words, a significant number of diabetes' patients have a disease that is manageable with the right nutritional and lifestyle advice.

In the UK, 3.9 million people have been formally diagnosed with diabetes. However, estimates that include undiagnosed cases push that figure upward to more than 4.8 million. If current trends continue, every year will see another half a million people on the diabetes spectrum. If Type-2 diabetes accounts for around 90% of the UK's cases (reflecting the global picture), Type 1 makes up about 8%, and rarer forms the remaining 2%. In the US, 29.7 million people have been diagnosed with diabetes (all types)—again with the breakdown reflecting the global picture that around 90% are Type 2. Understanding the role of diet, and particularly the role of dietary fiber, is crucial in both the prevention and management of this condition.

Types of diabetes

Type-1 diabetes is an autoimmune condition, where the body's immune system mistakenly attacks insulin-producing cells in the pancreas. This means it cannot be prevented or managed through lifestyle changes alone. Type-2 diabetes, on the other hand, is a chronic condition where the body *becomes resistant* to insulin or the pancreas doesn't produce enough of it. As a result, glucose from the carbohydrates we eat cannot be moved out of the bloodstream and into the body's cells for energy effectively. The pancreas tries to compensate for this by producing more insulin. Over time the response becomes less successful and blood-glucose levels remain too high.

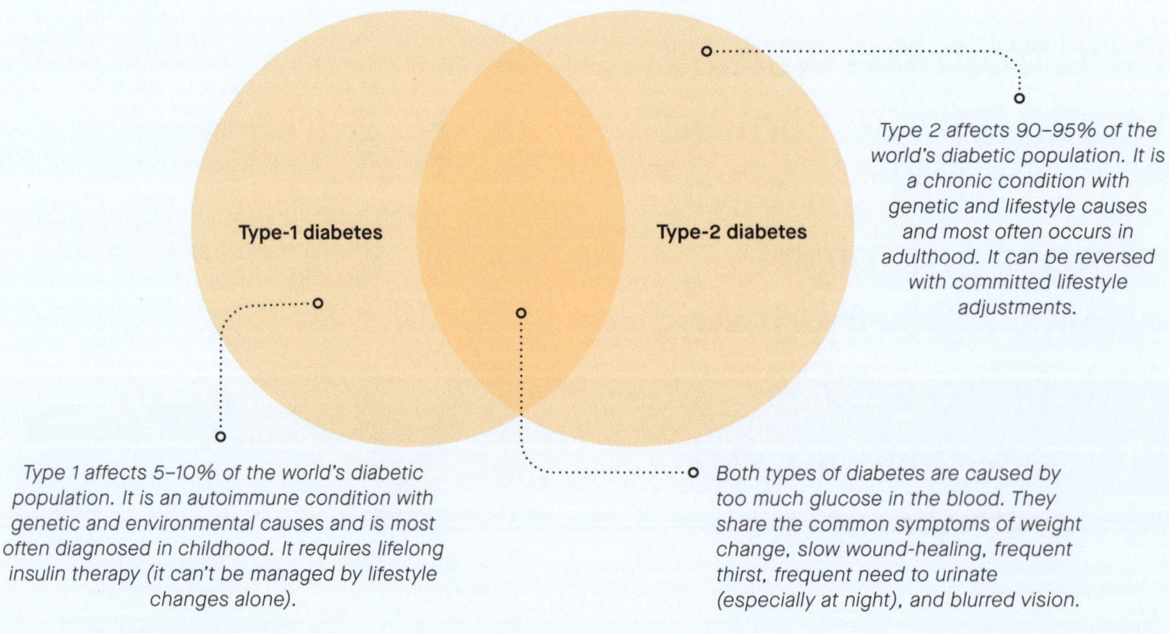

Type 2 affects 90–95% of the world's diabetic population. It is a chronic condition with genetic and lifestyle causes and most often occurs in adulthood. It can be reversed with committed lifestyle adjustments.

Type 1 affects 5–10% of the world's diabetic population. It is an autoimmune condition with genetic and environmental causes and is most often diagnosed in childhood. It requires lifelong insulin therapy (it can't be managed by lifestyle changes alone).

Both types of diabetes are caused by too much glucose in the blood. They share the common symptoms of weight change, slow wound-healing, frequent thirst, frequent need to urinate (especially at night), and blurred vision.

Fiber for blood-sugar stability

Historically, those with Type-2 diabetes have been advised to adopt a low-carbohydrate diet. However, newer evidence suggests that, in fact, higher-carbohydrate diets are more effective, because the stress of restrictive eating and frequent weight cycling leads to poorer metabolic outcomes, including impaired glucose uptake, increased liver fat, and reduced insulin secretion. Instead of eliminating carbohydrates, then, a balanced diet that includes high-fiber, nutrient-dense carbohydrates (page 40) may lead to improved outcomes. These foods are rich in phytonutrients and have a lower glycemic index, meaning they produce a slower, more stable rise in blood glucose. Furthermore, fiber slows gastric emptying and glucose absorption, reducing post-meal blood-sugar spikes. Finally, high-fiber diets are associated with improved insulin sensitivity, lower fasting glucose levels, and reduced risk of even developing Type-2 diabetes. Overall, for individuals living with diabetes, increasing daily fiber intake to between 25g and 35g may support better blood-sugar control and long-term metabolic health.

Diabetes and the gut

Research underscores the pivotal role of the gut microbiome in regulating metabolic health and blood-glucose control. As we know, a fiber-rich diet increases levels of short-chain fatty acids (SCFAs). These strengthen the intestinal lining, reduce inflammation, and improve insulin sensitivity, changes associated with enhanced glucose metabolism and reduced insulin resistance. By nurturing a more diverse and stable gut microbiota, dietary fiber may act as a natural modulator of metabolic function.

Recent science

A 2023 randomized, placebo-controlled trial found that a prebiotic, fiber-enriched nutritional formula significantly improved both HbA1c (a key marker of blood-sugar control) and quality of life in individuals with Type-2 diabetes, also promoting growth of beneficial SCFA-producing gut bacteria. In a 24-week pilot trial, consuming 20g of a diverse prebiotic fiber supplement each day led to a modest but statistically significant reduction in HbA1c among pre-diabetic adults with baseline HbA1c under 6%. Large cohort data from the Melbourne Collaborative Cohort Study (2023) revealed a 25% lower incidence of Type-2 diabetes among participants with higher cereal fiber intake (although this effect appeared to be partly mediated by body mass index). Furthermore, a 2024 meta-analysis highlighted

For individuals living with diabetes, increasing daily fiber intake to between 25g and 35g may support better blood-sugar control and long-term metabolic health.

that fiber intake measurably improved glycemic control in individuals with Type-2 diabetes. These findings suggest that integrating high-fiber foods and prebiotic supplements can support blood-sugar regulation, enhance insulin sensitivity, and protect against diabetes.

So, while diabetes remains a growing global challenge, the evidence is clear: increasing fiber intake is one of the most effective, accessible, and empowering dietary strategies we have to support blood-sugar control and enhance quality of life for those with diabetes.

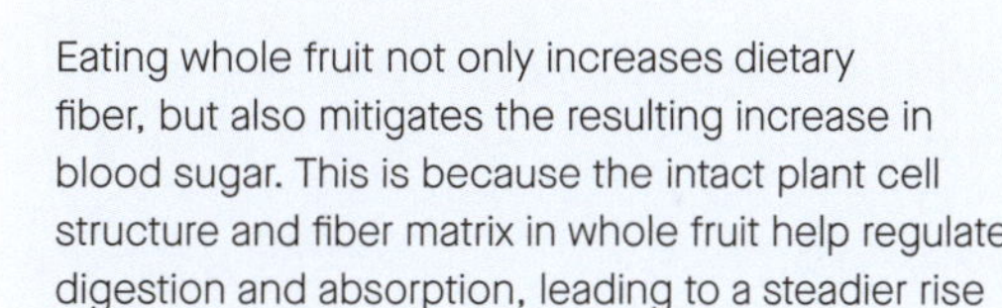

Eat the whole fruit

Eating whole fruit not only increases dietary fiber, but also mitigates the resulting increase in blood sugar. This is because the intact plant cell structure and fiber matrix in whole fruit help regulate digestion and absorption, leading to a steadier rise in blood glucose.

Eating 6 medium oranges = 12–15g of dietary fiber

150ml fresh orange juice from 6 medium oranges = 1g of dietary fiber

Can fiber help flush out plastics and heavy metals?

Environmental toxins, such as plastics and heavy metals, pose a growing concern for health. They are substances (natural and synthetic) in our air, water, soil, and food. Plastics can take anywhere from 20 to over 500 years to degrade, but even then they don't disappear—they break down into microplastics, which enter the food chain and so our body. While not a concern for most of us, research suggests that heavy metals (lead, mercury, and so on) may disrupt the balance of the gut microbiome. Amazingly, though, fiber is emerging as a way the body could tackle both.

The plastics problem

The rate at which plastic decomposes depends on the type, environmental conditions, and how it is discarded.

Microplastics are found in food packaging, clothing fibers, personal care products, and household items, meaning they can easily end up in the air we breathe and the food and drink we consume. Unsurprisingly, microplastics have now been detected in everything from bottled water and table salt to household dust.

Estimates suggest that the average adult may ingest between 39,000 and 52,000 microplastic particles each year. These figures seem alarming enough, but gaps in current testing methods suggest that our actual exposure is (worryingly) likely to be far greater.

Where do dietary plastics come from?

Everyday sources of dietary plastics include food packaging, plastic wrap, tea bags, plastic-lined coffee cups, and reheating leftovers in plastic containers. But before panic sets in, this doesn't mean you need to throw out all the plastic boxes you own. It's more about being aware of where exposures come from and making small, achievable swaps where possible, like reducing single-use plastics or choosing glass or stainless steel for hot-food storage.

Heating food in plastic containers can cause harmful chemicals such as bisphenol A (BPA) and phthalates to leach into the food, especially when the plastic is not labeled as microwave-safe. These chemicals are known endocrine disruptors, meaning they can interfere with hormone function and have been linked to reproductive and metabolic health issues. Repeated heating may increase the risk of exposure over time, especially when using old plastic containers, where tiny flakes of the container walls can find their way into the food inside.

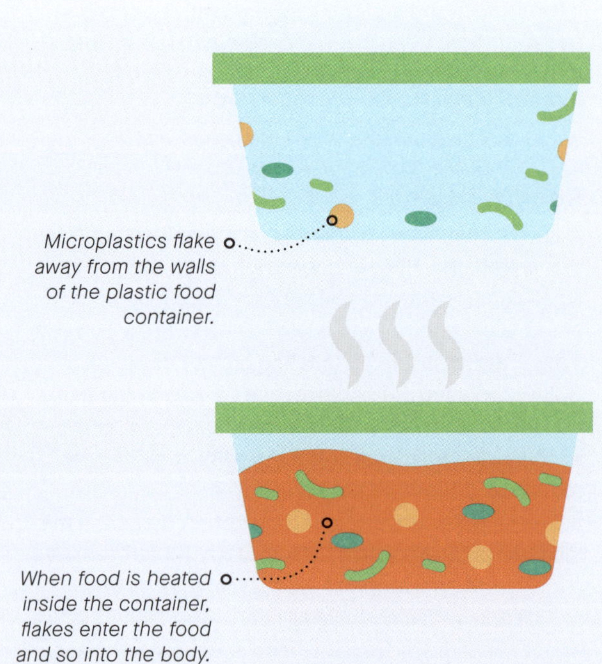

Microplastics flake away from the walls of the plastic food container.

When food is heated inside the container, flakes enter the food and so into the body.

What happens to microplastics in the gut?

Recent studies show that, once ingested, microplastics don't just remain in the gut: they can cross biological barriers in the body. They have been detected in the bloodstream, lung tissue, placenta (of pregnant women), breast milk, and even brain.

Alarmingly, one 2024 study estimated that in individuals with prolonged high exposure, brain tissue could contain up to 0.5% plastic by weight. While this area of research is still evolving, it raises important questions about how microplastics interact with the body and what steps we can take to reduce their accumulation.

What's the fiber solution for plastics?

Incredibly, emerging research suggests that our dietary fiber intake may offer a surprising line of defense against these marauding microplastics. A review conducted in 2024 explored how different types of dietary fiber, particularly soluble fibers, such as beta-glucan and pectin (page 43), may help limit microplastic accumulation in the body.

One proposed mechanism for this, demonstrated by animal and cell models, is that dietary fiber may reduce the transportation of plastic particles across the gut barrier and into blood and lymph circulation. The theory is that soluble fiber forms a thick, gel-like matrix in the gut, creating a viscous environment that helps trap unwanted substances, such as bile acids and toxins—but also potentially microplastics. The trapped particles then move through the digestive system so that we excrete them via the stool. In other words, they are prevented from crossing into the bloodstream or lymphatic system. Some early human research along these lines is beginning to show promise—with studies suggesting that high-fiber diets may lower levels of plastic-associated chemicals in blood and urine. While these studies are still limited in scale and are in their infancy—we still need much more research to be sure—the potential is significant.

The problem with heavy metals

Heavy metals such as mercury, cadmium, arsenic, and lead occur naturally in the environment but have become more widespread through industrial pollution, and contaminated water and soil. These metals can accumulate in plants, fish, and animal products—and that means that our diet is often our main source of exposure to them. As alarming as this might sound, in most developed countries overall exposure is generally low, and well below safety thresholds. However, in some parts of the world where soil or water contamination is higher, levels can be slightly more concerning.

What happens to heavy metals in the gut?

Once inside the body, heavy metals are not easily broken down or excreted. Over time, they can build up in the body's tissue and may begin to have adverse effects on our organs, such as the liver, kidneys, and brain. More recently, research has shown that they may also disrupt the gut microbiota (the community of microbes that support digestion), immunity, and metabolic health. High exposure to certain metals has been linked with changes in the diversity and function of gut bacteria, increased inflammation, and damage to the intestinal barrier that acts to regulate what passes from the gut into the bloodstream and helps protect the body from toxins and pathogens.

What's the fiber solution for heavy metals?

Recent studies have suggested that people who consume more dietary fiber tend to have lower blood concentrations of heavy metals. Certain fibers—especially soluble types such as pectin, beta-glucan, and resistant starch—can bind to heavy metals in the gut, reducing how much heavy metal is absorbed into the bloodstream and promoting its removal through the stool. Fiber may also help by supporting a more resilient gut microbiota, counteracting some of the damage heavy metals cause to intestinal cells and beneficial bacteria. However, as with plastics, this research is very much still in its infancy and we need to know a lot more before we can confirm how different fiber types influence heavy-metal absorption in humans. Nonetheless, it raises an exciting possibility that a diet rich in varied fiber sources could help the body defend itself not just against toxins from food, but from the environment too.

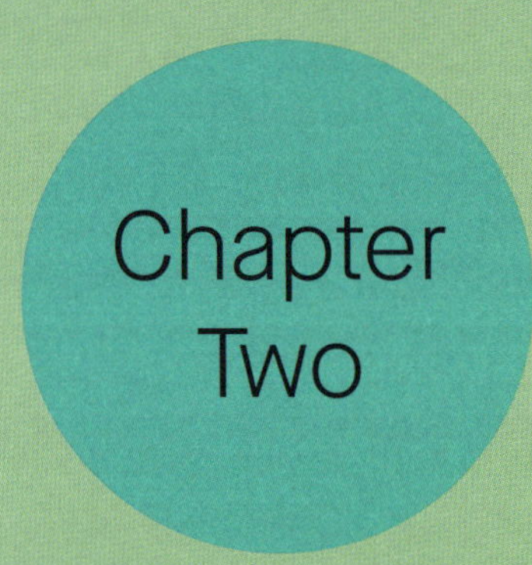

The
30:30:30

The 30:30:30 Fiber Formula is a simple yet transformative framework that brings together three evidence-based habits to nourish the body and support a healthy gut: 30 different plants a week, 30 chews per mouthful, and 30g of fiber a day.

Research shows that eating around 30 different plant foods each week—from fruits, vegetables, and grains to nuts, seeds, and herbs—supports a more diverse gut microbiome. This diversity is linked to better digestion, stronger immunity, and even long-term protection against chronic disease. Variety, not perfection, is what matters most. Then, taking the time to chew each mouthful—around 30 times—aids digestion, enhances satiety, and reduces bloating. Finally, the goal of 30g of fiber remains the benchmark for optimal gut and digestive health.

This chapter provides the practical advice you need—whatever your lifestyle or health goals—to put the 30:30:30 Fiber Formula into practice.

fiber formula

The 30:30:30 formula

The 30:30:30 formula is a simple yet powerful way to structure eating habits for long-term health. The aim is for 30g of fiber per day, 30 different plant foods each week, and 30 chews per mouthful.

Each "30" is backed by research, and together they offer a practical framework for supporting gut health, weight management, and overall well-being.

Taken together, the 30:30:30 formula empowers individuals with a framework that is evidence-based, practical, and flexible. It is not a diet of restriction, but a lifestyle approach that celebrates variety, balance, and awareness of key nutritional and dietary needs.

30 grams of fiber per day

Despite being one of the strongest dietary predictors of good health, fiber remains the most underconsumed nutrient globally, with average intakes in the UK, US, and elsewhere falling far short of recommendations (page 18–19). A large 2019 meta-analysis in *The Lancet* found that consuming 25–30g of fiber daily was associated with reductions in cardiovascular disease, Type-2 diabetes, colorectal cancer, and overall mortality. Importantly, different types of fiber play distinct roles: soluble fibers (like oats, beans, and psyllium) improve blood-glucose control and cholesterol, while insoluble fibers (whole grains, vegetables, and nuts) promote regular bowel movements and support gut motility. Emerging studies also highlight the importance of fermentable fibers (inulin, resistant starch), which feed beneficial gut microbes, producing short-chain fatty acids, such as butyrate. These, in turn, strengthen the gut barrier and reduce inflammation (page 13).

30 plant foods per week

The idea of eating 30 different plants weekly comes from the American Gut Project, one of the largest microbiome studies to date. This research has shown that dietary diversity (rather than just the total amount of fiber we consume) is strongly linked to a healthier gut microbiome. As we've seen, plants in this context include fruits, vegetables, herbs, spices, legumes, nuts, seeds, and whole grains, each offering a unique make-up of fiber and phytochemicals in their different forms. Recent reviews have shown that people who consume a more diverse range of plants have greater microbial diversity, which in turn supports immune function, metabolic health, and even mental well-being through the Gut–Brain axis (page 27). Practically, this could mean adding another type of fruit to your snack list, adding chickpeas to a salad, or sprinkling seeds over breakfast oatmeal, which are all small changes that contribute to that weekly plant tally.

The 30:30:30 formula empowers individuals with a framework that is evidence-based, practical, and flexible.

30 chews per bite

Mindful eating is increasingly recognized as a tool for improving digestion and regulating appetite. Studies suggest that chewing each bite around 30 times slows eating speed, enhances satiety signals, and reduces overall food intake without feelings of deprivation. It also encourages us to engage all five senses (taste, smell, sight, touch, and even hearing) to fully appreciate our food. Mechanistically, thorough chewing helps break food down into smaller particles, making nutrients more accessible for digestion, while also allowing gut hormones, such as GLP-1 (page 42) and others, to signal fullness more effectively. Beyond physiology, chewing slowly creates space to connect with the eating experience improving satisfaction, reducing mindless snacking, and helping reestablish healthier relationships with food.

Bonus 30: 30-minute meals

The idea that meals should take no more than 30 minutes to prepare gives a bonus boost to the other 30s.

Studies consistently highlight time as one of the biggest barriers to healthy eating. By focusing on quick, whole-food meals, such as stir-fries, grain bowls, or hearty salads, it becomes easier to integrate fiber-rich, plant-diverse foods into daily life without the overwhelming task of lengthy cooking. When you're planning your meals for the week, try to choose those that are quick and easy.

The recipes in this book primarily concentrate on nutritional content over cooking time (although, of course, the faster you chop, the quicker the recipes will be, and there are plenty of options that anyway fall within 30 minutes). However, to get you started with looking for clever hacks and time-savers, while still boosting fiber, I have also included a recipe section dedicated to "Bonus 30" meals (pages 134–153). As you get used to incorporating more fiber into your diet, and it becomes habit, you can start to find other exciting ways to keep the cooking time down while pushing the fiber content up!

Favorite speedy recipes

- Green lima bean mac and fiber cheese (page 137)
- Harissa-spiced hispi wedges with date and almond tabbouleh and mint yogurt (page 141)
- Persian herb and grain stewed lentils and caramelized onions (page 153)

How much fiber is in my food?

The rise of ultra-processed and convenience foods has led to a decline in home cooking, particularly in Western countries like the UK and the US. As a result, in some places average fiber intake has dropped to around 18–19g per day, well below the recommended 30g for optimal health.

As we've learned, fiber is typically found in the more wholesome parts of our diets—fruits, vegetables, grains, pulses, legumes, and whole grains—but it can also be surprisingly present in foods like dark chocolate, popcorn, and coconut chips.

This book features 60 delicious recipes, each containing at least 8g of fiber per serving, making it easier for you to reach your 30g-a-day target—all while celebrating variety, flavor, and nourishment by enjoying 30 different plant foods per week. However, knowing where to find other fiber-rich foods will help you integrate more fiber into your everyday life in ways beyond the recipes themselves. Once finding the fiber superheroes becomes a habit—once you're simply pulling them instinctively from the shelves during your weekly shopping trip—hitting your 30g target is going to be easier than ever. Over the following pages, we'll look at some general know-how on recommended intakes by age, how to pick the best loaf of bread, and how to be gentle on your gut as you increase your fiber intake. We'll also provide the key to your fiber fix: the tables showing which foods are most fiber-rich.

Once finding the fiber superheroes becomes a habit ... hitting your 30g target is going to be easier than ever.

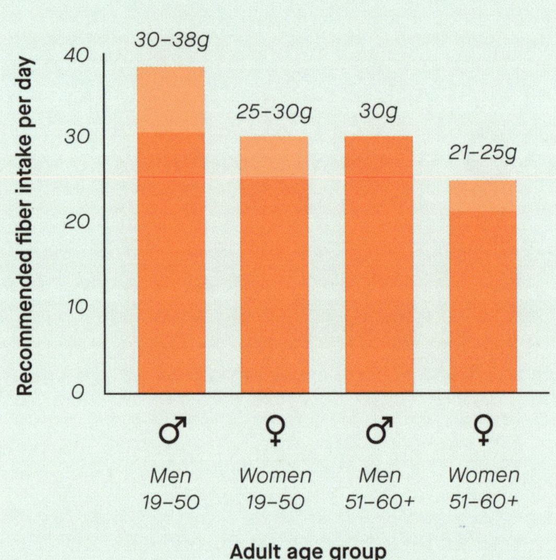

Daily fiber recommendations by age

The daily fiber needs for males and females at around age 18 is about 30g and 25g respectively (page 76). But changing fiber needs doesn't stop there. This table shows the recommended daily fiber intake for adults from the age of 19 onward.

Note that while we can talk in averages, men and women have different needs throughout their lives, and individual needs will vary from person to person. In older age, fiber needs tail off as our metabolism slows down.

Adjusting to more fiber

Increasing the variety of plant-based foods in your diet naturally boosts your fiber intake. While this is beneficial for long-term gut health, a sudden increase can lead to temporary digestive symptoms such as gas, bloating, diarrhea, or constipation. To help your body adjust more comfortably, bear in mind the following tips.

 **Sit tall and chew thoroughly** Good eating posture supports the natural flow of digestion. Chewing well ensures food reaches your stomach in a form that's easier to process.

 **Keep your body active** Gentle movement, such as stretching or yoga, can stimulate digestion and help reduce bloating or discomfort.

 **Take it slowly** Introduce new plant foods one at a time. Give your digestive system time to adapt before adding another.

 **Stay well hydrated** Drinking fluids is essential for helping fiber move smoothly through the digestive tract, and for supporting digestion (page 75).

The best loaf

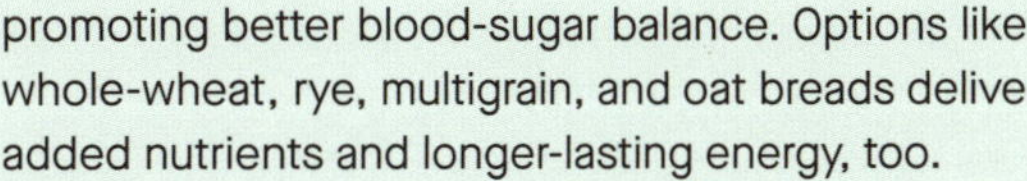

Breads made with whole grains, seeds, or oats offer significant fiber advantages over loaves of white bread. They can aid digestion and support heart health, while promoting better blood-sugar balance. Options like whole-wheat, rye, multigrain, and oat breads deliver added nutrients and longer-lasting energy, too.

 **White** Containing minimal fiber (around 2.7g per 100g), white bread falls short of being a fiber source.

 **Whole-grain and high-fiber white** Providing around 6–7g fiber per 100g, whole-wheat and high-fiber white are a fiber source in public-health guidelines.

 **Multigrain or seeded** These loaves often offer the highest fiber levels (up to about 10g), depending on the added seeds and grains. **Chia seeds** are standout—they are one of the highest fiber sources known, offering around 34g per 100g. **Other nuts and seeds**, such as almonds, pumpkin, and sunflower (all great bread toppings) provide moderate fiber and essential nutrients, even if servings are small.

 **Rye** Containing about 6g fiber per 100g, often has a lower glycemic response (the rate at which it releases sugar into the bloodstream) than other breads, making it a good option.

 **Sourdough** Made with whole-wheat flour, sourdough offers similar fiber to whole-wheat (about 6g per 100g), while white sourdough provides only about 3g. Both forms offer fermentation-related gut benefits (page 29).

 **Oat bread** Made with oats or a mixture of oats and whole-wheat flour, oat bread offers around 5–6g fiber per 100g. The oats' soluble fiber (beta-glucan; see page 39) can help support heart health and steady blood-sugar levels. They give a moist texture and a slightly nutty flavor.

The fiber tables

The following tables are organized from most fiber-rich to least—according to food group and then each food itself. Everything is measured to 100g so that you can instantly compare which foods can boost the fiber content in your diet and which might be best left on the shelf.

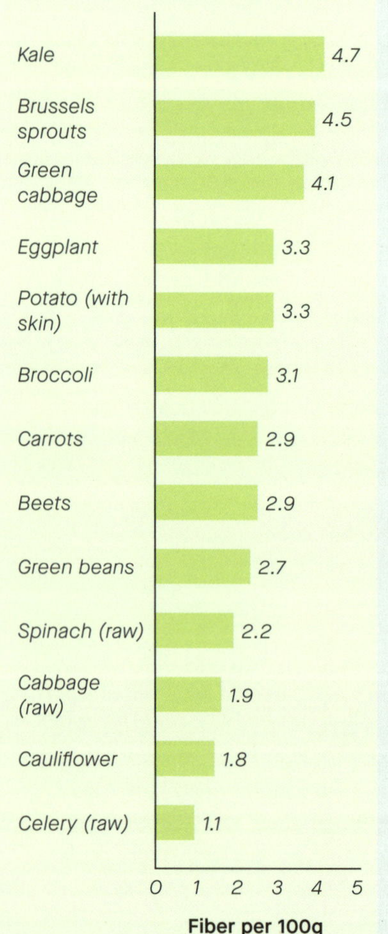

Fiber in vegetables

(per 100g; about 1 cup cooked veggies or 1½ cups raw)

	Fiber per 100g
Kale	4.7
Brussels sprouts	4.5
Green cabbage	4.1
Eggplant	3.3
Potato (with skin)	3.3
Broccoli	3.1
Carrots	2.9
Beets	2.9
Green beans	2.7
Spinach (raw)	2.2
Cabbage (raw)	1.9
Cauliflower	1.8
Celery (raw)	1.1

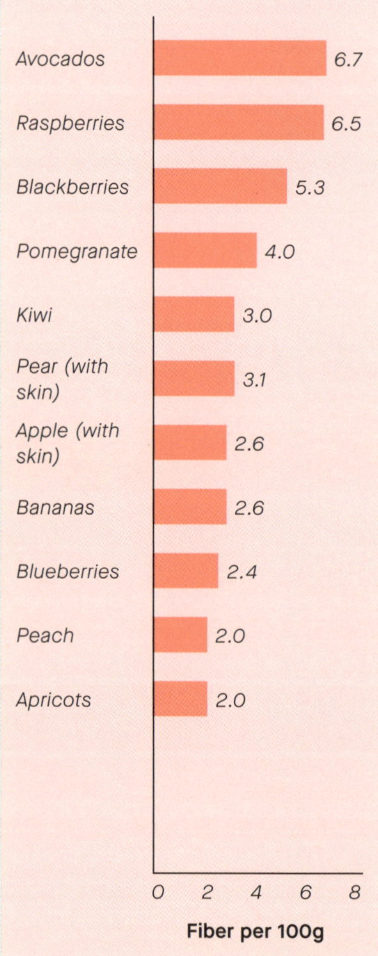

Fiber in fruit

(per 100g; about ¾–1 cup fruit)

	Fiber per 100g
Avocados	6.7
Raspberries	6.5
Blackberries	5.3
Pomegranate	4.0
Kiwi	3.0
Pear (with skin)	3.1
Apple (with skin)	2.6
Bananas	2.6
Blueberries	2.4
Peach	2.0
Apricots	2.0

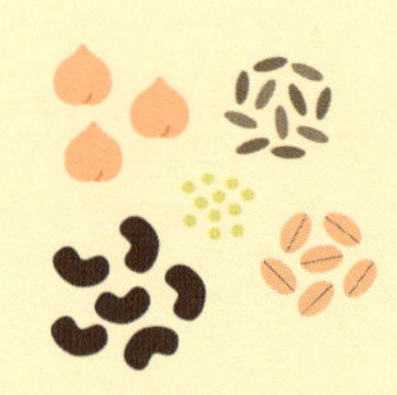

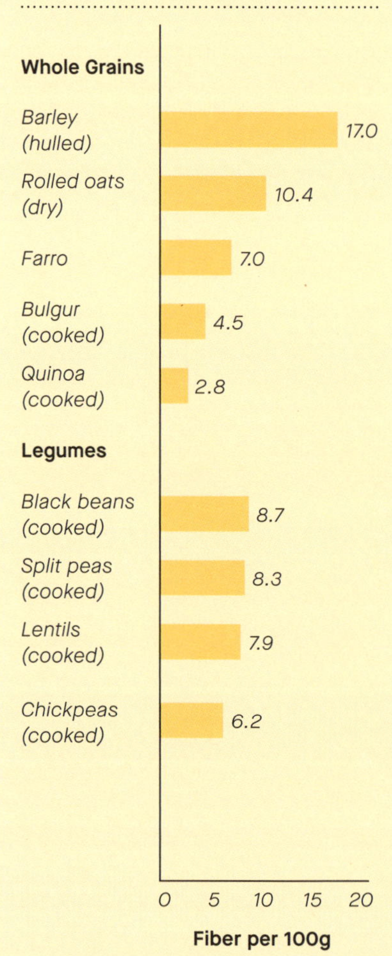

Fiber in whole grains and legumes (per 100g; about ½ cup cooked grains)

Whole Grains

	Fiber per 100g
Barley (hulled)	17.0
Rolled oats (dry)	10.4
Farro	7.0
Bulgur (cooked)	4.5
Quinoa (cooked)	2.8

Legumes

	Fiber per 100g
Black beans (cooked)	8.7
Split peas (cooked)	8.3
Lentils (cooked)	7.9
Chickpeas (cooked)	6.2

Fiber in nuts and seeds

(per 100g; about ½–¾ cup nuts and seeds)

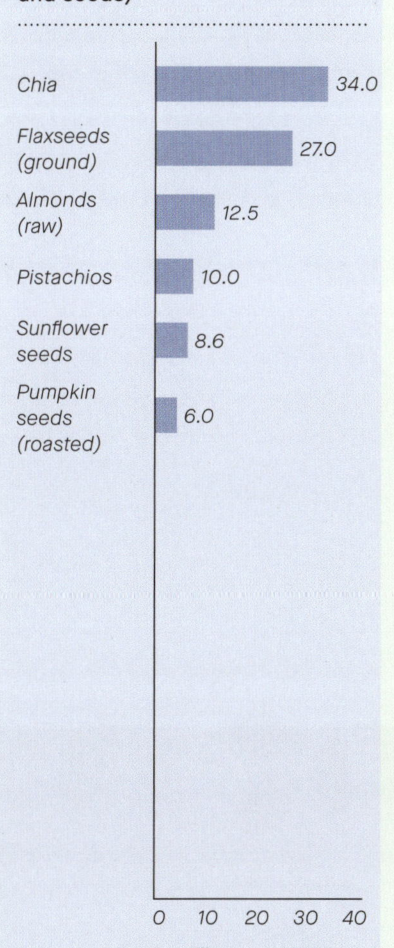

Fiber in bread

(per 100g; about 3 slices)

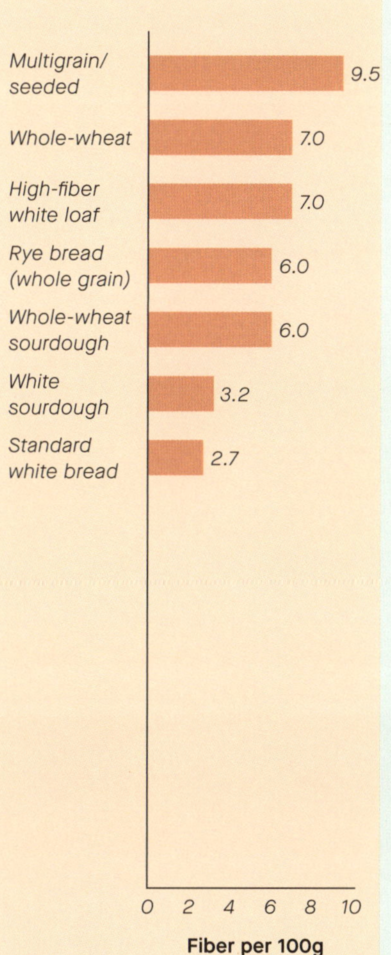

Fiber surprises

(per 100g)

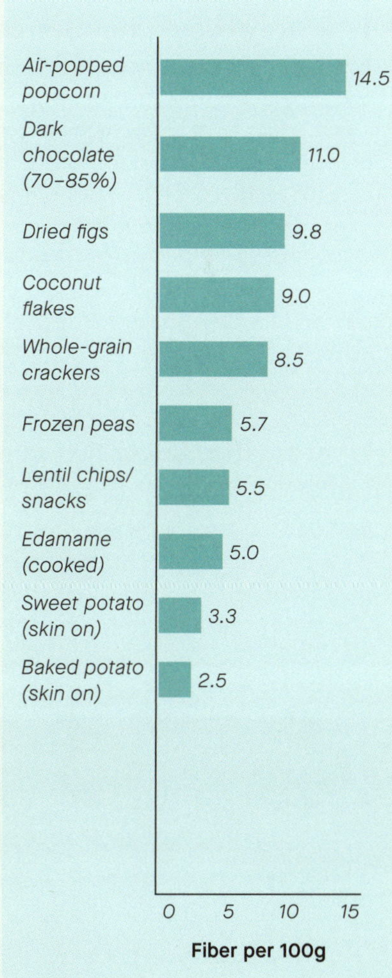

How do I hit 30 plants a week?

I often share the 30:30:30 approach in clinical practice and professional work as a simple yet effective way to make a concerted effort to enhance gut health and improve fiber intake. At first people wonder how on earth they may reach the target of 30 different plants in just one week, but—with a few tips, techniques, and know-how—it's easier than you may think.

Over the following pages, I've highlighted the practical techniques you can use to hit your 30-a-week target not just easily and with lots of flavor, but with positivity—and hopefully even joy! First, though, the answer to a question that my clients so frequently ask me ...

Why 30-a-week, not 5-a-day?

Five-a-day campaigns focus solely on our intake of fruit and vegetables. The 30-a-week system focuses on "plant points" that highlight the importance of the range of plant-based foods you're eating, rather than just the number. In this context, a "plant" refers to any food grown from the ground, not just fruits and vegetables.

In other words, it includes whole grains, legumes (like beans and pulses), nuts, seeds, herbs, and spices too.

Why is this important? Your gut microbiome is home to trillions of bacteria that thrive on different plant compounds. By consuming a wide variety of plant-based foods, you help cultivate a rich and diverse microbial ecosystem—your "gut garden."

Research from the American Gut Project shows that people who eat 30 or more different types of plant foods per week have a significantly more diverse gut microbiome than those who eat 10 or fewer.

Scoring plant points

One of the best ways to ensure you're getting a broad range of plant-based foods is to count plant points. Every distinct type of plant you consume earns a point (this isn't related to the amount you eat, but rather the variety of the foods you're eating), making it easier and more engaging to track variety in your diet.

A useful tool for this is the "Super Six"—six core plant food groups that all contribute to your plant-point total (see panel, below).

What are the "Super Six" core plant foods?

Incorporating a mixture of these food groups into your diet throughout the week helps you reach the 30-plant-point goal to support a healthier, more resilient gut.

Vegetables

Fruit

Whole grains

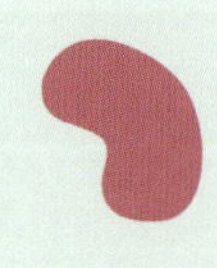

Legumes

Nuts & seeds

Herbs & spices

60 "Super Six" starter wheel

To get you started, this wheel of 60 plants provides double inspiration for how to rack up the 30 plants on your plate. The list is by no means exhaustive (the world of edible plants is vast), but it's a good starting point for readily available fiber nutrition.

Fruits
Apples, Bananas, Berries (such as blueberries or raspberries, each scoring 1 point), Grapes, Kiwi, Mango, Oranges, Pears, Pomegranate, Watermelon

Legumes (beans and pulses)
Black beans, Borlotti beans (aka Cranberry beans), Lima beans, Navy beans, Chickpeas, Lentils (red, green, Puy, etc.—each counts as one), Kidney beans, Peas (split peas, garden peas), Pinto beans, Soybeans

Vegetables
Asparagus, Beets, Broccoli, Carrot, Cauliflower, Zucchini, Bell pepper, Kale, Red cabbage, Sweet potato

Whole grains
Barley, Brown rice, Buckwheat, Bulgur, Millet, Quinoa, Rye, Spelt, Whole oats, Whole-wheat pasta

Note: refined grains (white bread, white rice, and so on) don't count!

Nuts and seeds
Almonds, Brazil nuts, Chia seeds, Flaxseeds, Hazelnuts, Pistachios, Pumpkin seeds, Sesame seeds, Sunflower seeds, Walnuts

Note: Nut butters count if made from the whole nut (that is, 1 portion of whole-almond butter = 1 almond point).

Herbs and spices
Basil, Cinnamon, Coriander/cilantro, Cumin, Ginger, Oregano, Mint, Parsley, Rosemary, Turmeric

Note: Fresh and dried forms of herbs and spices count, but each herb or spice counts only for ¼ point—so you need to add up 4 different herbs or spices in your food to make 1 point (page 83).

Making room for more plants: simple, supportive tips

Adding more plant-based foods to your meals doesn't have to be complicated. With a few gentle changes and a bit of curiosity, you'll soon find yourself naturally enjoying a more colorful, fiber-rich plate. Start slow, be kind to your body, and remember: every plant counts.

Fill your plate with color and variety

Aim to fill half your plate with vegetables whenever you can. Choose a mixture of colors—each color brings different flavors and nutrients. Try snacking on a rainbow of raw vegetables—add hummus, guacamole, or fresh salsa to put even more variety in your week.

Rethink the role of meat

You don't have to cut out meat entirely, but think of it as a side or garnish rather than the main focus of the meal. This simple shift makes more room on the plate for plant foods, and so those all-important plant points.

Choose high-fiber foods with heart-healthy fats

Healthy fats from plants are a wonderful addition to your diet. Olives, avocados, nuts, seeds, and nut butters offer flavor, satiety, and nourishment all in one.

Try a meat-free meal each week

Pick one night a week to go vegetarian—build your meals around fiber-rich beans, lentils, whole grains, and greens. You might even discover a new favorite!

Start your day with whole grains

Breakfast is a great opportunity to include more plant-based variety. Try oatmeal, buckwheat, barley, or quinoa topped with fruit, nuts, or seeds for a delicious, filling start to the day.

Go for your greens

Leafy greens like kale, spinach, arugula, or Swiss chard are full of fiber and nutrients. Eat them raw, or when you cook them, steam, stir-fry, broil, or braise to retain their flavor and goodness. Try mixing a few different kinds into your meals throughout the week.

Build a meal around a salad

A large bowl of leafy greens can be the foundation of a satisfying and nourishing meal. Add vegetables, fresh herbs, beans, lentils, tofu, tempeh, or mycoprotein to make it hearty and filling. See the salad recipes in the Lunches chapter, on pages 110–133, to help.

Enjoy whole fruit for dessert

Swap out sugary treats for nature's own sweets. A juicy peach, a slice of watermelon, or a handful of berries can make the perfect end to a meal—fresh, light, sweet (in a good way), and satisfying.

Start small, build slowly

Making changes to your diet is a journey, not a race. Begin with small, manageable steps. Try the "1-2-3" plant-based plate (below).

What is the "1-2-3" plant-based plate?

When building a meal, aim to include …

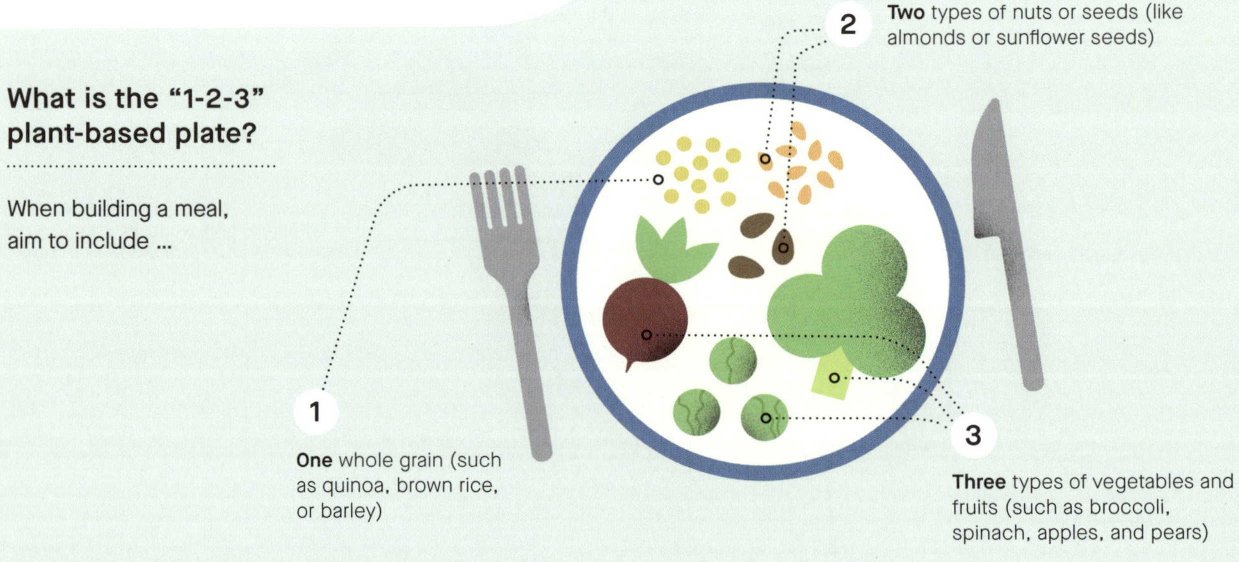

Should I use fiber supplements as a boost?

Ideally, we should get our daily fiber from whole plant foods because these foods offer not only fiber, but also essential nutrients and plant compounds that supplements simply can't provide. That said, fiber supplements can play a role for some people, particularly those with restricted diets, chronic constipation, or certain health conditions. They may also offer short-term support during times of digestive imbalance. Remember, though, they should never replace a diverse, fiber-rich diet—and they can come with side effects. Supplements can cause bloating, gas, or discomfort if introduced at high dosages too quickly, or taken without enough fluids, and they may not be suitable for everyone.

The following table highlights some of the most readily available supplements and their action on the body. Always consult your doctor or a registered dietitian before starting a fiber supplement, especially if you have digestive issues, take regular medications, or are pregnant. All supplements should be introduced gradually with plenty of water and under professional supervision. And remember—they are not a substitute for real food!

Fiber type	Study highlights (2020–2025)	Main benefits	Common drawbacks
Psyllium + pectin	>10 g/day improved stool output and frequency (RCT meta-analysis)	Constipation relief, cholesterol lowering	Gas; bloating if introduced too quickly
FOS (Inulin-type)	Improved frequency, softened stools; few side effects for most	Prebiotic, gentle laxative effect	Bloating, not ideal for IBS-sensitive guts
Acacia fiber	Helped with IBS symptoms and microbial diversity in two trials	Prebiotic effect, better tolerated than inulin	Less impact on metabolic markers
Inulin + FOS	Boosted memory and cognitive function in older adults	Brain health (potential gut–brain axis effect)	No effect on muscle strength
Oat beta-glucan	Lowered synthetic chemical levels (PFAS) in blood after 4 weeks of use in healthy adults	Detox support, cholesterol, and blood-glucose control	Early stage research; long-term effects unknown

What healthy swaps can I make?

The simplest way to approach increasing your fiber intake is to make small food swaps—replacing foods you consume every day with more fiber-rich alternatives.

If you're an omnivore, a good first step is to turn your meat-based dishes into half beans or pulses and half meat (such as on page 162). For families, there are so many amazing swaps that quickly accumulate to increase everyone's intake. The table below gives a list of everyday swaps (with added benefits) to help you work toward maxing out the fiber potential of each day.

Pasta
Swap out white for whole-wheat or legume-based pasta.
- *Adds protein with very little change in taste or texture*
- *Try the recipe on page 137*

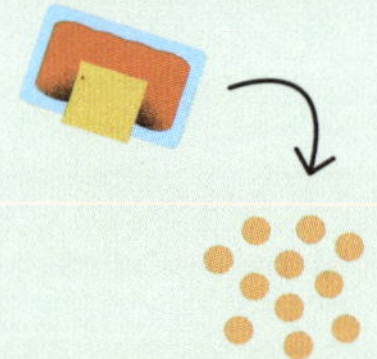

Ground meat
Swap half for lentils, grains, or beans in chili, meatballs, etc.
- *Provides plant protein while reducing saturated fat*
- *Try the recipe on page 177*

Cookies
Swap out for oat-based cookies or homemade fiber-rich alternatives.
- *Less sugar, and a slower release of energy*
- *Try the recipe on page 193*

Bread
Swap out white for whole-grain, seeded, or rye bread.
- *Doubles the fiber content; feeds your gut microbiome*
- *Try the recipe on page 173*

Rice cakes
Go for chickpea crackers or a small handful of nuts and seeds instead.
- *Boost of healthy fats, and long-lasting energy*
- *Try the recipe on page 185*

White chocolate
Swap out for dark chocolate with at least 70% cocoa solids.
- *More antioxidants; less added sugar*
- *Try the recipe on page 194*

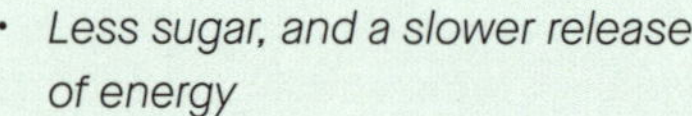

Rice
Try brown rice, quinoa, pearl barley, spelt, or bulgur wheat.
- *B-vitamins, better blood-sugar control, deliciously nutty*
- *Try the recipe on page 169*

Chips
Swap for air-popped popcorn or roasted chickpeas.
- *Fewer ultra-processed ingredients*
- *Try the recipe on page 181*

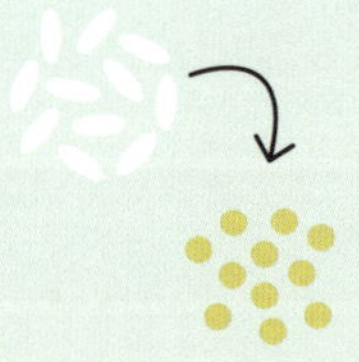

Flour
Use whole-wheat flour.
- *Nutrient-rich; slow sugar release*
- *Try the recipe on page 201*

Jelly
Substitute homemade fruit compôte.
- *More omega-3s; far less sugar*
- *Try the recipe on page 91*

Leave the skin on

One of the simplest ways to boost your daily fiber intake is to leave the skin on fruits and vegetables wherever possible. The skin of foods like potatoes (see table below for the potato lowdown), carrots, apples, pears, and cucumbers are rich in insoluble fiber, which helps support healthy digestion and regularity. Instead of peeling, give the produce a good scrub to remove dirt and enjoy the extra nutrients and fiber on your plate. Even vegetables like zucchini and eggplants offer more fiber when eaten with their skins. This easy swap reduces waste and supports a more satisfying, gut-friendly plate with minimal effort.

What about vegan cheese?

Common commercial varieties of vegan cheese, made from refined oils and starches like coconut oil, potato starch, or tapioca (such as those from Violife or Sheese) are usually fiber-free. In contrast, vegan cheeses made from whole-plant ingredients, such as cashews, almonds, tofu, or oats, may provide a small amount of fiber—typically 0.5–2g per 30g serving. For those looking to boost fiber intake, choosing artisanal or homemade vegan cheeses—made with legumes, nuts, or seeds—can be a better option. These retain more of the fiber naturally found in whole plant foods and can contribute modestly to your daily fiber goals.

Preparation type	Skin on/off	Processing level	Fiber (per 30g)	Fiber (per 150g)
Chips (from sliced potatoes)	Skin off (usually)	Processed	~1.2g	~6.0g
Baked potato (with skin)	Skin on	Minimally processed	~1.0g	~5.0g
Potato wedges (with skin)	Skin on	Minimally processed	~0.8g	~3.5–4.0g
Roast potatoes (with skin)	Skin on	Processed	~0.7g	~3.5g
Chips (from potato flakes/starch)	Skin off	Ultra-processed	~0.6g	~3.0g
Roast potatoes (without skin)	Skin off	Processed	~0.4–0.5g	~2.0–2.5g
French fries (oven or fried)	Skin off	Processed	~0.4–0.5g	~2.0–2.5g
Boiled potatoes (peeled)	Skin off	Minimally processed	~0.4g	~2.0g

Can I get fiber from my drinks?

From smoothies and juices to coffee, green tea, and even fruit-infused water, can the drinks we consume contribute to our fiber intake? Yes ... a little. While it's essential to prioritize whole foods as the primary source of dietary fiber, some drinks can offer a small fiber boost, depending on how they're prepared.

We should all think of drinks primarily as tools for hydration, but in some cases—like a blended smoothie or even a fiber-rich hot chocolate (opposite)—they can provide a top-off. Importantly, though, proper hydration helps your body absorb fiber from all your food—there's more about this on the following pages.

Plant-based "milks"

Oat, soy, and almond milks vary widely. Oat milk can have around 1–2g fiber per 1 generous cup (250 ml), soy milk about 1g, almond milk usually less than 1g. The benefit of soy milk over the other types is that it contains more protein.

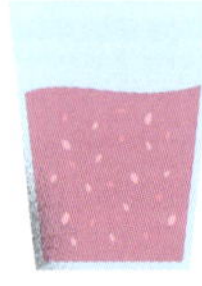

Fruit smoothies

Smoothies on average provide 3–5g of fiber per 1 generous cup (250ml) serving, depending on the fruit and whether the smoothie includes whole fruit or just juice. But, eating whole fruit is generally more beneficial than drinking it as a smoothie (page 67). This is because whole fruit contains intact fiber, especially insoluble fiber, which slows digestion and promotes feelings of fullness. When fruit is blended into a smoothie, some of this fiber, particularly the physical structure that aids in slowing sugar absorption, is partially broken down. While smoothies still contain fiber, the mechanical blending can reduce the effectiveness of fiber's benefits by speeding up sugar absorption and potentially leading to quicker blood-sugar spikes. Additionally, it's easier to consume larger amounts of fruit (and therefore more sugar) in smoothie form, which may impact dental health, calorie intake, and feelings of satiety.

Coffee and tea

Neither coffee nor brewed black or green tea have any fiber at all per cup (where a cup is 250ml). Matcha tea, which is drunk with the whole-leaf powder (rather than being brewed then strained) can offer about 1g of fiber per serving (or 1 teaspoon of powder gives around 2g of fiber). The fiber in fruit teas is generally negligible, if present at all.

While it's essential to prioritize whole foods as your primary source of dietary fiber, some drinks can offer a small fiber boost, depending on how they're prepared.

Dark chocolate hot chocolate

I am a huge fan of a dark chocolate hot chocolate, so imagine how excited I was to learn that dark chocolate, rich in cocoa flavonols, has been shown to potentially support stem-cell activity related to vascular repair. Bear with me while I give you the caveats for this first: there is, though, currently no strong evidence that dark chocolate directly increases stem cells in other tissues or broadly promotes stem-cell regeneration. So, while initial findings are promising, we need more human studies to confirm these effects and their health implications. Now for the really good news: when it comes to fiber there is much more evidence. While the fiber content of hot chocolate is typically low (around 1g per 1 cup/250ml), final fiber varies based on the recipe. The use of milk powder, cocoa solids, and whether or not there is added fiber in the final drink make a difference. The fiber content of a dark hot chocolate depends mainly on the cocoa content, but here's how you can make your hot chocolate work for you in this and other ways.

Cocoa powder (unsweetened, dark) contains about 6–8g of fiber per 1oz (28g) of powder.

A standard serving for hot chocolate uses about 1–2 tablespoons (5–10g) of cocoa powder, providing roughly 1–3g of fiber.

Additional ingredients like sugar or whipped cream add little or no fiber.

If prepared with milk or a plant-based milk (which generally has minimal fiber), the fiber mainly comes from the cocoa.

So 1 generous cup (250ml) of dark hot chocolate might provide around 1–3g of fiber, depending on how much cocoa you use and its fiber density. If you want a higher fiber result, using more pure, high-fiber cocoa powder or adding ingredients like ground flaxseed or oat bran can boost the fiber content to make the hot chocolate work harder.

What can the labeling tell me?

Most people know to check food labels for fat, sugar, and salt—but fiber? Not so much. Despite its critical role in digestive, heart, and even mental health, fiber is often the forgotten nutrient. Add in the confusion of ultra-processed foods and the fact that nutrition labels differ slightly from country to country, it's no wonder so many people are unsure where to begin.

Top 5 cheat sheet

Here are a top-five tips for knowing you're on the right track with the fiber content of the food you buy—regardless of where you are in the world!

 Products high in fiber but low in free sugars are a good bet: a cereal with 7g fiber and under 5g sugar per 100g is generally a nutritious choice.

 Foods with more than 3g fiber per serving are good; foods with more than 5g fiber per serving are excellent.

 Look for fiber-rich foods at the top of the ingredients list—that indicates that there are proportionally more of them in the product you're buying.

 Consider the labeling in light of what you actually see—the closer a food is to its natural state, likely the greater its overall nutritional value.

 Avoid "low carb" or "net carb" marketing that may subtract fiber content to appear lower-carb—it can be misleading.

Above all, it's worth remembering that it's always better to swap ultra-processed foods for whole-food versions—cooking the staples, such as rice or potatoes, yourself makes a real difference.

 **Traffic lights: the UK**

In the UK, the front-of-pack traffic-light system flags levels of fat, saturated fat, sugars, and salt, but not fiber.

 **Nutri-Score: the EU**

The Nutri-Score system (in countries such as France, Spain, and Germany) gives foods an A–E letter rating and a color based on overall nutritional quality, awarding positive points for fiber, protein, and fruit or vegetable content.

 **NutrInform battery: Italy**

Italy's plain-looking system presents nutrients as battery icons that show how much energy, fat, saturated fat, sugar, and salt each portion contributes to daily intakes.

 **The keyhole and the heart: Scandinavia**

Scandinavian countries use the Keyhole symbol to mark healthier choices higher in whole grains and fiber. Finland also uses a heart symbol to identify foods that are lower in salt and saturated fat and higher in fiber, helping consumers quickly spot heart-healthy options.

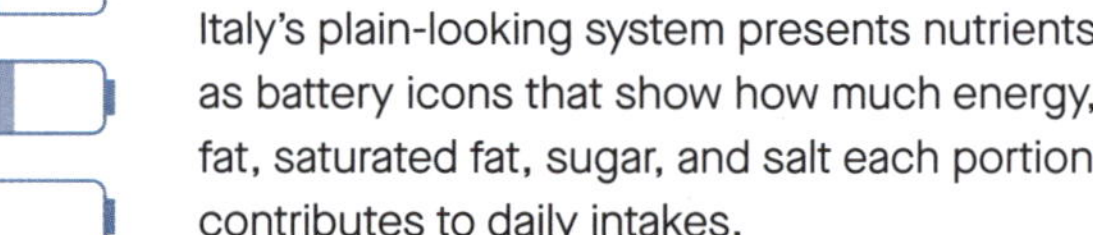

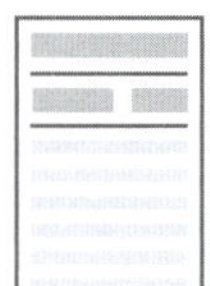 **Nutrition Facts Label: the US**

The US Food and Drug Administration (FDA) uses the Nutrition Facts Label—a straightforward table identifying the fat, cholesterol, and sodium, and breakdown of total carbohydrates into dietary fiber, total sugars, and added sugars. To be defined as a "healthy food," products must contain meaningful amounts of ingredients such as fruits, vegetables, or grains, and include at least one "nutrient to encourage" (fiber, potassium, calcium, iron, or vitamin D), while limiting added sugar, salt, and saturated fat.

A word on chicory root

In many cases, manufacturers increase fiber content by adding isolated ingredients such as inulin, a soluble fiber commonly extracted from chicory root. While inulin can contribute to overall fiber intake and support gut health, products that rely heavily on it may still be low in other beneficial nutrients and high in sugars, refined starches, or additives. For this reason, it is important to look beyond the front-of-package claims and consider the overall nutritional quality of the food you buy.

The pros and cons of fiber labeling

The pros of putting fiber information on a label are:
- Labels provide quick insights into how fiber-rich a food might be.
- Labels help guide healthier choices on the go.
- Labels help identify marketing spin versus actual nutritional value.

The cons of putting fiber information on a label are:
- Labels aren't always easy to interpret.
- Fiber isn't highlighted on front-of-package marketing in every country.
- Some foods contain added fibers that don't have the same benefits as whole-food sources.

Labeling in the UK

On most UK labels, fiber is listed in the "Carbohydrates of which sugars/fiber" section of the nutrition panel. Terms like "multigrain" or "made with whole grains" don't guarantee high fiber—check the actual grams of fiber to be sure. Also, look out for the following:

1. Fiber per serving
- Look at the portion size ("per bar," "per slice," and so on) to see actually how much fiber you'll be eating.
- With that label in mind, aim for 8g fiber per meal and 3–4g per snack.

2. The ingredients list
- Look for whole grains, seeds, nuts, legumes, fruit/vegetable powders, oats, bran, chicory root (inulin), or psyllium: good fiber sources.
- The closer a fiber-rich food is to the top, the more of it there is.

3. Misleading claims
- Some "health" foods (such as protein bars) may have very little fiber or rely on added fibers (polydextrose, inulin) for texture.

Labeling in the US

The US Food and Drug Administration recognizes fiber as a nutrient lacking in the US diet, but there is no front-of-package labeling to flag high-fiber foods. Fiber content can usually be found in one of these ways:

1. Fiber per serving
- Fiber is listed under "Total Carbohydrate" on the Nutrition Facts Label.
- Fiber is expressed in grams per serving.
- It is often shown as % Daily Value (%DV)—based on a 28g-per-day reference point. For example: 5g fiber = 18% DV.

2. Types of fiber
- Occasionally, you'll see soluble and insoluble fiber broken down separately, but it's not an FDA requirement.

3. The ingredients list
- Look for fiber-rich ingredients, such as whole-grain wheat, oats, and barley; added fibers such as inulin or chicory-root fiber; and psyllium husk, flaxseed, and chia seeds.

Can I trust the marketing?

Marketing health—whether through nutrient buzzwords or statements, or diet trends (see panel, below)—is big business. As soon as "high in fiber" pops up on a sticker, the food itself must be healthy and bursting with fiber, right? What do these marketing claims actually mean?

In both Europe and the US, the use of nutrition and health claims on food packaging is strictly regulated to ensure accuracy and to protect consumers. In the EU, claims are governed by Regulation (EC) No 1924/2006 and must be scientifically substantiated. The European Food Safety Authority (EFSA) evaluates the evidence, and the European Commission approves claims for inclusion in the EU Register. In the US, the Food and Drug Administration (FDA) regulates claims under the Nutrition Labeling and Education Act (NLEA) of 1990. Claims are categorized as authorized, qualified, or structure/function, with varying levels of scientific scrutiny. While authorized health claims require FDA approval, structure/function claims do not, but they still must be truthful and not misleading.

Popular claims in the EU and US

Nutrition claims in the EU describe the content of a nutrient in the food. In the US these are defined by the FDA and describe levels of nutrients:

- "High in fiber" (EU)—at least 6g fiber/100g food
- "Source of fiber" (EU)—at least 3g fiber/100g food
- "Excellent source of fiber"(US)—20% or more of the Daily Value (DV) per serving
- "Good source of fiber" (US)—10–19% of the Daily Value (DV) per serving

Health claims link a nutrient to a beneficial effect on the body. They must be authorized (by the FDA in the US), and carry a qualifying statement if evidence is limited:

- "Fiber contributes to normal bowel function"
- "Plant sterols may reduce blood cholesterol"
- "Beta-glucan from oats can help maintain normal blood-cholesterol levels"
- "Soluble fiber from oats, as part of a diet low in saturated fat and cholesterol, may reduce the risk of heart disease"

Function claims require no preapproval but must be truthful, such as "Fiber helps support digestive health."

The diet business

So many diets are marketed promising long-lasting health and well-being. Here are four of the most popular and how they might affect your fiber intake.

Juice diets remove the fiber-rich pulp from fruits and vegetables, leaving a concentrated sugar solution with no fiber. This can lead to blood-sugar spikes and hunger crashes, and over time may contribute to sluggish digestion and a less diverse gut microbiome.

Carnivore diets eliminate all plant foods, delivering next to zero dietary fiber, and stripping the diet of critical nutrients.

Intermittent fasting isn't inherently harmful, and may be beneficial for some, but long fasting windows can reduce overall fiber consumption over the course of the day. If you don't prioritize fiber-rich foods during your eating windows, your digestion can slow down and your stools may harden and become difficult to pass.

Ketogenic diets, by design, restrict carbohydrate intake, cutting out a significant source of fiber (page 12). Many keto followers also lean on well-marketed, processed "keto snacks," which are often virtually fiber-free.

Can I have too much fiber?

In many Western countries, the real issue isn't getting *too much* fiber, it's not getting *enough*. With this in mind, it's unlikely you'll consume too much fiber unless you suddenly change your diet or rely heavily on supplements without proper hydration or adjustment time.

Extremely high fiber intakes, typically above 70g per day, may interfere with the absorption of essential minerals such as iron, zinc, and calcium. That's because some typically high-fiber grains, nuts, and seeds are also rich in compounds called phytates. These can bind minerals together and make them harder for the body to absorb and use. Individuals with sensitive digestive systems or conditions like Irritable Bowel Syndrome (IBS) may find that some types of fiber, especially insoluble or fermentable ones, worsen their symptoms. In rare cases, very high intakes may cause intestinal blockages, particularly in individuals with slowed gut motility. Certain foods high in prebiotic fibers, like Jerusalem artichokes and legumes, can be especially fermentable and may produce excess gas if not introduced gradually. For these reasons, consume a diverse mixture of plant foods, rather than relying on one kind, stay well hydrated (below), and increase fiber intake little by little.

Minimizing the side effects of increased fiber

It's really hard to eat "too much" fiber, but increasing your fiber intake too quickly can be a problem if your digestive system isn't used to processing this vital nutrient. Common symptoms include gas, bloating, and cramping. To minimize side effects of an increased fiber intake, do three simple things:

 Increase fiber gradually over several days or weeks, not all at once.

 Drink plenty of water (see panel, below).

 Listen to your body—some people with IBS or a sensitive gut may need to be more cautious.

The importance of water

Eating large amounts of fiber without drinking enough water can lead to uncomfortable digestive symptoms such as bloating, gas, cramping, and even constipation. That's because fiber is like a sponge—absorbing water so that the fiber softens and swells. That effect keeps our stools (page 27) easy to pass, preventing blockages and aiding digestion. Aim to drink 6–8 glasses of water each day, and if your stools are hard to pass, address your diet and potentially increase your water intake. (If this persists, speak to a dietitian or doctor.) Note that even though tea and coffee are diuretics, they can still count toward daily fluid intake.

What are the trends—and the myths—about fiber?

Wellness trends gained traction in the 1970s in the US, driven by alternative health and self-care philosophies. In the 1990s, lifestyle magazines began to promote wellness as aspirational, linking it with beauty, fitness, and luxury. Today, social media—fueled by branded content—has brought a "wellness" explosion. Today's wellness trends reflect both its countercultural origins and its evolution into a multibillion-dollar industry.

There has been a move on social media toward fiber as the next great "hack"—from bowls of pastel-hued oats to so-called detox drinks. Some practices are harmless and can support increased fiber intake, but others distort the science or rely on unsupported claims. Below and opposite are some of the most prominent fiber-related wellness trends, with assessments of their validity and whether they genuinely benefit health or simply capitalize on cultural wellness phenomena.

Green powders

Often seen as a shortcut to better health, green powders are concentrated blends of dried and ground vegetables, herbs, algae, and grasses. They're promoted for their high vitamin and mineral content and often boast long lists of nutrients. However, they typically contain virtually no fiber and are not a substitute for the complex texture, bulk, and nutritional matrix of fruits and vegetables in their natural state.

Worryingly, these products are not always subject to strict regulation, and the accuracy of their nutrient claims can be difficult to verify, particularly when the powders are bought online from lesser-known brands that may lack independent testing or quality control. While these powders may help fill the gap on days when fruit and vegetable intake is low, they cannot replace real food and won't improve your fiber levels.

Sea moss

This trendy seaweed is promoted as a gut and skin savior, but the actual scientific evidence for that claim is extremely limited. While it does contain some vitamins and minerals, claims around detoxification, immunity, or fiber-related benefits are largely unproven. Like any single "superfood," sea moss is unlikely to offer much without a balanced, fiber-rich diet around it.

Gut cleansers

Often marketed as teas, powders, or juice fasts, these products usually promise to "reset" or "clean out" your digestive system. In reality, the gut is not a pipe that needs cleaning! These cleanses rarely contain much fiber at all and can even disrupt digestion if they lack solid food or hydration. In addition to this, full juice cleanses typically exclude most other essential nutrients from the diet, including protein, healthy fats, and fiber—making them nutritionally unbalanced and unsustainable in the long term.

Chia-seed water

TikTok's "internal shower" drink has brought chia seeds newfound popularity. The claim is simple: 1–2 tablespoons of chia seeds soaked in a glass of water, then drunk, are a natural laxative to "flush out the gut" and support weight loss. It's true that chia seeds are nutritionally dense (1 tablespoon provides roughly 5g of dietary fiber, alongside small amounts of protein, omega-3 fatty acids, and micronutrients). Hydrated, they can bulk and soften stools to help relieve mild constipation in those with low fiber intake. However, the online claims are far broader than evidence supports. The idea that chia water "melts fat" or significantly suppresses hunger is misleading. The plumped seeds may give a brief sense of fullness, but the volume needed to meaningfully blunt appetite is impractical, and the calories from those additional seeds negates any supposed weight-loss benefit.

Fiber maxxing

Popular in certain online wellness spaces, this involves aggressively increasing fiber through powders, seeds, and fortified snacks. While increasing fiber intake is something we all need to do, suddenly ramping up intake can cause bloating, cramps, or constipation, especially without adequate hydration (page 73). A gradual increase in fiber intake from whole foods is far more effective (and sustainable).

Adaptogenic mushrooms

These fungi, such as lion's mane, are gaining popularity for their supposed cognitive and gut benefits. While they do contain beta-glucan (a type of soluble fiber; page 39), the quantities in powders or capsules are often too small to meaningfully impact fiber intake. We need more research before anyone should be recommending them for gut health.

Colorful oatmeal and smoothie bowls

Aesthetically pleasing, often topped with fruit, seeds, and nut butters, these bowls can absolutely support fiber intake when made up of whole grains and with a variety of toppings. However, their benefit depends on the ingredients, not the "Instagrammability"! A colorful bowl is only as nutritious as what's in it.

The "plant points" trend

Encouraging a wide variety of plant foods each week (such as aiming for 30+ types) is a positive trend backed by research for the American Gut Project. Greater diversity in plant intake supports a more diverse gut microbiome, especially when whole grains, legumes, vegetables, fruits, nuts, and seeds are involved. This one gets a checkmark! You can find out more about plant points on page 62. We've even created our own tracker to help you keep a record of how you're doing on points every week (page 83).

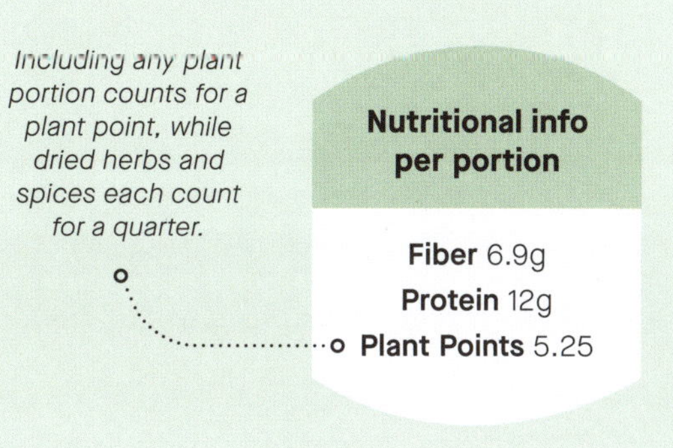

How much fiber should I feed my children?

Fiber is not a nutrient that directly drives growth in the way protein, calcium, or essential fats do. However, it plays a supportive role in children's diets, shaping the environment in which healthy growth and development can occur. As a result, getting enough of it is really important for growing children.

At the simplest level, we know that a fiber-rich diet encourages healthy, regular bowel movements. That, in itself, helps children maintain a healthy appetite, ensuring they are able to eat enough of the other nutrients that are essential for general growth and development. Nutritional needs throughout our lives, though, are not linear. During your child's first decades, adapting their intake appropriately for their age supports the growth of their bones, the development of their immune system, and their changing energy levels. The diagram below shows how those needs change from birth to adulthood.

Changing fiber needs in children

At birth, babies have all the nutrients they need from their mother's breast milk or from specially balanced formula milk. Once babies begin to eat solid foods, they need small amounts of fiber from the soft fruits, vegetables, and cereals we use in their purées. After that, the fiber needs of girls and boys change as they grow, including according to gender.

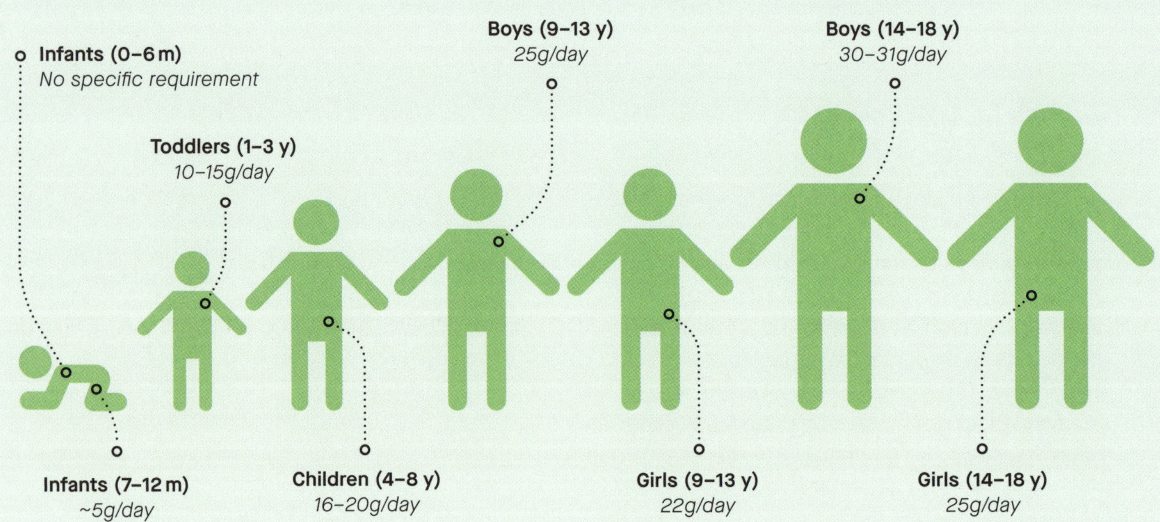

Fiber and growing bones

Over the years, a belief has emerged that eating a fiber-rich diet could impair bone health or limit growth in children. There has been a question as to whether foods rich in fiber also contain "anti-nutrients" such as phytates and oxalates. These are naturally occurring compounds found in fiber-rich foods that can bind to minerals such as calcium, iron, and zinc, theoretically reducing how much of those good nutrients the body absorbs. In practice, though, this is not the case. The European Food Safety Authority has concluded that the impact of phytates and oxalates on calcium absorption is negligible, and there is no evidence of adverse effects on bone health from eating fiber-rich foods. In fact, several studies suggest the opposite may be true: prebiotic fibers, which feed beneficial gut bacteria, may in fact improve calcium absorption and support bone-mineral density in children. This is particularly important as bone mass accumulates rapidly in childhood and adolescence, laying the foundation for lifelong bone health.

Fiber and a developing immune system

By supporting digestive health, fiber is essential for the development of the immune system. The gut microbiota, shaped partly by fiber intake (page 11), plays an important role in how minerals are absorbed and how the immune system develops. Evidence shows that children who consume adequate fiber benefit, like adults, form a more diverse gut microbiota and greater production of short-chain fatty acids, which help regulate immune function and inflammation. These effects are thought to reduce the risk of allergies and other immune-related conditions later in life.

Fiber and childhood energy needs

While they are growing, and particularly during growth spurts, children generally need more calories per kilogram of body weight than adults (note. that's not more calories overall—children's overall calorie needs are lower until they reach late teenagehood). For this reason, parents may be concerned that filling, high-fiber foods can reduce overall energy intake if consumed in large amounts. But, like everything, balance is key. Fiber should form a part of meals that are also rich in the healthy calories needed for energy (for all the running, playing, and learning—and for all the growing), and the nutrients needed to support growth. A bowl of oatmeal with nut butter and fruit, for example, provides fiber alongside protein, healthy fats—and healthy energy.

Top tips for parents

- **Start with small swaps** Making regular, fiber-rich swaps is a great way to get more fiber into your children (page 66)—but make one swap at a time so the boost in fiber is gentle (and the changes are more likely to fall under the radar!).

- **Mix it up** Combine high-fiber options with familiar favorites to smooth the transition.

- **Make it fun** Get children involved in baking or topping their own yogurt bowls—they're more likely to eat what they help prepare.

- **Offer water** Encourage water alongside higher-fiber foods to avoid constipation.

- **Lead by example** Children copy what they see: if you eat fiber-rich foods, your children are more likely to follow!

- **Pair it with vitamin C** Serve fiber with vitamin C–rich foods to maximize iron absorption.

- **Look for a balanced plate** Include fiber in meals that also provide energy, protein, calcium, and healthy fats so as not to crowd out calories.

- **Think variety** A wide mixture of fruit, vegetables, pulses, and whole grains ensures children get many different types of fiber and a broad range of nutrients to support their growth and development.

- **Persevere** It can take up to 10 exposures before children accept vegetables or higher-fiber foods, especially those with slightly bitter flavors. Keep offering them in different ways and don't worry if they're rejected at first. A love for those new flavors will—most likely—come.

How do I get my child to eat more fiber?

Adding fiber-rich foods to your child's diet doesn't have to be tricky (or a battle!)—sometimes it's about weaving them, little by little, into food children are already likely to recognize and love.

Here are some ideas for every meal of the day. And don't forget to check out the parent-friendly tips on the previous page and the everyday swaps we can all make on page 66, too.

Breakfast

Cereals ⟶ Choose whole-grain cereals (shredded wheat, bran flakes, rolled oats, and so on). Add berries or even a sprinkle of chopped dark chocolate.

Yogurt ⟶ Stir oats, grated apple or other fruit, and a spoonful of seeds or nuts (if age appropriate) into a plain yogurt bowl for a quick high-fiber breakfast.

Pancakes ⟶ Make pancakes with whole-wheat flour and chopped dark chocolate. Top them with juicy berries and a spoonful of plain yogurt.

Toast ⟶ Instead of toast for scrambled or a poached egg, try sweet corn fritters made with whole-wheat flour; or serve up soft-boiled eggs with whole-wheat bread slices (eggs give a filling protein start to the day, too). If you're looking for something to spread on whole-wheat toast, swap out regular jelly for a fruit compôte (page 91).

Lunch

Sandwiches ⟶ Opt for whole-grain or 50/50 rolls and wraps packed with favorite fillings—and added grated vegetables for extra crunch and fiber.

Bits & dips ⟶ Pack a lunchbox with veggie sticks (slices of carrot, cucumber, and pepper all travel well) or flaxseed crackers (see page 285; a great alternative to white breadsticks) with a cup of homemade hummus or bean-based dip (page 186).

Soup ⟶ Make a little flask (for takeout) or bowl of veggie soup (so easy to pack with fiber and different plant foods) served with a side of a whole-grain or 50/50 roll—or even whole-wheat vermicelli noodles for slurping through.

Muffins ⟶ Swap out sugary chocolate or blueberry muffins for carrot, banana (page 96), or zucchini versions, naturally sweetened with fruit and with extra veggie count.

Snacks

Fruit $\longrightarrow$ A small handful of dried apricots, figs, or goji berries packs in the dietary fiber (add some nuts, if age appropriate and permitted); or dip some apple slices or orange segments in dark chocolate and leave to set. (Plus, remember, fresh fruit with the skin on—apples, pears, plums—is still the best and simplest form of fiber and the perfect snack!)

Beans $\longrightarrow$ A handful of roasted chickpeas or fresh fava beans is crunchy, savory, and naturally high in fiber.

Cookies $\longrightarrow$ Homemade pancakes or oat cookies (see page 193) instead of snack bars can be fiber superstars. Sweeten with pieces of dried fruit in the mixture if you like.

Supper

Burgers $\longrightarrow$ Swap out meat burgers for bean burgers with all the toppings (letting everyone stack their own makes the process fun)—and (of course) serve it all up on a whole-grain (or 50/50) bun!

Shepherd's or cottage pie $\longrightarrow$ Try this with a topping of 50/50 mashed potatoes (keep the skin on) and blended lima beans; sweet potato topping is a good option, too. Plus, you can use lentils in the filling, just as you can for Bolognese or chili (page 165).

Fishsticks $\longrightarrow$ Make homemade fishsticks or breaded chicken nuggets with whole-wheat breadcrumbs.

Pizza $\longrightarrow$ Make mini pizzas on whole-wheat tortillas or pita breads with all their favorite veggie toppings!

Sweet treats

Ice cream $\longrightarrow$ Blend creamy Greek yogurt with a handful of frozen berries for an instant, fruit-packed "ice cream." Stir through some whole blueberries or raspberries at the end to keep some of the fiber intact.

Smoothies $\longrightarrow$ Blend a handful of oats, chia seeds, or ground flaxseeds with fruit and yogurt. Blended fruit isn't as fiber-rich as whole fruit (page 51), but with the oats and seeds added to the mixture, you're winning here!

Banana split $\longrightarrow$ Try a banana sliced lengthwise with a filling of thick Greek yogurt (instead of ice cream). Scatter over some raspberries or chopped strawberries and sprinkle over some grated dark chocolate—add some seeds if your child is old enough.

Your weekly plant tracker

You now know that increasing the diversity of plants in your diet is one of the simplest ways to improve fiber intake. You also know that counting plant points will enable you to keep track of your fiber-fueled nutrition every day. Here, we're giving you the tools to put that into practice.

A recap: the "Super Six" plant foods

Remember, the Super Six plant foods are not just limited to vegetables (page 62). They are made up of:

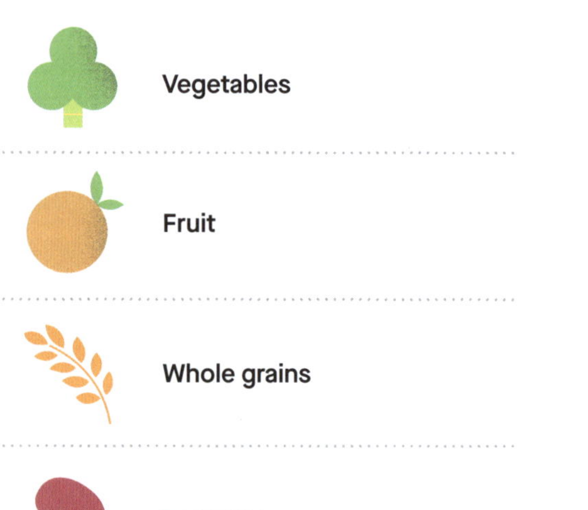

Vegetables

Fruit

Whole grains

Legumes

Nuts & seeds

Herbs & spices

This weekly plant tracker is designed to help you to see at a glance how varied your weekly diet really is. Each time you eat a different plant food, simply check the relevant box on the grid.

At first, you may find that you easily hit your varied vegetable or fruit quota, but need to up your legumes and nuts and seeds to bring some balance and variety. When you start out, embrace the challenge and don't let the goal hinder you. It's fine if some weeks you add in new plant foods and others you stick to established favorites. Over time, as you discover new recipes and new plant sources of fiber, hitting 30 different sources of plant fiber will become easier, more varied, and more enjoyable. Before you know it, the variety of plant foods you eat each week will simply be a natural part of your diet. Feel free to copy the grid from the book to keep it on hand wherever you are during mealtimes.

Of course, as an aside, the aim is not to stop eating, say, vegetables once you have checked all the variety boxes in a week—the aim of the tracker is to encourage you to increase *types* of plant foods that may be lacking in your diet, never to reduce the amount of those that you're already eating. More is definitely more!

10 plant foods for 5g of fiber

As a handy guide, each of the following will give you 5g of fiber. If you eat just six of them in one day, you've reached your goal of 30g of daily fiber!

- 9 oz (250g) vegetables
- 1 tablespoon chia seeds
- 1½ tablespoons hemp seeds
- 3 oz (80g) raspberries
- 3½ oz (100g) frozen peas
- 2¾ oz (75g) cooked lentils
- 3½ oz (100g) avocado
- 1 thumb-sized piece of ginger (1 in/2.5 cm)
- 1 medium pear
- 2½ oz (70g) black beans

Super-Six weekly tracker

Use this grid to track the variety of super-six foods in your diet. Score one point for every different kind of vegetable, fruit, whole grain, legume, nut, or seed you eat, checking off the boxes as your points accumulate. Single herbs and spices count as one quarter point each. Once you're scoring at least 5 points each week in each super-six category, you're hitting your target of 30 different plant foods for the week.

The Super Six	Week beginning ...					Bonus points	
Vegetables 1 vegetable type = 1 point	☐	☐	☐	☐	☐	☐	☐
Fruit 1 fruit type = 1 point	☐	☐	☐	☐	☐	☐	☐
Whole grains 1 grain type = 1 point	☐	☐	☐	☐	☐	☐	☐
Legumes 1 bean/pulse type = 1 point	☐	☐	☐	☐	☐	☐	☐
Nuts & seeds 1 type of nut, seed, or whole nut butter = 1 point	☐	☐	☐	☐	☐	☐	☐
Herbs & spices 1 herb or spice type = ¼ point (check 4 small boxes to score 1 point)	☐☐☐☐	☐☐☐☐	☐☐☐☐	☐☐☐☐	☐☐☐☐	☐	☐

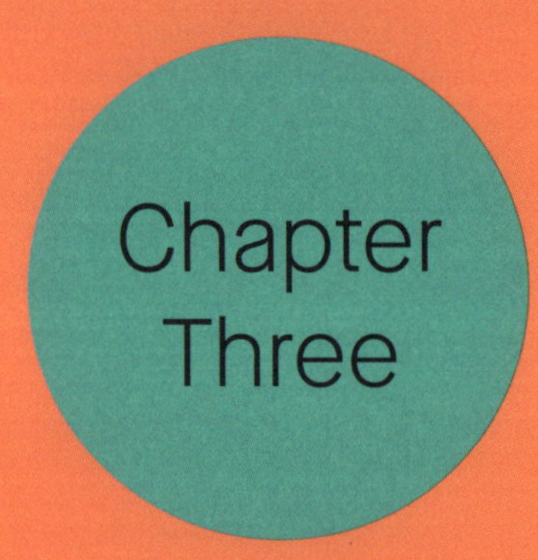

Recipes
for a

This chapter brings everything together: the science, the habits, and the joy of food through recipes that fit real life. The dishes are designed not only to help you reach your target of 30g of fiber a day, but also to show that doing so doesn't have to involve complicated cooking or endless hours at the stove—they are here both to nourish and to inspire confidence in the kitchen.

Each recipe comes with totals for plant points and fiber. Even the smallest ingredients contribute to your weekly totals. I have also included the protein to demonstrate how easy it is to achieve optimal protein count without trying.

Many of the recipes have been tested at home with my own family, so whether you're cooking for yourself, your children, or after a long working day, these dishes are not only healthy and delicious, but practical crowd-pleasers too.

Some recipes are air-fryer friendly. Look out for the symbol at the top of the page and refer to the recipe introduction or notes for alternative cooking instructions.

fiber-filled life

How the recipes work

These recipes are built around my 30:30:30 formula, aiming for around 30g of fiber a day, 30 different plants a week, and chewing each bite about 30 times—which is more about how you eat than what you cook. There's also a chapter with meals that can be made in around 30 minutes. All the recipes aim to make reaching your daily fiber and plant-diversity targets as simple and enjoyable as possible.

Building up to 30g of fiber a day

Each recipe includes grams of fiber per portion or serving, so you can mix-and-match meals, snacks, and desserts to build toward 30g across the day. You don't need every recipe to be "perfect" on its own—think of your day as a whole:

- Breakfast, lunch, and dinner: aim for around 6–10g of fiber per meal
- Snacks and desserts: use these as extra top-offs of fiber and plant points

Throughout the week, notice the variety too—different whole grains, pulses, nuts, seeds, fruit, and vegetables all count toward your 30 plants.

Understanding the nutrition panel

At the start of each recipe, you'll find a simple nutrition snapshot. For most recipes this will include:
- Fiber (g)—the star of the show, helping you track toward 30g a day
- Protein (g)—to support fullness, muscle maintenance, and steady energy
- Plant points—how many different plant ingredients that portion contributes

These figures are estimates, based on standard ingredients and typical supermarket values. They're there to guide, not to dictate, and they're not intended as a clinical or medical tool.

Servings, portions, and plant points

Some dishes are listed as "Serves 4–6" or similar. Where there's a range like this, the nutrition per portion has been calculated using the higher number of servings (that is, 6). That means the fiber and other nutrients shown are a conservative minimum. If you eat a larger portion (for example, it feeds 4 instead of 6), you'll get a little more than stated.

Similarly, plant points are calculated per portion, based on the recipe as written. If you're cooking for smaller or larger households, or stretching recipes with extra sides, your exact intake will naturally shift a little.

Ingredient swaps and variations

Real life doesn't always match a shopping list, and this book is going global, so I've given swaps and suggestions wherever I can.

- Can't find fresh herbs? Use dried and adjust to taste.
- Don't have a particular bean? Substitute another canned bean or a lentil.
- Different whole grain available locally? Use what you can find.

Any time you swap ingredients, use different brands, or follow a suggested variation, the fiber, protein, and energy values will change slightly, and your plant-point count may go up or down. That's completely normal; the important thing is to keep leaning toward whole, minimally processed plant foods most of the time.

Sides, serves, and extras

Unless clearly stated, the nutrition panel does not include sides or serving suggestions (for example, "serve with an arugula salad" or "add steamed greens"). These extras are a good opportunity to boost fiber and plant points, but they will also alter the macro content positively.

Think of the nutrition panel as the fact-check for your base recipe. If you add:
- an extra handful of leafy greens,
- a spoonful of seeds, or
- a side of beans or lentils ...

... you will increase both your nutritional intake and your plant points accordingly.

Oils, fats, and a few kitchen notes

Where I've used oils, I recommend cold-pressed canola oil or extra-virgin olive oil for everyday cooking and dressings. These provide unsaturated fats that support heart health and help you absorb fat-soluble vitamins from all those plants.

You don't need fancy equipment to cook from this book. Basic pans, baking sheets, and a decent knife will take you a long way. An air fryer is sometimes offered as an option for speed and crispness, but it's not essential.

Use all of the recipes as a flexible framework, not a set of rules. The aim isn't perfection, it's to make high-fiber, plant-rich eating feel possible, pleasurable, and sustainable in the real world.

Equipment

You don't need a fancy kitchen to cook from this book, just a few basics you'll reach for again and again:

- Zester: for adding fine citrus zest to dressings, marinades, and baked dishes
- Grater: ideal for grating vegetables into sauces, fritters, and loaves, and for hard cheese
- Rolling pin: for rolling doughs and flattening things like breads or fiber-boosted snacks
- Potato masher: for mashed potatoes, of course, but also for roughly crushing beans and pulses
- Small food processor: handy for blending nuts, seeds, dips, pestos, and quick crumble toppings
- Hand-held blender: perfect for blending soups and sauces right in the pan
- Stand blender: useful for smoothies, sauces, and ultra-smooth soups
- Spatula: for folding batters, scraping every last bit from the bowl, and reducing food waste

Use what you already have. These bits and pieces for your kitchen will make high-fiber cooking faster and easier, but there is always a workaround.

Cook's notes

To keep things simple, the recipes in this book follow a few consistent assumptions:

Herb and vegetable prep

- We use fresh herbs throughout, but you can substitute with dried: start with about 1 tsp dried per 1 tbsp chopped fresh and adjust to taste. All fresh parsley is flat-leaf.
- All onions and garlic are peeled, unless otherwise stated.
- Scrub vegetables, like carrots, sweet potatoes, and potatoes, but leave them unpeeled (to max the fiber).

Eggs and dairy

- All eggs are medium size.
- Butter is unsalted.
- In most baking, eggs can be swapped out for flax eggs (1 tbsp ground flax + 3 tbsp water per egg, left to thicken).

Oils and fats

- Olive oil and canola oil are the default, unless otherwise stated.
- Extra-virgin oils are best kept for finishing dishes or salad dressings, rather than high-heat cooking.

Nuts, seeds, and seasoning

- Store opened packets of nuts and seeds in sealed bags in the freezer to keep them fresh and reduce rancidity.
- Salt is fine sea salt. If you're using salt flakes, you'll need a little more by volume (season to taste).
- Chiles are with their seeds, unless otherwise stated.

Grains, legumes, pulses, and cans

- Soak dried pulses and legumes overnight before cooking, and rinse grains thoroughly before use.
- Many recipes use cans and pouches of grains and pulses for convenience, but cooking your own is even better.

Easy ingredient swaps

- Chickpea for yellow split pea flour, or vice versa.
- Marmite can be swapped out for light soy sauce in some recipes to provide a similar umami depth (this will slightly alter the salt content).
- Any substitution or brand change will gently shift the fiber, protein, and energy values, and may nudge your plant-point count up or down. If you're keeping dishes largely whole-food and plant-rich, you're on the right track.

Breakfast represents a wonderful opportunity to boost fiber intake: cereals and grain-based foods contribute the majority of fiber to the average diet. Choosing whole grain, plant-rich options that genuinely nourish makes this meal really count.

In this section, I've reimagined breakfast as achievable, exciting and, of course, fiber-rich. Whether it's a fig granola (my personal favorite) or carrot pancake with ginger, or a high-fiber smoothie blend, these recipes are designed to sustain energy, support gut health, and keep you fuller for longer. You'll also find air-fryer and prep-ahead options, because real life rarely allows for elaborate mornings.

Starting out with a fiber-rich breakfast supports digestion and blood-sugar balance, setting you up for a good day. It also helps build a thriving microbiome, paving the way for lifelong health! Breakfast, then, when built on the right ingredients, isn't just the first meal of the day; it's your first opportunity to close the fiber gap.

Breakfasts

Nutty barley, cinnamon & dried fig granola

 **Makes** 800g    **Prep** 5 min    **Cook** 40 min   

5½ oz (150g) barley flakes

4¼ oz (120g) spelt, rye, or rolled oats (or use more barley flakes)

5½ oz (150g) mixed nuts, roughly chopped (I use a mixture of almonds, hazelnuts, pecans, and walnuts)

1¼ oz (35g) puffed quinoa (or use more barley flakes)

5½ oz (150g) mixed seeds (I use 4½ oz/125g pumpkin and sunflower, and the remainder sesame and flaxseeds)

2 tbsp psyllium husk

2½ tsp ground cinnamon

scant ½ cup/3½ oz (100g) mild olive oil, coconut, or other mild oil

⅓ cup/3½ oz (100g) maple syrup

5½ oz (150g) dried organic figs, chopped

Sea salt

A wholesome, crunchy start to the day, this is a celebration of one of my favorite fruits. Figs are such an underrated ingredient in granolas; they add natural sweetness, a soft chew, and a lovely boost of calcium. Top tip: this isn't an overly sweet recipe, so if you prefer a little more sweetness, simply add an extra drizzle of maple syrup before baking.

1. Preheat the oven to 325°F (160°C) and line your largest baking sheet with parchment paper.

2. Mix all the dry ingredients together in a large bowl until evenly combined.

3. In a pitcher, combine the oil and maple syrup, and stir through a pinch of salt. Pour the mixture over the dry ingredients and stir until everything is nicely coated.

4. Spread out the granola mixture in an even layer on the lined baking sheet and bake for 35–40 minutes, stirring occasionally so the granola cooks evenly, until golden.

5. Leave the granola to cool on the baking sheet, then stir in the figs. The granola will crisp up further as it cools.

6. Store it in an airtight container at room temperature for up to 1 week.

Note You can cook this in your air fryer too. Heat the air fryer to 325°F (160°C) and air-fry for 10–12 minutes, tossing occasionally. You may need to cook the granola in a few batches, depending on the size of your air fryer.

Grape & fennel seed baked oats

 **Serves** 6

 **Prep** 10 min

 **Cook** 45 min

- 2½ oz (75g) shelled pecans, raw almonds, walnuts, or hazelnuts, or a mixture
- 7 oz (200g) rolled oats
- 2 tbsp psyllium husk
- 1 tsp baking powder
- ½ tsp sea salt
- scant 2 cups/15 fl oz (425 ml) milk of choice
- 3½ tbsp maple syrup or honey
- 1 tsp vanilla essence (optional)
- 2 flax eggs (2 tbsp ground flax with 6 tbsp water, soaked for 10 minutes) or regular eggs
- 3 tbsp olive oil, or melted coconut oil or butter
- 10½ oz (300g) black seedless grapes or frozen blueberries
- 2 tsp fennel seeds
- 2 tsp demerara (or soft brown) sugar
- Skyr, or Greek or coconut yogurt, to serve

This dish is beautifully versatile: it's perfect as a nourishing breakfast but it makes a great dessert too! Serve it with a spoonful of kefir for extra gut-friendly goodness.

1. Preheat the oven to 350°F (180°C) and line an 8 in (20 cm) square brownie pan or baking dish with parchment paper.

2. Put the nuts in the pan and toast them in the oven for 8–10 minutes until golden.

3. Meanwhile combine the oats, psyllium husk, baking powder, and salt in a bowl. Once the nuts are ready and cool enough to touch, chop them and add to the bowl.

4. In a separate bowl, whisk together the milk, maple syrup, vanilla (if using), flax eggs or eggs, and olive oil, then add this into the oats mixture.

5. Spread two-thirds of the grapes or blueberries on the bottom of the pan, then cover them in the oat mixture. Evenly distribute the remaining fruit on top, then sprinkle with the fennel seeds and the sugar. Place in the oven for 40–45 minutes until golden and firm, then allow to cool for a few minutes before slicing and serving with skyr or yogurt. Also delicious cold.

Blueberry & mango frozen smoothie bowl

 **Serves** 2    **Prep** 10 min

3½ oz (100g) frozen blueberries (or your favorite berry)

3½ oz (100g) frozen mango or frozen pineapple

1 fresh or frozen ripe banana

1 tbsp chia seeds and/or ground flaxseed

2 tbsp peanut butter, almond butter, or tahini

1 pitted date or 2 dried figs

scant ⅔ cup/5 fl oz (150–175 ml) milk of choice, or kefir (adjust for thickness)

To serve

1 kiwi, peeled and sliced, or ½ apple or pear, cored, and diced

2 tsp pumpkin seeds and/or sunflower seeds

2 tsp smooth or crunchy peanut butter

2 tsp chia, flaxseed, and/or hemp seeds

Optional extras

2 tbsp high-fiber granola (page 88) or puffed quinoa

1 tbsp coconut flakes

2 tsp chopped nuts (such as almonds, walnuts, hazelnuts, macadamia, or pecans)

2 tbsp skyr or Greek yogurt

The burst of color in this smoothie bowl is a sign of its goodness—its vibrant purple hue comes from polyphenols, powerful plant compounds that support long-term health. You can, though, use whatever frozen fruit you have to hand (freezer staples are brilliantly cost effective in recipes like this one). Blackberries, raspberries, or mixed berries all work beautifully and provide good amounts of fiber. Have fun experimenting to find your favorite combo.

1. Blend all the smoothie ingredients together, adding more milk as needed until you have a thick and creamy mixture.

2. Top with kiwi, apple or pear, pumpkin and/or sunflower seeds, peanut butter, and chia, flaxseed or hemp seeds, and any of your chosen optional extras, and serve.

Prune & walnut banana muffins

 **Makes** 12    **Prep** 15 min    **Cook** 25 min

Nutritional info per serving

Fiber 4.1g
Protein 7.8g
Plant Points 8.25

1 orange

4¼ oz (120g) pitted prunes

1¾ oz (50g) raisins or golden raisins

2 large ripe bananas

½ cup/4½ oz (125g) skyr, or Greek or coconut yogurt

3½ oz (100g) smooth peanut butter

4½ tbsp olive or canola oil

generous 2 tbsp (30g) muscovado, dark brown, or coconut sugar

2 flax eggs (2 tbsp ground flax with 6 tbsp water, soaked for 10 minutes) or regular eggs

1¼ cups/5¾ oz (160g) whole-wheat, spelt, or oat flour

1 tsp baking powder

½ tsp baking soda

½ tsp sea salt

1 tsp mixed spice

1¾ oz (50g) walnuts, finely chopped, plus 12 large halves, to decorate

We've all heard the classic advice: if you're feeling constipated, eat more prunes! That's because prunes contain sorbitol (a natural sugar alcohol) and insoluble fiber, both of which help keep the digestive system moving smoothly. In addition, they are a wonderfully versatile ingredient, adding natural sweetness, moisture, and richness to baking. Combined with fiber-rich flaxseeds (if you use flax eggs, which I recommend) and crunchy walnuts, these muffins are a delicious way to boost fiber without feeling like you're "being healthy"—even children love them!

1. Preheat the oven to 400°F (200°C). Line a 12-hole muffin pan with paper cups or grease generously.

2. Zest the orange into a blender, then cut the orange itself in half. Place the prunes in a bowl and squeeze over one orange half and top off with boiling water so that the prunes are just covered. Put to one side to soak for 10 minutes. Cover the raisins or golden raisins in boiling water and put to one side for at least 5 minutes. Squeeze the other orange half into the blender with the zest.

3. Drain the prunes, then place them in the blender along with the bananas, skyr or yogurt, peanut butter, oil, sugar, and flax eggs or eggs. Blend until completely smooth.

4. In a large bowl, combine all the remaining ingredients (except the walnuts for decoration). Pour in the blended mixture and stir gently until just combined. Drain the raisins, add them to the batter, and fold through, being careful not to overmix.

5. Spoon the mixture into the muffin cases, then top each muffin with a piece of walnut. Bake for 20–25 minutes until risen and an inserted skewer comes out clean. Transfer to a rack to cool. Delicious warm, or will last 4 days in an airtight container.

Barley oatmeal with blackberry, apple & bay leaf compôte

 **Serves** 4    **Prep** 5 min    **Cook** 12 min

3½ oz (100g) barley flakes

3½ oz (100g) rolled oats

1 tbsp chia seeds

2 cups/17 fl oz (500 ml) milk of choice

¼ tsp sea salt (optional)

¼ tsp ground nutmeg and/or ground cinnamon, plus extra to serve

4 tbsp almond or smooth or crunchy peanut butter, to serve

For the blackberry compôte

9 oz (250g) fresh or frozen blackberries

1 small apple, cored and chopped into small chunks

1 bay leaf

2 tbsp maple syrup, plus extra to taste if needed

Barley works beautifully in oatmeal, offering a naturally nutty flavor and a slightly chewy texture. Although soaking oats overnight can increase their resistant starch, it isn't essential here: barley flakes cook quickly and deliver a creamy consistency in just 15 minutes. For an extra nutritional boost, stir chia seeds into the oatmeal, or add them to the compôte to create a lovely jam-like texture.

1. Soak the barley and oats in 2 cups/17 fl oz (500 ml) of water for at least 15 minutes, but ideally overnight if you have the time.

2. Place the soaked barley and oats (along with their soaking liquid) in a pan with the remainder of the oatmeal ingredients, except the almond or peanut butter, and bring the liquid to a rapid simmer. Turn down the heat to a gentle simmer, and cook the oatmeal for 10–12 minutes, stirring often, until it is tender and creamy.

3. Meanwhile, make the compôte. Place the blackberries, apple, bay, maple syrup, and 1½ tablespoons of water in a small pan and gently bring to a boil. Turn down the heat to a simmer and keep cooking until the apple is tender and the blackberries are defrosted (if using frozen) and beginning to break down. Crush a few berries to release their juice. Have a taste and add a little more maple syrup if you prefer. Set the compôte aside and keep it warm until the oatmeal is ready.

4. Divide the oatmeal between your serving bowls and spoon over a few tablespoons of the compôte. Top each serving with a tablespoon of almond or peanut butter and a little pinch of extra nutmeg or cinnamon, then serve.

Carrot pancakes with ginger, honey & turmeric yogurt

 **Serves** 4    **Prep** 15 min    **Cook** 15 min

2½ tsp cider vinegar or lemon juice

scant 1⅓ cups/10¾ fl oz (315 ml) milk of choice

2¾ oz (80g) raisins or golden raisins

scant 1⅓ cups/5¾ oz (170g) whole-wheat flour

½ cup/2¼ oz (60g) all-purpose flour

1 tsp ground cinnamon

1 tbsp ground flaxseed or ground chia

about ½ tsp baking soda

2 tsp baking powder

2 flax eggs (2 tbsp ground flax with 6 tbsp water, soaked for 10 minutes) or 2 small eggs

4 tsp melted coconut or olive oil

1 tsp maple syrup

1 large ripe banana, mashed

4½ oz (125g) carrot, scrubbed and grated

Sea salt

2 tbsp mixed seeds, to serve

For the spiced yogurt

1¼ cups/10½ oz (300g) skyr, or Greek or coconut yogurt

½ tsp ground turmeric

2 tsp grated fresh ginger

2 tsp maple syrup or honey

I love experimenting with flavors, and this recipe was inspired by the abundance of carrots I always seem to have in the fridge. They are wonderful grated into pancake batter, bringing natural sweetness and a soft texture. If you're using flaxseeds rather than chia, you may need to add a little extra baking soda to help the pancakes rise beautifully. Adding herbs or spices to a yogurt topping is an easy way to boost plant points.

1. Combine the vinegar and milk in a bowl and set it aside for 5–10 minutes until it begins to curdle (this will be less obvious with nondairy milks). Separately, pour boiling water over the raisins in a bowl and leave to soak for 5 minutes.

2. Meanwhile, combine all the dry ingredients with a pinch of salt (you may need a touch more baking soda if you're using flaxseeds over chia).

3. Whisk the flax eggs or eggs, 1 teaspoon of the oil and the maple syrup into the mashed banana and stir in the carrot.

4. Drain the raisins, then add these into the egg/banana mixture. Add this to the curdled-milk mixture. Fold the wet ingredients into the dry until just combined—try not to overmix. Rest the batter for 10 minutes to hydrate the flour.

5. While the batter is resting, make the spiced yogurt. Pour the yogurt into a bowl. Combine the turmeric, ginger, and honey and swirl the mixture through. Refrigerate until you're ready to eat.

6. Once the batter has rested, place a nonstick skillet over medium heat and add a drizzle of oil. Wipe it around with a paper towel to create a thin coating. Once hot, in batches, spoon the batter into the pan, about 2 tablespoons per pancake, leaving space between each pancake so they can spread slightly. Once small bubbles form after 2–3 minutes, gently flip each pancake over and cook the other side for 1–2 minutes. Keep warm in a low oven while you cook the rest, adding oil and wiping between batches as needed, then serve with the yogurt and sprinkled with the seeds. An extra drizzle of honey is nice, too.

Coconut, kale & turmeric-baked eggs with quinoa

Nutritional info per serving

Fiber 8.1g
Protein 26g
Plant Points 6.5

 **Serves** 2    **Prep** 15 min    **Cook** 20 min

2½ oz (70g) white, black, or red quinoa, rinsed

1 tbsp coconut oil

½ tsp black mustard seeds

4–5 fresh or dried curry leaves (optional)

½ tsp cumin seeds

½ tsp fennel seeds

Thumb-sized piece of ginger, finely minced

1 small garlic clove, finely minced

½–1 green chili (depending on heat), sliced

4 scallions, sliced

5½ oz (150g) kale, stems removed and chopped

2 tomatoes, chopped

¾ tsp ground turmeric

2 tbsp tamari or light soy sauce

scant 1 cup/7 fl oz (200 ml) coconut milk

4 eggs

Big handful of cilantro, leaves and stems chopped

Sea salt

Lime wedges, to serve

This breakfast is savory-meets-sweet, and inspired by a trip abroad where I first tasted baked eggs infused with coconut and spice. It's packed with color, flavor, and plant diversity, and you can easily make it vegan by leaving out the eggs. Save time by using a pouch of precooked quinoa: mixed packs with red, black, and white seeds not only make life easier, but add extra plant points and a variety of fibers. If you want to make this vegan, swap out the eggs for tofu.

1. Place the quinoa in a pan with ⅔ cup/5¼ fl oz (160 ml) of water and a pinch of salt. Bring to a simmer and cook for 15 minutes until tender and the water has cooked away (add more if necessary). Cover with a dish towel and leave for at least 5 minutes to steam dry.

2. Meanwhile, place a large, wide oven-proof skillet (with a lid) over medium heat and melt the coconut oil. When hot, add the mustard seeds and as soon as they start popping, add the curry leaves (if using), cumin, and fennel seeds and fry for 30 seconds or until the curry leaves turn translucent.

3. Turn the heat down to low and add the ginger, garlic, chili, and scallions and a big pinch of salt. Fry for 2 minutes until the onion is softened. Stir in the kale, tomato, turmeric, tamari, and a splash of water and keep stirring until the kale begins to wilt, about 2–3 minutes.

4. Pour in the coconut milk and cooked quinoa and stir to combine. You want it to be quite saucy, so add a splash of water if it seems dry.

5. Heat up the broiler to high and make 4 small hollows in the mixture. Crack an egg into each hollow and cover with a lid. Simmer over low heat for 2–3 minutes, then take off the lid and place under the grill for 2–3 minutes until the whites are set and the yolks are cooked to your liking. Scatter over the cilantro and serve with lime wedges.

Chickpea pancakes with onion, tomatoes, cilantro & coconut sambol

Nutritional info per serving

Fiber 8.5g
Protein 13g
Plant Points 6.25

 **Serves** 4    **Prep** 20 min    **Cook** 10 min

1¾ cups/7 oz (200g) chickpea flour

½ tsp baking powder

¼ tsp ground turmeric

¾ tsp garam masala

¾ tsp sea salt

3½ oz (100g) cherry tomatoes, chopped

¾ small red onion, chopped (remaining ¼ used below)

2 handfuls of cilantro, leaves and stems chopped, plus extra to serve

4 tsp coconut or olive oil, to fry

For the coconut sambol

¼ small red onion, chopped

¼ tsp hot chili powder

1 green or red chili, chopped

2¼ oz (60g) dried, shredded coconut

Zest and juice of 1 lime

Sea salt and freshly ground black pepper

A coconut sambol is a vibrant Sri Lankan-style relish made with grated coconut, fresh herbs, and lime, the perfect partner for this savory chickpea pancake. If you can't find fresh coconut, use shredded instead. A fried egg on top will make it more substantial, or try sliced avocado if you're vegan or want more plant points. And if you like a bit of heat, feel free to add a touch of chili.

1. Whisk together the chickpea flour, baking powder, spices, salt, and generous 1 cup/9 fl oz (250 ml) of water and put to one side for 20 minutes to thicken up.

2. Meanwhile, prepare the sambol. Combine the sambol ingredients with 4 tablespoons of water, a good pinch of salt, and plenty of pepper. Mix well with your hands, scrunching them up a little, then put the mixture to one side.

3. Stir the chopped tomatoes, onion, and cilantro into the rested batter.

4. Place a medium nonstick skillet over medium heat and warm 1 teaspoon of the oil. When hot, add a quarter of the batter and spread it around with the back of a spoon so it's about ⅛ in (3 mm) thick. Leave the pancake to cook for 2–3 minutes, or until you see small bubbles appearing on the surface. Then, gently flip it over. Cook the other side for 2–3 minutes, adding more oil if it feels like it needs it, until dark golden and a bit crunchy on the edges. Slide the pancake out of the pan onto a plate, and keep warm while you make the remainder.

5. Eat while nice and hot, with the sambol, a little extra cilantro, and a fried egg if you want.

Potato farls with smashed avocado, feta & mint

 **Serves** 4

 **Prep** 15 min
+ chilling

 **Cook** 40 min

1 lb (450g) starchy potatoes (such as Yukon Gold), scrubbed

2¼ oz (60g) butter, plus a little to grease the pan

¾ cup/3½ oz (100g) whole-wheat flour, plus extra to dust

2 tbsp ground flaxseeds

Sea salt and freshly ground black pepper

For the smashed avocado

2 avocados

Juice of ½ lemon

Small handful of mint leaves, chopped

2½ oz (70g) feta, crumbled

Pinch of dried red pepper flakes, to serve (optional)

Soft and golden, these Irish griddle breads make a lovely alternative to toast. Prepare a batch at the weekend—they will keep beautifully for easy breakfasts throughout the week, and the cooling and reheating increases the resistant starch. If you have leftover potatoes in the fridge, use those instead of boiling from scratch.

1. Cut the potatoes into large, even-sized chunks and place them in a pan of cold, salted water. Cover the pan with a lid and bring the water to the boil. Cook for about 12–15 minutes, or until the potatoes are tender, then drain them in a colander. Set the colander over the pan and leave the potatoes to dry for 10 minutes.

2. Return the dry potatoes to the pan and mash them until smooth. Ideally, refrigerate them for 12–24 hours at this point, but if you're short on time, spread the mash over a plate to help it cool quickly, then place it in the fridge until cold.

3. When you're ready to make and cook the farls, first stone and peel the avocados. Place the flesh into a bowl and crush it with a fork to a coarse consistency. Stir in the lemon juice, mint, and feta and season lightly to taste (it might not need salt—the feta is salty). Put to one side until you're ready to eat.

4. Melt the butter, then stir it with the flour and flaxseed into the cooled potato. Season with a little pepper, taste, and adjust the salt if necessary. Combine until you have a pliable and not-too-sticky dough.

5. Dust your hands with flour. Transfer the dough to a lightly floured surface and shape it into a ball. Cut the ball in half and set one half aside. Using a rolling pin, roll the other half into a rough circle approximately 6–6½ in (15–17 cm) in diameter. Cut the circle into 4 equal wedges.

6. Warm a large nonstick skillet over medium heat and grease it lightly with butter. When the butter is hot, add the farl quarters and cook them for 3 minutes until golden on the underside. Very gently turn over the wedges and cook on the other side for about 7–8 minutes, until heated through and golden. Transfer the cooked farls to a warm oven while you repeat with the remaining potato dough.

7. Divide the farls between 4 serving plates and serve with equal amounts of the smashed avocado and feta, and a pinch of chili flakes, too, if you like.

Crispy chickpea fried eggs with garlic yogurt & herbs

 **Serves** 2

 **Prep** 5 min

 **Cook** 20 min

1 × 14 oz (400g) can chickpeas, drained and rinsed

1 tbsp sesame seeds

2 tbsp olive or canola oil

¼ tsp dried oregano

½ tsp Turkish chili flakes or pinch of chili powder

4 eggs

A few mint leaves, chopped, or a sprinkle of dried mint, to serve

1 tsp sumac (optional), to serve

For the garlic yogurt

½ small garlic clove, minced

generous ½ cup/ 5½ oz (150g) skyr, or Greek or coconut yogurt

Small handful of dill, chopped, to serve

Sea salt and freshly ground black pepper

Using Turkish chili flakes brings an authentic warmth to this Turkish twist on classic fried eggs, but regular chili works just as well, if that's what you have. Likewise, feel free to substitute dried mint for the fresh if that's easier. One tip: be patient before you start frying your chickpeas—make sure they're thoroughly dried, so that you get the desired crispy crunch in the finished dish.

1. Make the garlic yogurt. Combine the garlic and yogurt in a bowl and season well with salt and pepper. Put to one side.

2. Gently pat dry the chickpeas in a dish towel.

3. Warm a large nonstick skillet (with a lid) over medium-low heat and add the sesame seeds. Toast for 1–2 minutes until beginning to color, then add the oil, chickpeas, and plenty of salt and pepper. Fry, stirring occasionally, for 7–9 minutes until the chickpeas begin to color and turn crisp. Be patient as it will happen eventually.

4. Once the majority of chickpeas are crispy, stir in the oregano and chili. Heat up the broiler to high and make 4 small hollows in the mixture. Crack an egg into each and cover with the lid. Simmer over low heat for 2–3 minutes, then take off the lid and place the pan under the grill for 2–3 minutes until the whites are set and the yolks are cooked to your liking.

5. Transfer the dish to plates and spoon over the yogurt. Sprinkle over the herbs and sumac, then serve.

Super high-fiber seeded nut & raisin loaf

 **Makes** 1 loaf

 **Prep** 5 min + resting

 **Cook** 1 hour 20 min

2½ oz (75g) dried red lentils, finely ground

2½ oz (75g) rolled oats

2½ oz (75g) sunflower seeds

2½ oz (75g) pumpkin seeds

2½ oz (75g) flaxseeds

1¾ oz (50g) almonds and/or hazelnuts, roughly chopped

2½ oz (75g) raisins (optional)

2 tbsp chia seeds

4 tbsp psyllium husks

1¼ tsp sea salt

3 tbsp coconut oil, melted, plus extra to grease

I'm the biggest fan of loaves. From banana bread to seeded bakes, I'm obsessed with them, and I try to include at least one in every book I write. This high-fiber loaf is one of my favorites: packed with nuts and seeds, naturally sweetened with raisins, and flour-free, it's made entirely from pantry staples. Soak the mixture overnight before baking to put it straight into the oven in the morning. It keeps beautifully all week. Leave out the raisins if you want it less sweet.

1. Grease a 1lb (450g) loaf pan (or silicone loaf mold) with a little coconut oil and line it with parchment paper (base and sides).

2. Combine all the dry ingredients in a mixing bowl (with or without the raisins) and stir in the coconut oil so everything is nicely coated, then stir in 1¾ cups/14 fl oz (400 ml) of water. Transfer the mixture to the loaf pan and smooth the top.

3. Leave the loaf mixture to soak for at least 2 hours (and up to 12 hours), until it feels stiff and thick.

4. Preheat the oven to 350°F (180°C). Bake the bread for 1 hour 10 minutes–1 hour 20 minutes until the top is golden and the loaf sounds hollow when you tap the bottom (briefly remove it to test, then return it to the pan). Leave the loaf to cool in the pan for 10 minutes, then transfer it to a rack to cool completely before slicing.

5. Store in an airtight container for up to 5 days. It's also delicious toasted.

With the juggle of work meetings, school pickups, and otherwise packed schedules, it's all too easy to opt for something quick and processed for lunch. This chapter brings the joy back to practical, time-sensitive midday eating. Think hearty grain salads, the best sandwich I have ever made, soups that actually fill you up, and rolls layered with color and crunch.

In our fast-paced lives, planning ahead is one of the simplest yet most powerful ways to look after both our health and our wallets. Preparing lunches in advance not only saves money but also helps us make more mindful choices, eat slowly, and digest properly. These recipes are designed to make that sequence easy: cook once, eat well all week.

Each ingredient adds something unique, from lentils offering resistant starch to nuts and seeds delivering healthy fats and prebiotic fiber. You'll also see that protein and fiber work best together, keeping hunger steady and energy balanced until dinnertime.

Lunches

Vegetable summer rolls with mango & edamame beans

Fiber 13g
Protein 9.2g
Plant Points 9.75

 **Makes** 12
Serves 4

 **Prep** 30 min

1 avocado, pitted, peeled, and sliced

1 not-too-ripe mango, peeled, pitted, and sliced

1 large broccoli stalk (about 3½ oz/100g), peeled and cut into matchsticks

1 large carrot (about 1½ oz/125g), scrubbed and cut into matchsticks

½ red bell pepper (about 2½ oz/75g), seeded and cut into matchsticks

3½ oz (100g) red cabbage, shredded

4 oz (115g) edamame beans, cooked

¼ oz (10g) cilantro and/or mint leaves

12 rice paper wrappers

Sea salt and freshly ground black pepper

For the dipping sauce

6 tbsp smooth or crunchy peanut butter

1 small garlic clove, minced

1 tbsp tamari or light soy sauce

Juice of 1 lime

1 tbsp maple syrup

A pinch of dried red pepper flakes

This rainbow-tastic dish is as vibrant as it is versatile: it's perfect for showing off the beauty of fresh, colorful ingredients and, rolled up tightly, makes a stunning platter for entertaining. The creamy peanut-butter dipping sauce adds delicious richness—and even more plant points.

1. First, make the peanut butter dipping sauce by combining all the ingredients with 2–3 tablespoons of water. Stir until fluffy, then set aside.

2. Lay out all the prepared vegetables and herbs in front of you.

3. Pour some room-temperature water into a wide shallow bowl large enough to contain each wrapper.

4. One at a time, submerge each wrapper into the water for 5–10 seconds until soft, then use two hands to carefully transfer it to a clean work surface or plastic cutting board. Place a slice of avocado and a slice of mango about one-third of the way up from the bottom of the wrapper and pile equal amounts of the rest of the ingredients on top, leaving the top one-third free for wrapping. Pull up the bottom part of the wrapper over the vegetables, making sure everything is tightly tucked in. Fold in the edges and keep rolling all the way to the top. Slice the filled roll in half and place the halves on a plate (alternatively, you can keep the rolls whole, if you like).

5. Repeat with the rest of the ingredients, then serve with the dipping sauce.

Roast cauliflower & chickpeas with green tahini & pink onions

 **Serves** 4    **Prep** 15 min    **Cook** 35 min

1 large or 2 small heads of cauliflower (about 1lb/14 oz [850g] altogether), stem trimmed

1 × 14 oz (400g) can chickpeas, drained and rinsed

4 tbsp olive or canola oil

1 tsp ground cumin

1 tsp ground coriander

½ tsp ground cinnamon

½ tsp smoked paprika

10½ oz (300g) cherry tomatoes, halved

Sea salt and freshly ground black pepper

For the pickled onion

1 small red onion, sliced

Juice of ½ lemon

1 tsp superfine sugar

For the green tahini

1 garlic clove, roughly chopped

6 oz (175g) tahini

Juice of 1 large lemon, plus extra if needed

3 tbsp olive oil

2 handfuls of parsley leaves, roughly chopped, plus extra to serve

Small handful of mint leaves, roughly chopped, plus extra to serve

Never let anyone tell you that cauliflower is bland. Roasting it with chickpeas brings out a gorgeous nuttiness. This simple vegetarian dish is perfect for sharing at the weekend, or for enjoying as a quick, nourishing weekday lunch.

1. Preheat the oven to 425°F (220°C).

2. Cut the cauliflower into large florets and slice the stem into large chunks, keeping any nice leaves. Place all the pieces, except the leaves, in a bowl along with the chickpeas, oil, and spices and season generously with salt and pepper. Use your hands to mix everything together until nicely coated, then spread out the mixture on your largest baking sheet (you may want to use 2 if it looks crowded).

3. Roast the mixture in the oven for 15 minutes, stir, add the cauliflower leaves (if using), and roast for a further 15–20 minutes, until the edges of the cauliflower are golden and crisp and the chickpeas have firmed up.

4. Meanwhile make the pickled onion. Place the onion in a small bowl, sprinkle over the lemon juice and toss with the sugar and a pinch of salt. Put to one side to pickle while the cauliflower mixture finishes roasting.

5. Put all the tahini ingredients and 4 tablespoons of water in a blender or small food processor with a big pinch of salt and pepper and blend until smooth. The mixture might initially be a little thick, so keep adding up to another 4 tablespoons) of water and blending until you have a lovely, fluffy dip. Adjust the seasoning. You may want to add more lemon juice, too.

6. Spread the tahini on the bottom of a big serving plate and tumble the roasted cauliflower and chickpeas on top. Arrange the tomatoes around the plate and scatter with the pickled onions and a few mint and parsley leaves. Serve warm or at room temperature.

Beet Waldorf grain salad

 **Serves** 4 (as a main)

 **Prep** 15 min

 **Cook** 10 min

2½ oz (75g) walnuts or pecans, halved

2 × 9 oz (250g) mixed-grain pouch (such as Good & Gather Whole Grain Blend)

3 tbsp walnut or olive oil

Juice of 1 lemon

1 × 9 oz (250g) cooked vacuum-packed beet, drained and chopped into ⅝–¾ in (1.5–2 cm) chunks

2 apples (I use Gala), scrubbed and chopped into ⅝–¾ in (1.5–2 cm) chunks

4½ oz (125g) red or black seedless grapes, halved

3 celery sticks, finely sliced, any leaves roughly chopped

1 Little Gem lettuce, separated into leaves

scant ½ cup/3½ oz (100g) skyr, or Greek or coconut yogurt

1 tbsp cider vinegar

1 tbsp Dijon or whole grain mustard

2 tsp chopped tarragon leaves

7 oz (200g) feta or vegetarian alternative, crumbled

Sea salt and freshly ground black pepper

This vibrant twist on a classic Waldorf salad heroes earthy, sweet beets. It's a quick, throw-together option for busy days—just chop your ingredients and stir through a mixed grain pouch for ease. Toasted walnuts bring not only crunch and flavor, but also a boost of gut-nourishing omega-3 fatty acids.

1. Start by toasting the walnuts in a large dry pan over medium-low heat for 5–7 minutes until beginning to color, then allow to cool.

2. Dress the grains with 1 tablespoon of the oil, the lemon juice, and some salt and pepper and spread them over the base of a large platter (or divide between 4 plates).

3. Pile the beet, apple, grapes, and celery on top of the grains and arrange the lettuce leaves around the edge of the salad.

4. Combine the remaining oil, along with the skyr or yogurt, cider vinegar, mustard, and tarragon in a small bowl and season lightly. Generously drizzle the dressing over the salad, tossing it if you wish, then scatter over the feta and toasted walnuts, and serve.

Turkish lentil & carrot soup with mint & chili

 **Serves** 4    **Prep** 10 min    **Cook** 35 min

5 tbsp olive or canola oil

1 large onion, chopped

2 carrots, scrubbed and
chopped

2 garlic cloves, chopped

1 tsp ground cumin

1 tsp sweet paprika

1½ tbsp tomato paste

7 oz (200g) dried red lentils,
rinsed

5½ oz (150g) sweet potato,
scrubbed and chopped

5½ cups/2 pints (1.25 liters)
hot vegetable or chicken
stock (bouillon)

1 tsp sea salt, plus extra to
season

2¼ oz (60g) bulgur wheat,
rinsed

Juice of ½ lemon, plus
wedges to serve

½ tsp Turkish chili flakes,
or ¼ tsp dried red pepper
flakes

Handful of mint leaves,
finely chopped, or
1 tsp dried mint

Freshly ground black pepper

It's easy to fall into a soup rut, but this Turkish-inspired red lentil, carrot, and mint version is a brilliant way to keep things interesting and rack up plenty of plant points, too. Adjust the liquid at the end according to how thick you like your soup, and blend more or less, depending on your preference for texture. It's a great make-ahead—it keeps well in the fridge for two to three days in an airtight container.

1. Place a large, deep pan over medium heat and warm 2 tablespoons of the oil. Add the onion, carrots, and a pinch of salt and cook, stirring, for 8–10 minutes until soft.

2. Add the garlic and, once fragrant (about 2–3 minutes), add the cumin, paprika, and tomato paste. Cook for a further 1–2 minutes before adding the lentils, sweet potato, stock, and 1 teaspoon of salt. Bring to a simmer and cook for 15–20 minutes until the lentils and sweet potato are soft.

3. Meanwhile, place the bulgur in a pan, cover in a scant ⅔ cup/5 fl oz (150 ml) of boiling water, add a pinch of salt and simmer for 8–10 minutes until the water has been absorbed. Add more water as needed. Stir in the lemon juice.

4. Combine the remaining oil, chili, and mint in a small bowl and set aside to use as a garnish.

5. Once the lentils are soft, use an electric immersion blender to purée the soup—either until smooth or stop halfway if you'd like a little texture. Stir in the cooked bulgur.

6. Check the seasoning, and transfer the soup to bowls. Spoon over the chili-mint oil and serve each portion with a lemon wedge.

Caldo verde soup with smoky lima beans

 **Serves** 4    **Prep** 10 min    **Cook** 35 min

3 tbsp olive oil

1 large leek, sliced

2 garlic cloves, sliced

1 × 20 oz (570g) jar or can lima beans

12 oz (350g) starchy potatoes, such as Yukon Gold, scrubbed and cut into ⅝–¾ in (1.5–2 cm) cubes

1 bay leaf

3½ cups/28 fl oz (800 ml) hot chicken or vegetable stock

10½ oz (300g) dark leafy greens, such as spring greens or kale, chopped and thickest stems discarded

Sea salt and freshly ground black pepper

For the smoky lima beans

2 tbsp olive oil, plus extra to serve

2 garlic cloves, chopped

½ tsp smoked paprika, plus extra to serve

Big handful of parsley leaves, chopped, to serve

Caldo verde is Portuguese for "green broth"—a comforting, rustic soup traditionally made with potatoes, kale, and chorizo. My version keeps all that hearty flavor but replaces the meat with paprika-spiked lima beans, creating a wholesome vegan twist. I like using jarred lima beans for their rich, velvety liquid, which helps thicken the soup, but canned beans work just as well.

1. Warm the olive oil in a large deep pan over medium heat and fry the leek and garlic with a pinch of salt for 5–7 minutes until soft and slightly colored.

2. Add half the lima beans and all the liquid in the jar or can. Pour the remaining half of the lima beans into a colander and rinse, then drain on paper towel and set aside.

3. Add the potatoes, bay leaf, and stock to the pan. Season with salt and pepper, then bring the soup to a simmer and cook for 15–18 minutes until the potatoes are soft.

4. Meanwhile, make the smoky lima beans. In a small nonstick skillet, warm the oil and garlic over low heat and leave for 2–3 minutes to allow the garlic to infuse into the oil. Turn the heat up to medium, add the reserved, rinsed lima beans, along with the paprika, and some salt and pepper, and continue cooking, for another 4–5 minutes, stirring occasionally so they get a nice crust all over, then take the pan off the heat and keep the beans warm.

5. Remove the bay leaf and use an electric immersion blender to purée the soup—either until smooth or stop halfway if you'd like a little texture. Add the greens and simmer for 5–6 minutes until tender but still bright green. Check the seasoning, then divide between your bowls to serve.

6. Top each bowl with smoky beans, a sprinkle of parsley, another pinch of paprika, and a drizzle of oil.

Crispy quinoa & kale salad with creamy cashew dressing

 **Serves** 4    **Prep** 15 min    **Cook** 45 min

4½ oz (125g) white, black, or red quinoa, rinsed

3 tbsp olive oil

5½ oz (150g) lacinato kale, stems discarded

1 tbsp cider vinegar

7 oz (200g) canned or frozen and defrosted, or fresh sweet corn

7 oz (200g) cherry tomatoes, halved

2 avocados, pitted, peeled, and chopped into ½ in (1cm) cubes

1 red bell pepper, seeded and chopped into ½ in (1cm) cubes

1¾ oz (50g) toasted pumpkin seeds

For the dressing

3½ oz (100g) cashews, soaked for at least 2 hours

Juice of 2 limes

1 tbsp cider vinegar

2 tbsp olive or canola oil

½ small garlic clove, chopped

10g cilantro leaves and stems

½ green chili, ideally jalapeño, seeded

1 tsp maple syrup

Sea salt and freshly ground black pepper

This Mexican-inspired salad is substantial enough to enjoy for lunch or dinner. It holds up beautifully without going soggy, making it also perfect for packed lunches or picnics. You can use a pouch of precooked quinoa to save time (if you can find it, black or red quinoa adds extra fiber and a lovely nuttiness). You'll need to soak the cashews for the dressing for at least 2 hours (or overnight) before you begin.

1. Preheat the oven to 375°F (190°C) and line a large baking sheet with parchment paper. Place the quinoa in a pan with 1¼ cups plus 1 tbsp/10½ fl oz (300 ml) of water, bring to a simmer and cook for 15 minutes until tender and the water has cooked away (add more water if necessary, until the quinoa is tender), then cover the pan with a dish towel for 5 minutes for the quinoa to steam-dry.

2. Stir in 2 tablespoons of the oil, spread the quinoa out in a thin layer on the tray, and place the tray in the oven. Bake, stirring once, for 25–30 minutes until the edges are golden and crisp. Leave to cool and get crispier.

3. Make the dressing. Drain the cashews from their soaking liquid and blend with 7 tablespoons (100 ml) of water and all the other dressing ingredients until bright green and smooth. Have a taste and adjust the seasoning with salt and pepper.

4. Place the kale in a large mixing bowl with the remaining tablespoon of oil, the cider vinegar, and a pinch of salt and use your hands to massage it until it begins to wilt, about 2–3 minutes.

5. Add the rest of the salad ingredients, season with salt and pepper and give everything a gentle toss. Transfer to a platter and scatter over the crispy quinoa. Generously drizzle the dressing over the salad, tossing it if you wish, then serve.

Coronation Brussels sprout salad with couscous & apricots

 **Serves** 4    **Prep** 15 min    **Cook** 20 min   

2 × 6 oz (170g) chicken breasts or skinless, boneless thighs (at room temperature)

1 lb 2 oz (500g) Brussels sprouts, 14 oz (400g) halved, 3½ oz (100g) finely sliced

3 tbsp olive or canola oil

4¼ oz (120g) giant whole-wheat couscous

1½ tbsp cider vinegar

1 oz (30g) chopped pecans or toasted almond flakes

2¼ oz (60g) dried pitted apricots, thinly sliced

For the sauce

1½ tbsp mild curry powder

1 small garlic clove, minced

1 tbsp olive or canola oil

generous 1 cup/9 oz (250g) skyr, or Greek or coconut yogurt

1½ tbsp red or white miso

2 tsp maple syrup or honey

1½ tbsp cider vinegar

Sea salt and freshly ground black pepper

Handful of parsley leaves, chopped, to serve

A twist on the classic Coronation Chicken, this salad is easily made vegan by swapping out the chicken for tofu, or leaving it out altogether. If you don't like Brussels sprouts, chopped hispi (pointed) cabbage works perfectly, and fresh orange makes a lovely alternative to dried apricots, although with a little less fiber.

1. Preheat the oven to 425°F (220°C).

2. Meanwhile, combine all the sauce ingredients in a bowl and season with salt and pepper to taste. Use 5 tablespoons of the sauce to marinate the chicken—rubbing it generously over the meat. Set aside.

3. Pour the halved Brussels sprouts onto a large baking sheet and drizzle with 2 tablespoons of the oil. Toss well, spreading them out into an even layer. Add the chicken to the baking sheet (if it feels tight on space, place the chicken in a separate baking sheet), season everything with salt and pepper and roast for 18–22 minutes, until the Brussels are dark, charred, and tender and the chicken is cooked through (165°F [74°C] on a meat thermometer at the thickest part)—return the baking sheet to the oven if not. Once it's cooked, rest the chicken for 10 minutes, then slice.

4. While everything is in the oven, bring a pan of salted water to the boil and cook the couscous according to the package instructions until tender. Drain it, then rinse it under cold water.

5. Toss the raw, sliced Brussels with the remaining oil and the cider vinegar and season with salt and pepper. Stir in the pecans or almond flakes and the apricots and put to one side.

6. Spread the remaining sauce over a big platter or divide it between your serving plates. Top with the cooked couscous, then the charred Brussels sprouts and the chicken. Finish with the shredded Brussels salad and a good sprinkling of parsley.

Note You can cook the chicken in an air fryer at 350°F (180°C) for 18–20 minutes until a meat thermometer registers 165°F (74°C).

Roast beet, carrot & blackberry salad with halloumi

 **Serves** 4    **Prep** 15 min    **Cook** 50 min

1 lb 2 oz (500g) bunch of beets, scrubbed, cut into 1 in (2–3 cm) wedges

14 oz (400g) sweet potatoes, scrubbed, cut into 1 in (2–3 cm) pieces

4 shallots, quartered, or 2 red onions, cut into eighths

2 tbsp thyme leaves

6 tbsp olive or canola oil

3 thick slices (about 10½ oz/300g) stale rye bread, torn into 1 in (2–3 cm) pieces

8 oz (225g) halloumi, cut into ⅝ in (1.5 cm) chunks

5½ oz (150g) fresh or defrosted frozen blackberries

1 tsp maple syrup or honey

2 tsp cider vinegar

2 carrots, scrubbed and shaved into ribbons with a peeler

2¼ oz (60g) arugula

Sea salt and freshly ground black pepper

This recipe showcases the incredible anthocyanins found in dark-colored fruits and vegetables (like beets and blackberries). Anthocyanins are powerful plant compounds that support brain health and help protect against inflammation. For a vegan option, swap the halloumi for a handful of toasted mixed nuts, which add crunch and extra plant protein. You can use precooked beets to save time. Soaking the halloumi helps reduce saltiness and keeps it tender during cooking. You won't need oil, as a nonstick pan works perfectly.

1. Preheat the oven to 400°F (200°C). Scatter the beets, sweet potatoes, shallots, and thyme into a roasting pan and toss with 3 tablespoons of the oil. Roast for 35–45 minutes, turning once or twice.

2. Meanwhile, toss the rye bread in a tablespoon of oil, spread it out on another lined tray and toast on the shelf under the vegetables for the final 20 minutes of the vegetable cooking time.

3. While the bread is baking, place the halloumi in a bowl, cover with boiling water, and leave for 20 minutes to soften.

4. Make the dressing next. Roughly crush 1½ oz (40g) of blackberries with a fork and stir in the maple syrup or honey, vinegar, and remaining 2 tablespoons of oil. Put to one side.

5. Once the vegetables are golden and the rye bread is crisp, allow them to cool slightly on the tray. Prepare a platter or 4 plates with the shaved carrots, arugula, and remaining blackberries.

6. Place a nonstick skillet over medium heat. Drain the halloumi and pat it dry with paper. Once the pan is hot, add the halloumi (you won't need any oil) and leave for 2 minutes before turning and cooking the other side for a further 2 minutes until nicely golden all over and hot through.

7. Transfer the roasted vegetables, rye croûtons, and halloumi to the prepared platter or plates. Drizzle over the dressing and serve immediately while the halloumi is still hot.

Crispy rice salad with shrimp, broccoli & avocado

 **Serves** 4    **Prep** 10 min    **Cook** 25 min

Nutritional info per serving

Fiber 7.9g
Protein 21g
Plant Points 9.5

2 × 9 oz (250g) pouch of cooked long-grain brown rice, or leftover rice

3 tbsp sesame oil or canola or mild olive oil

1 tbsp tamari or light soy sauce

½ head (about 7 oz/200g) broccoli, head, and stem roughly chopped

3½ oz (100g) edamame beans

1 ripe avocado, pitted, peeled, and diced

12 radishes, sliced

3 scallions, sliced

Big handful of mint leaves, shredded

5½ oz (150g) cooked shrimp or firm tofu

1½ oz (40g) roasted peanuts, chopped, to serve

For the dressing

1½ tbsp sesame oil

1 tbsp sesame seeds, toasted

2 tbsp mild olive oil

2 tbsp tamari

1 tbsp maple syrup

Juice of 1½ limes

Sea salt and freshly ground black pepper

This vibrant salad is all about texture: crisp rice, creamy avocado, and tender shrimp. Make it vegan by swapping the shrimp for baked tofu, which soaks up the dressing beautifully. This recipe scales effortlessly, too—for smaller portions, skip the oven and crisp the rice in a hot pan with a drizzle of oil. Just don't overcook it if you want to keep that lovely soft but still firm texture.

1. Preheat the oven to 400°F (200°C) and line a baking sheet with parchment paper. Toss the rice in the oil so it's evenly coated and spread it out in an even layer on the lined baking sheet. Bake it in the oven for 20–25 minutes, stirring occasionally until golden and crisp, but with a little chew. Once golden, drizzle over the tamari or soy sauce and toss well before leaving to cool.

2. Place the chopped broccoli and edamame in a steamer (or in a bowl in the microwave, and cover with plastic wrap/plastic wrap). Cook them for 4–5 minutes until the broccoli is al dente and the edamame are tender, then leave to cool.

3. When the vegetables are cool, place them in a bowl along with the avocado, radishes, scallions, mint, and shrimp or tofu. Combine the dressing ingredients and season with salt and pepper. Add the dressing and the crispy rice, and season to taste with salt and pepper. Toss gently to combine.

4. Divide the mixture between your serving plates, sprinkle with the peanuts, and serve.

Baked chickpea & carrot falafels with tahini sauce

 **Serves** 4

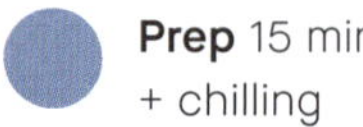 **Prep** 15 min
+ chilling

 **Cook** 30 min

2½ oz (75g) carrots, scrubbed and coarsely grated

1 × 14 oz (400g) can chickpeas, drained, rinsed, and thoroughly dried

1 onion, chopped

3 garlic cloves, chopped

Handful of parsley, chopped

Handful of cilantro, chopped

1 tsp ground cumin

1 tsp ground coriander

1 tsp sea salt

½ tsp baking powder

2–4 tbsp chickpea flour or all-purpose flour

4 tbsp canola or olive oil

For the tahini sauce

3½ oz (100g) tahini

½ small garlic clove, minced

Juice of 1 lemon

1 tbsp olive oil

For the salad

1 tbsp pomegranate molasses or juice of ½ lemon

1½ tbsp olive oil

Seeds from ½ pomegranate

1 cucumber, chopped

14 oz (400g) cherry tomatoes, halved

Sea salt and freshly ground black pepper

These are a lighter, more delicate take on traditional falafels, which are made with soaked dried chickpeas. They are ideal for children or adults on the go, as they make a great lunchbox option with that creamy whipped tahini sauce in a cup for dipping.

1. Place the carrot in some paper towel and wring out all the liquid. Set aside.

2. Put all the remaining falafel ingredients except the flour and oil into a blender and blend until finely chopped—you want plenty of texture but the mixture needs to be fine enough that it will stick together.

3. Transfer the mixture to a bowl and stir in the carrots and 2 tablespoons of the flour. Grab a handful of the mixture and if it feels like it's not sticking together, add a little more flour. Test again, and keep adding up to another 2 tablespoons of flour until you are satisfied the mixture will hold. Chill and rest the mixture in the fridge for 30 minutes.

4. Meanwhile, preheat the oven to 400°F (200°C) and line a baking sheet with parchment paper. Grease the paper generously with 2 tablespoons of the oil.

5. About 1 tablespoon at a time, scoop out portions of the chilled mixture and form each one into a patty. You should get 16 patties altogether. Place them on a baking sheet as you go. Use a pastry brush to brush the top and side of each patty with the remaining 2 tablespoons of oil.

6. Bake the falafels for 12–15 minutes until golden, then gently turn them over and cook the other side for 10–12 minutes, until they are cooked through and golden. Leave to rest and firm up for 5 minutes.

7. Meanwhile, to make the tahini sauce, stir together the tahini, garlic, lemon juice, and oil. It will seize up, but slowly start whisking in 4–5 tablespoons of water until you get a lovely, creamy sauce, the texture of thick yogurt. Season to taste and add more lemon if you want it perkier or more oil if you want it richer.

8. To make the salad, whisk together the molasses or lemon juice and oil, then add the other ingredients. Season lightly and toss.

9. Serve the warm falafel with the tahini for dipping or drizzling, and the salad on the side. On top of warm flatbreads is delicious.

Green goddess avocado sandwich

 **Makes** 2    **Prep** 5 min

4 slices whole-wheat or rye bread

1 large ripe avocado, pitted, peeled, and thinly sliced

Handful of sprouts, cress, or microgreens

Handful of baby spinach

8–10 slices cucumber

2 tbsp sauerkraut (or pickled onions; see page 114)

4 romaine, Little Gem, or butter lettuce leaves

For the sauce

½ tbsp capers in brine, well-drained

A few pinches of parsley leaves

A few pinches of dill leaves

½ small garlic clove, peeled

½ tsp Dijon mustard

1 tbsp olive oil

5 tbsp skyr, or Greek or coconut yogurt

Sea salt and freshly ground black pepper

I can honestly say this is one of the best sandwiches I've ever made; it's also one my clients have loved for years. The magic lies in the sauce: a silky blend of avocado, parsley, dill, garlic, and Dijon mustard. Use dried herbs if that's what you have—the result is still wonderfully creamy, tangy, and packed with flavor.

1. Make the sauce first. Chop the capers and herbs together and sweep them into a bowl. Grate in the garlic and stir in the mustard, oil, and skyr or yogurt. Season to taste.

2. To assemble, thickly spread all the slices of bread with the sauce, then top 2 slices of bread with the avocado, sprouts, spinach, cucumber, sauerkraut, and finally the lettuce. Place the other bread slices on top (sauce side downward) and firmly press together before cutting in half and eating immediately.

This chapter celebrates real, everyday meals built around the simple goal of getting more plants, more fiber, and more color onto your plate in around just 30 minutes—these recipes are the "Bonus 30" we introduced on page 57. They demonstrate that nutritious cooking doesn't have to be complicated or time-consuming. Rather, they prove that wholesome, homemade food can be about quick, clever fixes without cutting any nutritional corners: adding tofu to a pasta sauce, blending beans into mac 'n' cheese, and so much more.

Each speedy meal supports balanced nutrition, combining fiber and protein with healthy fats and slow-release carbohydrates for sustained energy, steady appetite, and positive mood.

30-minute dinners

Green lima bean mac & fiber cheese

 **Serves** 4

 **Prep** 10 min

 **Cook** 20 min

5½ oz (150g) lacinato kale or spinach, stems removed as necessary

10½ oz (300g) whole-wheat macaroni

2 tbsp olive or canola oil

1 large leek, sliced

2 garlic cloves, sliced

2 × 14 oz (400g) cans lima beans

¼ nutmeg, grated

5½ oz (150g) Cheddar, Red Leicester, Gouda, and/or Gruyère (ideally a mixture), grated

2½ oz (75g) Parmesan (or vegan substitute), grated

Sea salt and freshly ground black pepper

Made with whole-wheat macaroni, a blend of lima beans, and healthy greens, this recipe boosts fiber without compromising the classic cheesy flavor you'd expect from such a guaranteed family favorite. It's delicious proof that comfort food can still be wonderfully nutritious.

1. Bring a pan of salted water to the boil and cook the green leaves for 5–6 minutes until tender. Scoop them out of the water into a large blender. Add the macaroni to the boiling water and cook according to the package instructions until al dente. Drain, reserving a cupful of the cooking water.

2. While the pasta is cooking, warm the oil in a pan over medium heat and fry the leek and garlic for 5–7 minutes, until softened and beginning to color.

3. Reserve 4¼ oz (120g) of the beans, then transfer the rest, including their liquid, to the blender with the greens. Add the nutmeg and plenty of salt and pepper and blend until you have a completely smooth, vibrant green sauce. Pour the sauce into a baking dish.

4. Heat your broiler to medium. Combine the Cheddar and/or other cheeses with the Parmesan and set aside. Stir the drained pasta into the baking dish along with all but 2 big handfuls of the mixed cheeses. Pour in the reserved beans and the cooked leek and garlic mixture, then stir well to combine, adding a few splashes of cooking water until the mixture reaches your desired consistency. Scatter over the reserved cheese mixture.

5. While the mixture is still hot, place the dish under the grill for 4–6 minutes, until the cheese is melted and delicious and the sauce is bubbling.

Grilled mackerel fillet with herby rice

 **Serves** 4  **Prep** 10 min  **Cook** 15 min

4 × 5½ oz (150g) skin-on mackerel fillets

1½ tbsp tamari or light soy sauce

1½ tbsp maple syrup or honey

For the salad

2½ oz (75g) dried, shredded coconut

1 small red onion, finely chopped

9 oz (250g) green beans, cut into ¾ in (2 cm) pieces

2 × 9 oz (250g) pouches of cooked basmati and wild rice

¾ oz (20g) cilantro, leaves and stems chopped

¾ oz (20g) Thai basil, leaves picked and chopped

½ oz (15g) mint, leaves picked and chopped

½ oz (15g) dill, tender fronds chopped

2½ oz (75g) roasted peanuts, roughly chopped

Zest and juice of 3 limes

Sea salt and freshly ground black pepper

½ cucumber, thickly sliced on the diagonal, to serve

This grilled mackerel comes with *nasi ulam*, a traditional Malaysian herby rice salad. It's the kind of recipe that rewards you with every mouthful. And, as a bonus, your gut bacteria will love the incredible plant diversity it brings to the table.

1. Marinate the mackerel. Pat the fillets dry with paper towel, then make several shallow diagonal cuts, being sure to only score the skin and not to cut into the flesh. Place the fillets in a small container, and rub with the tamari or soy sauce and maple syrup or honey. Leave the fish to marinate in the fridge while you get on with everything else.

2. Place the coconut in a small dry pan over medium-low heat and toast it, stirring often, until it begins to turn golden, about 3–4 minutes. Transfer the coconut to a plate and leave it to cool.

3. Place the onion in a small bowl and cover with cold water—this takes the edge off.

4. Bring a small pan of salted water to the boil and cook the beans until al dente (about 3–4 minutes). Drain them and rinse under cold water until cool.

5. Combine the cooled toasted coconut, green beans, drained onion, and the rest of the salad ingredients (except the cucumber to serve) in a salad bowl and season with salt (it will need a bit) and pepper.

6. Heat up your broiler until very hot (alternatively, you can cook the fish in an oiled skillet). Place the mackerel fillets on a foil-lined tray, skin-side up. Spoon over any leftover marinade, then place them under the grill for 2–4 minutes until the skin is crispy and bubbly. Gently turn the fillets over and cook the other side for 1–2 minutes, until the flesh is opaque (check if you're unsure).

7. Serve the mackerel alongside the rice salad and the slices of cucumber.

Harissa-spiced hispi wedges with date & almond tabbouleh & mint yogurt

Fiber 15g
Protein 19g
Plant Points 9

 **Serves** 4    **Prep** 10 min    **Cook** 30 min

1 tsp cumin seeds

1 tsp coriander seeds

1 tsp caraway seeds

½ tsp dried red pepper flakes

1 small garlic clove, minced

1 tsp sea salt

2 tbsp tomato paste

2 tbsp olive or canola oil

1 tbsp maple syrup or honey

Zest of 1 lemon, plus wedges

2 hispi cabbages, quartered

For the bulgur wheat

6¼ oz (180g) bulgur wheat

¾ oz (20g) parsley, leaves
  and stems chopped

2¼ oz (60g) roasted skin-on
  almonds, chopped

2 scallions, chopped

2¼ oz (60g) dried pitted
  dates or apricots, chopped

Juice of 1 lemon

2 tbsp olive oil

Sea salt and freshly ground
  black pepper

For the mint yogurt

½ small garlic clove, minced

Handful of mint leaves,
  chopped

generous ¾ cup/7 oz (200g)
  skyr, or Greek or coconut
  yogurt

This dish is a flavor explosion: smoky, sweet, nutty, and fresh all at once. It might sound elaborate, but it is wonderfully simple to bring together and a fantastic way to transform humble cabbage into something special. For meat eaters, the recipe is equally delicious made with a roasted chicken leg in place of the cabbage.

1. Preheat the oven to 425°F (220°C). Line a baking sheet with parchment paper.

2. Place all the seeds in a small skillet over medium heat and dry-fry, stirring often, for 2–4 minutes until they begin to smell fragrant. Pour them into a pestle and mortar (or spice grinder) along with the chili flakes and grind until fine. Add the garlic with a big pinch of salt and grind to a paste, then stir in the tomato paste, oil, maple syrup or honey, and lemon zest. Season with pepper, then rub the mixture over the hispi quarters.

3. Transfer the cabbage to the lined baking sheet and roast for 20–25 minutes until the edges are nicely charred and the center is tender but still has a little bite.

4. While the cabbage is in the oven, bring a pan of salted water to the boil. Rinse the bulgur and add it to the pan, cooking until tender (about 9–12 minutes; check the package for exact timings). Drain it into a sieve and place it over the hot pan to steam dry so it's nice and fluffy once cooled (still a little warm is fine, too).

5. Once the bulgur is ready, transfer it to a mixing bowl and add the rest of the salad ingredients. Season to taste with salt and pepper.

6. To make the mint yogurt, combine all the yogurt ingredients in a bowl and season to taste with salt and pepper.

7. Divide the cabbage wedges equally between your serving plates and serve alongside the tabbouleh and a spoonful of mint yogurt. Add lemon wedges for squeezing over.

Creamy artichoke, green olive & parsley pasta

 **Serves** 4    **Prep** 10 min    **Cook** 15 min

14 oz (400g) whole-wheat rigatoni (or pasta shape of choice)

2 × 10 oz (280g) jars of artichokes in oil, quarters or halves, drained (oil reserved if you like)

1 small lemon

3 tbsp olive oil (or use reserved artichoke oil, if it's 100% oil)

2 garlic cloves, finely chopped

A pinch of dried red pepper flakes, plus extra to serve

½ oz (15g) parsley, leaves and stems chopped

1¾ oz (50g) pitted green olives, roughly chopped

1½ oz (45g) Parmesan (or vegan substitute), grated, plus extra to serve

Sea salt and freshly ground black pepper

This is a really elegant pasta—not only full of fiber, but full of flavor, too. Artichokes preserved in oil rather than brine will taste best—and if yours have vinegar added, reduce the amount of lemon to compensate. Try not to keep heating the sauce after you've added the Parmesan as it will become lumpy.

1. Bring a large pan of salted water to the boil and cook the pasta according to the package instructions until al dente.

2. Meanwhile, place a large nonstick skillet over medium-high heat (you'll be adding your pasta to it, so the bigger the better). When the pan is very hot, add the artichokes cut side down (no need to add extra oil), and cook untouched for 4–5 minutes, turning once until they are nicely browned and a little crispy.

3. Zest the lemon into a blender and cut the lemon in half. Turn the heat under the artichokes down to medium and add the oil to the pan along with the garlic and chili flakes. Cook, stirring gently, for 1–2 minutes until the garlic begins to smell fragrant and feel sticky, then squeeze in the lemon juice from both halves of the lemon to stop the garlic cooking. Turn off the heat and season generously with salt and pepper.

4. Transfer half the artichokes to the blender with the zest. Add 6½ tablespoons of water and blend until you have a smooth purée. Scoop the purée into the pan with the rest of the artichokes.

5. Drain the pasta, reserving a generous cup of the cooking water. Return the artichoke pan to a very low heat and stir in the parsley, olives, and drained pasta. Toss gently to combine. Take the pan off the heat, stir in the Parmesan (or alternative) and a few good splashes of the reserved pasta water and keep stirring—the cheese will melt and emulsify with the oil and water into a silky sauce. Add more pasta water as needed until the sauce is glossy and coats the pasta beautifully. Transfer the pasta to your serving plates, and top with a little extra Parmesan (or alternative), if you like.

Kimchi fried spelt with sesame fried eggs

 **Serves** 2    **Prep** 10 min    **Cook** 10 min

2 tbsp mild olive or canola oil

3½ oz (100g) kale, thick stems discarded, shredded

3 scallions, thinly sliced, white and green parts separated

1 large carrot, scrubbed and coarsely grated

½ sweet potato (about 4 oz/115g), scrubbed and coarsely grated

2½ oz (75g) frozen peas, defrosted

3 tbsp kimchi, roughly chopped, plus 1 tbsp kimchi juice (and optional extra juice to serve)

1 × 9 oz (250g) pouch of cooked pearled spelt (or use a mixture of grains, pearled barley, and brown or black rice)

1 tbsp tamari or light soy sauce

For the eggs

2 tbsp sesame seeds

2 tsp sesame oil

2 eggs

Kimchi is a wonderfully beneficial fermented food that supports gut health. If you think you're not a fan, this dish—with its balance of tangy, savory, and nutty flavors—is here to convert you. The recipe makes a satisfying weekend brunch or a quick midweek dinner.

1. Warm the oil in a large skillet over medium heat and stir-fry the kale for 2–3 minutes, adding a few tablespoons of water to help it along, until it begins to wilt.

2. Add the spring-onion whites, along with the carrot, sweet potato, peas, and kimchi and stir-fry for another 2–3 minutes until the carrot and sweet potato are beginning to soften.

3. Add the tablespoon of kimchi juice, and the grains and tamari or soy sauce and keep cooking and stirring until the grains are hot and everything is nicely combined. Turn off the heat and keep warm while you cook your eggs.

4. Warm up a small nonstick skillet over medium-low heat. Sprinkle in the sesame seeds and toast for 1–2 minutes or so until they begin to color. Pour the sesame oil over the seeds, then crack in the eggs and fry them until they are cooked to your liking.

5. Divide the spelt between your serving plates and spoon them over with a teaspoon of kimchi juice if you like. Top each portion with an egg and a sprinkling of the scallion greens.

Gigli with red pesto & tofu sauce

Nutritional info per serving

Fiber 13g
Protein 26g
Plant Points 5.5

 **Serves** 4    **Prep** 2 min    **Cook** 15 min

1 lb (450g) spelt gigli or other whole-wheat pasta shapes

8 oz (225g; drained weight) roasted and skinned jarred red bell peppers (in brine)

2½ oz (75g) sun-dried tomatoes

10½ oz (300g) silken tofu

1½ oz (40g) skin-on or blanched almonds or sunflower seeds

1 garlic clove, minced

4 tbsp olive oil

4 tbsp nutritional yeast, plus extra to serve

Sea salt and freshly ground black pepper

Handful of basil leaves, to serve (optional)

Tofu is such an underrated ingredient and, in this dish, it makes the sauce luxuriously smooth while adding a great source of plant-based protein. The homemade red pesto is quick to blend, and bursting with extra plant points and fiber. Even my children adore this one!

1. Bring a pan of salted water to the boil and cook the pasta according to the package instructions until al dente.

2. Meanwhile, place all the other ingredients except for the basil in a blender with plenty of salt and pepper and blend until smooth. Have a taste and adjust the seasoning if you like.

3. Drain the pasta and return it to the pan. Over low heat, pour over the sauce and stir well to combine.

4. Divide the pasta between your serving plates, tear over a few basil leaves, and sprinkle with a little extra nutritional yeast to serve.

Cod en papillote with arugula & sunflower seed pesto

 **Serves** 4    **Prep** 10 min    **Cook** 25 min

4 tbsp extra-virgin olive oil, plus extra to grease

4 x about 5½ oz (150–160g) cod (or other meaty white fish) fillet, skin removed

1 lemon

2 × 14 oz (400g) cans navy or other white beans, drained and rinsed

1 × 10 oz (280g) jar of artichokes, in oil or brine, drained and quartered

8½ oz (240g) cherry tomatoes, halved, larger ones roughly chopped

A few rosemary or thyme sprigs

For the arugula and sunflower seed pesto

½ small garlic clove, minced

2¼ oz (60g) arugula

2¼ oz (60g) sunflower seeds

4 tbsp olive oil

Zest and juice of ½ lemon

¼ tsp sea salt, plus extra to season

Freshly ground black pepper

"En papillote" simply means cooking in parchment paper, a gentle method that locks in flavor and moisture. You can easily swap the cod for other fish, or make it vegan with hispi (pointed) cabbage (just allow a little extra cooking time). Serve the dish simply—with spinach or kale—and save any leftover pesto for spreading over bread to make sandwiches the next day.

1. Preheat the oven to 400°F (200°C). Cut 4 squares of foil, each 16 in (40 cm) square. Place a sheet of parchment paper (also 16 in/40 cm square) on top of each foil square to make double-layered bases. Lightly grease the parchment with a little oil.

2. Sit a piece of fish in the middle of each piece of oiled parchment and season with salt and pepper. Zest some lemon over each piece. Thinly slice the lemon into rounds and divide the rounds between the cod pieces.

3. Divide the rest of the ingredients between the cod portions, finishing with a tablespoon of olive oil over each. Season generously, then pull up the edges of the paper to make a dome and crimp the edges of the foil—you want to trap the cooking steam. Place the parcels on a tray and put them in the oven for 20–25 minutes, by which time the fish should be cooked through.

4. Meanwhile, place all the ingredients for the pesto in a blender or small food processor with 1–2 tablespoons of water and pulse until finely chopped. Season with pepper and more salt to taste.

5. Carefully open the cod parcels (don't delay in opening as the fish will overcook) and transfer the fish to serving plates. Spoon over the pesto according to taste, and serve with some kale or spinach on the side.

Persian herb & grain stewed lentils with caramelized onions

Nutritional info per serving

Fiber 14g
Protein 14g
Plant Points 7.25

 **Serves** 4    **Prep** 15 min    **Cook** 20 min

2 tbsp olive or canola oil

1 onion, chopped

2 carrots, scrubbed and chopped

2 tsp sea salt, plus extra to season

3 garlic cloves, chopped

½ tsp ground cumin

½ tsp ground coriander

¼ tsp ground turmeric

½ tsp freshly ground black pepper, plus more to taste

1 × 9 oz (250g) pouch of mixed grains, barley, or long-grain brown rice

1 × 14 oz (400g) can navy, kidney, or pinto beans, or lentils, drained and rinsed

4⅓ cups/1¾ pints (1 liter) hot vegetable or chicken stock (bouillon)

7 oz (200g) fresh or frozen spinach

¾ oz (20g) parsley, leaves and stems chopped

¾ oz (20g) cilantro, leaves and stems chopped

¾ oz (20g) dill, chopped

Skyr, or Greek or coconut yogurt, to serve

For the caramelized onions

2 tbsp olive or canola oil

2 onions, thinly sliced

1½ tsp dried mint

Perhaps more a soup than a stew, this is a bowl packed with vibrant greens. Use any grains or pulses you have to hand—precooked mixed-grain pouches make it even easier, but if you have only dried lentils in the cupboard, they will, of course, work too—simply add them as for the precooked, but with a little extra water, then simmer until tender before adding the herbs and spinach. Don't be put off by the long ingredient list—the dish is simple to pull together and feels like a hug in a bowl.

1. Warm the oil in a deep pan over medium-low heat and add the onion, carrots, and 1 teaspoon of the salt. Fry for 10–12 minutes, then add the garlic and fry for another 2 minutes until fragrant.

2. Add the spices and cook, stirring, for 30 seconds to toast them, then add the grains, pulses, stock, and remaining teaspoon of salt and bring to a simmer for 5–8 minutes. Add the spinach and herbs and continue simmering for another 2 minutes until the spinach has wilted. Taste and adjust the seasoning.

3. While the onion and carrot are cooking, make the caramelized onions. Put a skillet over medium-low heat and add the oil, onions, and a pinch of salt. Cook very slowly, for about 20 minutes, stirring only occasionally to prevent sticking, until dark golden and caramelized, adding a splash of water if they stick. Stir through the mint. Set aside.

4. Transfer the stew to bowls, and serve with a big spoonful of yogurt and the caramelized onions.

Eating more fiber doesn't mean leaving your
all-time favorites behind. Classics are the dishes
so filled with nostalgia they never fail to sustain,
comfort, and bring a smile. From a bubbling fish
pie to a plate of perfectly sauced meatballs
or a hearty burger on a Friday night, these are
the recipes that connect us to family, tradition,
and memory. With a few simple tweaks, they can
also be fiber-fueled to support your gut health.

There is something for everyone in this chapter,
including plenty of meat-free options: a vibrant
chickpea ratatouille bursting with Mediterranean
flavor; a chunky chili packed with antioxidants;
a luxurious mushroom spelt "risotto"; and my
beloved whole-wheat baked eggplant Milanese
with its golden, crisp coating. They are all
wholesome twists on well-loved classics.

Fiber
favorites

Stuffed potato skins with cashew sauce

 **Serves** 4

 **Prep** 10 min
+ soaking

 **Cook** 1 hour 10 min

6 potatoes (about
5½–6 oz/150–170g;
such as Maris Piper)

2 tbsp olive or canola oil

Freshly ground black pepper

½ tsp sea salt

2 tbsp toasted pumpkin
seeds, to serve

For the sweet corn filling

10½ oz (300g) frozen sweet
corn, defrosted

2 scallions, chopped

1 green chili (ideally
jalapeño), chopped

Big handful of cilantro,
leaves and stems chopped

1¾ oz (50g) feta, crumbled,
or vegetarian alternative
(optional)

2½ tbsp skyr, or Greek or
coconut yogurt

Juice of 1 lime

1 tbsp olive or canola oil

For the cashew sauce

3½ oz (100g) cashews

1 tbsp cider vinegar

2 tbsp olive or canola oil

½ garlic clove, chopped

½ tsp garlic granules

1 tsp smoked paprika, plus
extra to garnish

1½ tbsp nutritional yeast

1 avocado, pitted,
peeled, and chopped,
to serve

These stuffed skins are inspired by *elotes*, a Mexican street food. You'll need to soak the cashews for at least 2 hours in advance, ideally overnight, to get a beautiful creaminess in the sauce. Speed up the cooking by air-frying or microwaving the potatoes, then roasting them; or air-frying at 400°F (200°C) for 5–8 minutes on each side. The recipe is also delicious made with sweet potatoes.

1. Soak the cashews for the sauce in generous ½ cup/4 fl oz (125 ml) water for at least 2 hours, or ideally overnight.

2. When you're ready to cook, preheat the oven to 400°F (200°C). Prick the potatoes all over with a fork, rub in ½ tablespoon of the oil and place them on a baking sheet. Bake for 1 hour (or for 35–40 minutes at 400°F (200°C) in your air fryer; or 8–10 minutes on full power in your microwave), turning them once during cooking.

3. Meanwhile, drain the cashews from their soaking liquid, and place them in a blender along with the rest of the sauce ingredients. Blend for 1–2 minutes until completely smooth, then put to one side while you make the remainder of the dish.

4. Remove the potatoes from the oven and increase the temperature to 475°F (240°C). When the potatoes are cool enough to touch, halve each one and scoop out the flesh, leaving a ¼ in (5 mm) layer around the inside (reserve the flesh for making mash, gnocchi, or the potato farls on page 104). Return the skins to the baking sheet, cut-side down and roast for 5 minutes, then turn them over, brush the cut side with the remaining olive oil, season with salt and pepper and roast for another 5–8 minutes, or until crispy.

5. While the skins are in the oven, make the sweet corn filling by combining all the ingredients in a bowl. Season with salt and pepper to taste. Put to one side until the skins are ready.

6. Once the potato skins are crispy, pile each one with the sweet corn salad, divide the avocado between them, then spoon over the cashew sauce. Sprinkle with the pumpkin seeds, garnish with paprika, then serve with extra sauce on the side.

Creamy white bean fish pie

Nutritional info per serving

Fiber 13g
Protein 38g
Plant Points 6.5

 **Serves** 4 generously

 **Prep** 10 min

 **Cook** 1 hour

1½ oz (40g) butter

2 small leeks, sliced

¼ cup/1 oz (30g) white spelt flour

1 bay leaf

scant 2 cups/16 fl oz (450 ml) whole milk

1½ tsp Dijon or English mustard

Zest and juice of 1 small lemon

12 oz (350g) mix of cod, smoked haddock, and salmon, cut into large chunks

1 × 14 oz (400g) can white beans, such as navy, lima beans, or flageolet

5½ oz (150g) frozen peas

Small bunch of parsley, chopped

For the potato mash

2 lb 4 oz (1kg) starchy potatoes (such as Yukon Gold), scrubbed and cut into large (1¼ in/3–4 cm) even-sized chunks

1½ oz (40g) butter

Sea salt and freshly ground black pepper

Fish pie is so perfect that I didn't want to tamper with it too much—it just needed a gentle nudge to increase the fiber. Blending in creamy white beans—navy, lima, or flageolet—add that extra goodness, as well as a beautiful texture to complement the flaky fish. I leave the skins on the potatoes, too, because that's where much of the fiber and so many of the nutrients are held.

1. Make the mash first to allow it time to cool. Place the potatoes in a large, deep pan of plenty of salted water and bring the water to the boil. Boil the potatoes for about 12–15 minutes, until tender, then drain them, reserving a cupful of the cooking water, and pour them back into the pan. Mash well, stirring in 4–6½ tbsp/2¼ fl oz–3½ fl oz (75–100 ml) of the reserved potato cooking water, along with the butter, at the end. Season to taste with salt and pepper and leave to cool.

2. Preheat the oven to 400°F (200°C). Melt the butter in a wide pan over medium heat. When hot, add the leeks and fry for 6–8 minutes, until sweet, softened, and beginning to color. Add the flour and the bay leaf and cook for a minute or two, stirring, then slowly add the milk, stirring constantly until you have a smooth roux.

3. Bring the roux to a simmer, stirring until it begins to thicken. Add the mustard, some salt and pepper to taste, and the lemon zest and juice. Add the fish, pushing it under the surface to submerge. Cook gently for 1–2 minutes, then gently fold through the beans, peas, and parsley, taking care not to break up the fish. Remove the pan from the heat and transfer the mixture to a 10 in (26 cm) baking dish.

4. Spoon the cooled mash over the fish, smooth the surface and score it all over with a fork. Place the dish in the oven and bake the fish pie for 25–30 minutes until the sauce is bubbling and the topping is golden.

Persian-style chicken with walnut, pomegranate & saffron rice

Nutritional info per serving

Fiber 9g
Protein 71g
Plant Points 6.25

 **Serves** 4    **Prep** 10 min    **Cook** 1 hour 10 min

7 oz (200g) walnuts

2 tbsp olive or canola oil, plus extra if needed

6–8 bone-in, skinless chicken thighs

2 onions, chopped

Seeds from 4 cardamom pods, ground

½ tsp ground turmeric

1 cinnamon stick or ½ tsp ground cinnamon

120g prunes, pitted and halved

2 cups/17 fl oz (500 ml) pomegranate juice

Seeds from ½ pomegranate, to serve

Big handful of parsley leaves, chopped, to serve

For the saffron rice

10½ oz (300g) brown basmati rice, soaked for 30 minutes

3 cardamom pods, lightly split

Pinch of saffron threads, soaked in 2 tbsp hot water (optional)

Fesenjān (the inspiration for this dish) is a traditional Persian stew made with a rich, tangy-sweet sauce of walnuts and pomegranate molasses (often known as "pheasant jam"). For a vegan twist, you can swap the chicken for roasted celery root, which soaks up the flavors just as well.

1. Start by toasting the walnuts in a large dry pan over medium-low heat for 5–7 minutes until beginning to color. Leave to cool, then transfer to a food processor and blend until they form a fine-breadcrumb texture. Make them as fine as you can, but be sure not to over-blend as you don't want a paste.

2. Warm the oil in a large heavy-based pan over medium heat. Pat the chicken dry with paper towel, season, then add the thighs to the hot pan, taking care not to overcrowd the space (cook in batches, if necessary). Sauté the chicken, untouched, for 6–8 minutes, turning once during that time, then remove to a plate. (Repeat for remaining batches, as needed.)

3. Add the onions and a big pinch of salt to the pan, scraping up any delicious stuck bits, and adding a dash more oil if the pan is too dry.

4. Fry the onions for about 10 minutes until soft and golden. Add the blended walnuts and cook for another couple of minutes, stirring constantly so they take on a little color. Stir in the spices, prunes, and pomegranate juice. Return the chicken to the pan, then pour in just enough water to cover the chicken. Season well.

5. Reduce the heat to very low—you should see only fine, gentle bubbles—and simmer for 35–45 minutes, stirring occasionally to prevent sticking, until the chicken is tender and falling off the bone.

6. While the chicken is cooking, make the rice. Pour the rice into a deep pan with the cardamom pods and a pinch of salt and cover with 3 cups/24 fl oz (700 ml) of water. Bring to the boil and simmer for 35–45 minutes (adding more water if needed), until the water has been absorbed and the rice is tender. Remove from the heat, pour over the saffron and its soaking liquid, stir, then cover with a lid for 10 minutes.

7. Run a fork through the rice and divide it between your serving plates. Top with the chicken and sauce, and sprinkle with the pomegranate seeds and parsley to serve.

Pasta e fagioli with squash

 **Serves** 4–6    **Prep** 10 min    **Cook** 35 min

3 tbsp olive oil, plus extra to serve

1 carrot, scrubbed and chopped

1 onion, chopped

2 celery sticks, chopped

9 oz (250g) butternut or any variety of squash, peeled, seeded, and chopped into ½ in (1 cm) cubes

2 tsp sea salt, plus extra to season

3 garlic cloves, chopped

1 rosemary sprig, leaves roughly chopped

1 bay leaf

¼–½ tsp dried red pepper flakes (optional)

3¼ cups/26 fl oz (750 ml) boiling water, vegetable or chicken stock (bouillon), plus about another generous 1 cup/9 fl oz (250 ml) water to cover

1 × 14 oz (400g) can plum tomatoes, rinsed and chopped; or 3 tomatoes, chopped

2 × 14 oz (400g) can cranberry or navy beans, drained and rinsed

7 oz (200g) lacinato kale, stems discarded, chopped

160g whole-wheat macaroni or other small pasta shape

Freshly ground black pepper

Handful of parsley, chopped, to serve (optional)

Fagioli (pronounced fah-joh-lee) is the Italian word for beans—so, this is, quite simply, "pasta and beans." If you're cooking with the intention of having leftovers or eating later, cook the pasta separately and add it to the bowls as you serve. This prevents the pasta from soaking up all the broth and becoming mushy, and also makes the dish quicker to pull together when you want to eat.

1. In a large, deep pan, warm the oil over medium heat. Add the carrot, onion, celery, squash, and 1 teaspoon of the salt and fry for 10–12 minutes until soft. Add the garlic, herbs, and chili (if using) and cook for 2 minutes until the garlic is tender.

2. Add the water or stock, tomatoes, and 1⅔ cans of beans. Use an immersion blender to blend the remaining beans into a purée, then add these to the pan. I like to also crush some of the squash against the side of the pan to thicken the sauce. Simmer for 10 minutes to allow the flavors to mingle, then add the kale, pasta, remaining teaspoon of salt, some pepper to taste, and enough boiling water to just cover the soup (I used a generous 1 cup/9 fl oz [250 ml]).

3. Simmer, stirring often, for approximately 8–10 minutes, until the kale is tender and the pasta is al dente (check the pasta package for exact timings). The soup should be thick and delicious, but do add more water to loosen if you like. Check the seasoning (it will need a lot), then transfer to bowls. Scatter over some parsley if you wish, drizzle with oil, and serve. The soup will continue to thicken as it sits, so add a little more water if you're not serving immediately.

Pork, lentil & ricotta meatballs in tomato sauce

 **Serves** 4    **Prep** 10 min    **Cook** 45 min

1½ oz (40g) whole-wheat breadcrumbs soaked in 4 tbsp water for 10 minutes; or 1 oz (30g) rolled oats soaked in 4–5 tbsp water, to soften

7 oz (200g) lean ground pork

5½ oz (150g) cooked green or brown lentils, drained thoroughly if from a can

2½ oz (75g) ricotta

1 garlic clove, minced

1½ tbsp ground flaxseed

1 egg, beaten

½ oz (15g) parsley, leaves and stems finely chopped; or 1 tsp fennel seeds or dried oregano

1 oz (30g) Parmesan, grated, plus extra to serve

For the tomato sauce

3 tbsp olive or canola oil

2 garlic cloves, finely sliced

2 × 14 oz (400g) can chopped tomatoes

1 × 14 oz (400g) can cranberry beans, drained and rinsed

Parmesan rind (optional)

Big handful of basil leaves, plus extra to serve

Sea salt and freshly ground black pepper

Thinking of ways to keep much-loved classics on the menu, just with a little extra nourishment, is what makes my job so interesting. These meatballs are my lighter, higher-fiber take on a family favorite. The lentils boost both the fiber and plant diversity, while the ricotta keeps everything tender and juicy.

1. Squeeze the water from the breadcrumbs (or drain the oats), then place all the ingredients for the meatballs in a mixing bowl and mix with your hands to combine. Shape them into 20 large walnut-sized balls. Place them in the fridge to chill while you prepare the tomato sauce.

2. For the sauce, place a wide pan (with a lid) over medium-low heat. Add the oil and the garlic and warm them together until the garlic begins to feel sticky and is coloring on the edges (don't let it burn), then add the tomatoes and beans. Half-fill the tomato can with water, give it a swirl and add the tomato-y water too. Then, put in the Parmesan rind if you have one, and season with salt and pepper. Simmer the sauce for 20–25 minutes, until slightly reduced and tasting delicious.

3. Reduce the heat to low, add the meatballs to the sauce, and partially cover the pan with the lid—you want the sauce to simmer very gently. Simmer for 20 minutes, carefully turning the meatballs after 10 minutes until they are evenly tender and cooked through. Cut one open if you're unsure. Tear in some basil leaves, and serve with extra grated Parmesan. Whole-wheat pasta, mashed potato, or brown rice are good on the side.

My champion chunky veggie & chocolate chili

Nutritional info per serving

Fiber 17g
Protein 16g
Plant Points 14

 **Serves** 4–6    **Prep** 15 min    **Cook** 1 hour 10 min

10½ oz (300g) sweet potatoes, scrubbed

2 red bell peppers, seeded

9 oz (250g) chestnut (brown) mushrooms

6 tbsp olive or canola oil

3 tsp smoked paprika

3 tsp ground cumin

1 onion, chopped

1 celery stick, chopped

1 carrot, chopped

3 garlic cloves, chopped

1 × 14 oz (400g) can red kidney beans, drained

1 × 14 oz (400g) can black beans, drained

1 × 14 oz (400g) can chopped tomatoes

1 tsp dried oregano

1 bay leaf

1 tsp chili powder

4 tbsp tamari or light soy sauce

½ tbsp maple syrup

1 oz (25g) 70% dark (semisweet) chocolate

For the guacamole

2 ripe avocados

1 small garlic clove, minced

1 tomato, chopped

1 scallion, chopped

Juice of 2 limes

Handful of cilantro, chopped

Sea salt and freshly ground black pepper

My kids love this dish so much that I make it again and again. It's packed with beans, pulses, and whatever vegetables I have on hand and it freezes well for up to three months. To save time, you can roughly blend the onion, celery, and carrot in a food processor. Add a tablespoon of Marmite or miso for a gut-friendly umami kick.

1. Cut the sweet potatoes and red peppers into 1 in (2–3 cm) chunks and quarter the mushrooms. Preheat the oven to 400°F (200°C).

2. Put the mushrooms, sweet potatoes, and peppers in your largest baking pan and pour in 4 tablespoons of the oil. Sprinkle in the paprika and cumin, season with salt and pepper, and toss everything together to nicely coat. Bake the vegetables for 25–30 minutes until tender.

3. About halfway through the vegetables' cooking time, warm the remaining oil in a large, deep pan and fry the onion, celery, carrot, garlic, and a big pinch of salt for 10–12 minutes until the onion is soft and sweet. Crush one quarter of the kidney beans, with a fork, then add all the beans to the pan with the rest of the ingredients, except for the chocolate. Fill one of the cans with water and add that too.

4. When the vegetables are ready, add them to the pan and simmer for 30–40 minutes, until the sauce is thickened and everything is soft and delicious, adding the chocolate for the final 10 minutes. Season with salt, pepper, and more chili powder if you want it spicier, or more maple syrup if you'd like it sweeter.

5. While the chili is cooking, make the guacamole. Peel and stone the avocados, then crush the flesh in a bowl with a fork until you reach your desired texture (or use an immersion blender if you want it really smooth). Stir in the other guacamole ingredients and season with salt and pepper.

6. Serve the chili with brown rice, or baked potatoes and coleslaw, and spoonfuls of the guacamole on top.

Chickpea ratatouille

 **Serves** 4    **Prep** 15 min    **Cook** 1 hour 15 min

6 tbsp olive or canola oil

1 large or 2 red small onions, thinly sliced

3 garlic cloves, thinly sliced

1 yellow bell pepper, seeded and thinly sliced

1 red bell pepper, seeded and thinly sliced

1 tsp sweet paprika

1 × 14 oz (400g) can chopped tomatoes

1 × 14 oz (400g) can chickpeas, drained and rinsed

1 tbsp sherry or cider vinegar

Small bunch of basil, leaves picked

1 lb 2 oz (500g) tomatoes, sliced into ¼ in- (4 mm-) thick rounds

1 eggplant, sliced into ¼ in- (4 mm-) thick half-moons

10½ oz (300g) zucchini, sliced into ¼ in- (4 mm-) thick rounds

1 tsp dried oregano

Sea salt and freshly ground black pepper

A vibrant twist on a classic ratatouille, this version uses chickpeas to make it more filling and higher in fiber, without losing that silky, slow-cooked feel. The key is slicing the vegetables thinly so they soften at the same pace, creating a rich, tomato-based stew packed with color and flavor. Finish with a drizzle of good olive oil.

1. Preheat the oven to 425°F (220°C).

2. Warm 3 tablespoons of the oil in a wide saucepan (ideally with a lid) over medium heat and fry the onion for 5–6 minutes until soft, then add the garlic, peppers and a pinch of salt and cook for another 5 minutes, until the peppers are soft. Add the paprika, tomatoes, and chickpeas and simmer for 5 minutes. Stir in the vinegar, tear in the basil leaves, and season with salt and pepper to taste.

3. Transfer the chickpea mixture to a 12 × 8 in (30 × 20 cm) baking dish. Arrange the tomato, eggplant, and zucchini slices, in overlapping rows, in the baking dish, alternating between vegetables. Sprinkle the top with oregano, salt and pepper, and finish with the remaining 3 tablespoons of oil. Cover with foil and bake for 45–50 minutes, removing the foil after 30 minutes, until the vegetables are tender and colored on the edges (check that the eggplant is tender by inserting a sharp knife—it should glide through).

4. Let the ratatouille sit for 5–10 minutes to absorb its juices before eating it warm or at room temperature. It would also be delicious with the arugula and sunflower seed pesto from page 150.

Pearl spelt & mushroom "risotto"

 **Serves** 4    **Prep** 15 min    **Cook** 1 hour 10 min

¾ oz (20g) dried porcini mushrooms

4 cups/35 fl oz (1 liter) boiling water

1 vegetable or chicken stock cube (bouillon)

1½ tsp Marmite (optional)

3 tbsp olive or canola oil

1 celery stick, chopped

1 leek, sliced

2 garlic cloves, chopped

7 oz (200g) chestnut (brown) or button mushrooms, chopped

7 oz (200g) oyster mushrooms, chopped (or use more chestnut)

9 oz (250g) pearl spelt or pearl barley, rinsed

1 tsp sea salt

5½ oz (150g) spinach leaves

1½ oz (40g) Parmesan (or vegan substitute), grated, plus extra to serve

Freshly ground black pepper

For the pesto

2¾ oz (80g) watercress

1 small garlic clove, roughly chopped

1½ oz (40g) roasted hazelnuts, almonds, or pistachios

1 oz (25g) Parmesan (or vegan substitute), grated

5 tbsp olive oil

Juice of ½ small lemon

This is an absolute winner—rich, comforting, and full of flavor. Using spelt or barley grains rather than rice is a wonderful way to bring more plant diversity—and more fiber—into a traditional dish. To speed up the cooking, you can roughly blend the mushrooms in a food processor and soak the grains the night before as this helps speed up the cooking. Always check the package for cooking times, as some spelt varieties vary.

1. Place the porcini in a large pitcher or bowl, cover in the boiling water, crumble in the stock cube, stir in the Marmite (if using), and leave the porcini to soak for at least 10 minutes.

2. Meanwhile, warm the oil in a large pan over medium heat. Add the celery, leek, and garlic and cook for 5 minutes, until the celery and leek are just softened. Add all the chopped fresh mushrooms and fry for 5–8 minutes until the mushrooms have softened. Scoop out the porcini from their soaking water (reserve the water), roughly chop them, and add them to the pan.

3. Add the spelt or barley, along with the mushroom soaking water and salt. Season with pepper, then cook for 40–50 minutes, stirring occasionally, and ensuring the grains are always covered in liquid (add more water, if needed) until they are tender.

4. Meanwhile, make the pesto. Place the watercress, garlic, and roasted nuts in the bowl of a small food processor and blend until finely chopped. Add the Parmesan (or alternative), oil, and lemon juice and season with salt and pepper. Blend again briefly, to combine, then transfer the pesto to a small bowl.

5. Once the spelt or barley is tender, add the spinach, stirring to wilt. Take the pan off the heat, stir in the Parmesan (or alternative), and check the seasoning, adjusting as necessary. Serve the "risotto" in bowls with a big dollop of pesto and a sprinkle of extra Parmesan, if you wish.

Black bean & beet burgers

 **Serves** 4　　 **Prep** 20 min　　 **Cook** 30 min

1 tbsp ground flaxseed

1 tbsp flaxseeds

about 3 tbsp olive or canola oil

1 small leek, finely chopped

2 garlic cloves, finely chopped

2 tsp Marmite

1 × 14 oz (400g) can black beans

1 beet, scrubbed and coarsely grated

½ sweet potato, scrubbed and coarsely grated

1¾ oz (50g) dried whole-wheat breadcrumbs

2 tbsp chickpea flour

2¼ oz (60g) defrosted sweet corn

1 tsp smoked paprika

½ tsp ground cumin

4 whole grain burger buns and toppings, to serve

For the burger sauce

½ garlic clove, minced

1½ tsp Dijon or yellow mustard

1 tbsp cider vinegar

scant ½ cup/3½ fl oz (100 ml) mild olive oil

1 tbsp tomato paste

¼ tsp smoked paprika

1 tsp maple syrup

1 small pickle, chopped

Sea salt and freshly ground black pepper

A brilliant alternative to processed meat, the beans and beets in these burgers create a rich, satisfying texture, and they're just as good topped with melted cheese as any burger with beef (use vegan cheese, if you need). Cook the burgers slowly over medium heat to ensure they cook through—if the heat is too high, the outsides will burn before the insides are ready.

1. First, make a flaxseed "egg." Mix the ground flaxseed with 3 tablespoons of water and leave to soak for at least 10 minutes. Stir in the flaxseeds and set aside.

2. Meanwhile, warm 1 tablespoon of the oil in a small pan over medium heat and fry the leek and garlic with a pinch of salt for 4–5 minutes until softened. Stir in the Marmite and leave it to melt in.

3. Drain the black beans, reserving the liquid. Pour the beans into a bowl and mash them lightly, leaving them with a little texture. Squeeze dry the beet and sweet potato, then stir them into the bowl with beans. Add the remaining burger ingredients, season well with salt and pepper and mix with your hands so everything is nicely incorporated. The mixture can be refrigerated and stored for up to 5 days at this point, or frozen in an airtight freezer bag for up to 3 months.

4. Shape the burger mixture into 4 equal balls, then flatten them into patties about 1 in (2–3 cm) thick. Place them in the fridge to firm up for at least 20 minutes while you prepare the burger sauce.

5. To make the sauce, first measure out 5 teaspoons of the reserved liquid from the black beans. Add this with the garlic, mustard, vinegar, and a big pinch of salt to a tall pitcher and blend with an immersion blender on the highest setting for 15 seconds until blended and frothy. Very slowly and with the blender still running, drizzle in the oil until fully incorporated. Move the blender up and down to get as much air into the mixture as possible. You'll soon find the sauce begins to thicken. Once thick, stir in the other ingredients and season with salt and pepper, and adding a little extra maple syrup or cider vinegar as needed. Refrigerate until you're ready to serve.

6. To cook the burgers, warm the remaining 2 tablespoons of oil in a large nonstick skillet over medium-low heat. Once the oil is hot, add the burgers and cook on each side for 6–7 minutes without moving, until a dark crust has formed (add more oil if you need to). Transfer each burger to a split burger bun and serve immediately drizzled with the sauce and loaded with the toppings of your choice (I like sliced tomato, sliced pickle, and sliced cheese).

Whole-wheat baked eggplant Milanese

 Serves 4

 **Prep** 20 min
+ salting

 **Cook** 30 min

2 large eggplants, cut lengthwise into ⅝ in (1.5 cm) slices (you should get about 8 slices)

3 tbsp olive or canola oil

5½ oz (150g) whole-wheat breadcrumbs

1½ oz (40g) Parmesan (or vegan substitute), grated, plus extra to serve

2 eggs, beaten with 1 tbsp milk, or 4 tbsp oat cream

⅓ cup/1½ oz (40g) whole-wheat flour, generously seasoned

280g whole-wheat spaghetti

Sea salt and freshly ground black pepper

Lemon wedges, to serve

Arugula salad, to serve

For the tomato sauce

3 tbsp olive or canola oil

3 garlic cloves, sliced

2 × 14 oz (400g) can chopped tomatoes

Big handful of basil leaves, plus extra to garnish

Inspired by my love of eggplant parmigiana, this version has a light, crispy twist—like a classic Milanese! Make your own breadcrumbs by pulsing day-old whole-wheat bread in a food processor. You could skip the salting step, but it really does help the coating stay crisp. For a quicker option, cook the Milanese in an air fryer at 350°F (180°C) until golden.

1. Spread some sheets of paper towel on plates or cutting boards, salt both sides of the eggplant slices and leave them to drain on the paper towel for 30 minutes.

2. Meanwhile, prepare the tomato sauce. Warm the oil and garlic in a pan over medium-low heat. Gently fry the garlic for 4–5 minutes until sticky and beginning to color on the edges. Add the tomatoes, and some seasoning, and bring to a simmer. Cook gently until reduced—the time it takes you to cook the eggplant should be long enough (add splashes of water to the pan if it ever looks dry).

3. Preheat the oven to 400°F (200°C) and line a baking sheet with parchment paper. Drizzle with 1½ tablespoons of the oil. Once the eggplant has released some liquid (you'll see droplets on the surface of the slices), rinse under the tap and pat the slices dry with paper towel. Mix the breadcrumbs with the Parmesan and spread them out on a plate. Pour the egg mixture into a shallow bowl and then the flour mixture onto another plate.

4. One by one, lightly coat the eggplant slices in the flour mixture, then gently dip them into the egg, and then into the breadcrumbs, pressing each slice to help the breadcrumbs stick. Place the slices on the oiled baking sheet and spray (or brush) the remaining oil over each one. Bake for 20–25 minutes, turning after 15 minutes, until the eggplant is golden and crisp on both sides.

5. While the eggplant slices are in the oven, bring a pan of salted water to the boil and cook the pasta according to the package instructions until al dente. Drain the pasta, reserving a cupful of the cooking liquid.

6. Rip the basil into the tomato sauce, then toss the sauce through with the cooked pasta, adding just enough pasta water to loosen—you want it nice and saucy.

7. Transfer the pasta to plates, sit a couple of eggplant slices on the side, and serve each portion with a lemon wedge, and some extra grated Parmesan (or alternative) and basil leaves over the top. An arugula salad is good with this, too.

Mushroom & bean stroganoff

 **Serves** 4    **Prep** 15 min    **Cook** 20 min

10½ oz (300g) chestnut (brown) mushrooms, halved, or quartered if large

7 oz (200g) mixed mushrooms, such as oyster, shiitake, eryngii and chanterelle, portobello, or more chestnut (brown) mushrooms, cut into large chunks

1 tbsp tamari or light soy sauce

3 tbsp olive oil

1 large leek or onion, sliced

2 garlic cloves, chopped

1 tsp thyme leaves

1 bay leaf

2 tsp smoked paprika

2 tbsp tomato paste

2 tsp cider vinegar

1 × 14 oz (400g) can kidney beans, drained and rinsed

1 × 14 oz (400g) can black beans, drained and rinsed

1½ cups/12 fl oz (350 ml) hot mushroom, vegetable, or chicken stock (bouillon)

1 ½ tsp Dijon mustard

1 tsp red or white miso, or Marmite

2–3 tbsp crème fraîche or cream (oat alternatives can also be used)

Sea salt and freshly ground black pepper

Handful of parsley, chopped, to serve

7 oz (200g) brown basmati rice, cooked, to serve

I've suggested canned beans here, but, if you can get them, jarred will add extra depth. For the best final flavor, I'm frying the mushrooms without oil first—it helps drive off moisture and intensify the results.

1. Place a very wide skillet or saucepan over medium-high heat and, once hot, add the chestnut mushrooms, cooking them untouched for 2 minutes. Stir, and cook for another 2 minutes until nicely browned. Scrape the mushrooms onto a plate and repeat with the mixed mushrooms—cooking them for less time or until brown. Then, return the chestnut mushrooms to the pan, add the tamari or soy sauce and simmer for 20–30 seconds until it bubbles away and is absorbed by the mushrooms. Scrape them all onto the plate and wipe out the pan.

2. Turn the heat down to medium and add the oil, leek or onion, and garlic and cook for a further 4–5 minutes, scraping up any delicious stuck bits, until the leek or onion is softened. Stir in the herbs, paprika, tomato paste, vinegar, beans, and stock. Season with salt and pepper to taste, then simmer for 5 minutes before returning the mushrooms to the pan along with the mustard and the miso or Marmite. Add a splash of water if the sauce seems a bit dry and simmer for a further 5 minutes to give the mushrooms some time to absorb the sauce.

3. Swirl the cream through the pan, sprinkle over the parsley, and serve with brown basmati rice.

Chicken & quinoa meatballs with white bean broth

 **Serves** 4    **Prep** 15 min    **Cook** 20 min

For the meatballs

4¼ oz (120g) cooked white quinoa

14 oz (400g) ground chicken

2¼ oz (60g) Parmesan, grated, plus extra to serve

1 egg, beaten

Big handful of parsley leaves, chopped

1 tsp fennel seeds

1 small garlic clove, minced

1 tsp sea salt, plus extra to season

2 tbsp olive oil

Freshly ground black pepper

For the broth

2 tbsp olive oil

2 small leeks or 1 large onion, chopped

1 large or 2 small fennel bulbs, finely chopped

2 garlic cloves, chopped

1 Parmesan rind (optional)

7 oz (200g) frozen peas

2 × 14 oz (400g) cans navy beans, drained and rinsed

5½ cups/2 pints (1.25 liters) chicken stock (bouillon)

2 big handfuls of mint leaves, chopped

2 big handfuls of parsley leaves, chopped

1 head of Little Gem lettuce, roughly shredded

Adding quinoa to these meatballs makes them so much lighter than using chicken alone. When in season, add asparagus or any fresh greens you have on hand to the broth—nourishing and endlessly versatile and comforting.

1. Combine all the meatball ingredients except the oil in a bowl, seasoning generously with pepper. Then, shape the mixture into 20 ping-pong-sized balls. Place these in the fridge while you prepare the broth.

2. In a large deep pan, warm the olive oil and fry the leeks, fennel, and a pinch of salt for 8 minutes, until the vegetables are softened. Add the garlic and cook for another 2 minutes until fragrant, then add the Parmesan rind (if using), peas, beans, and stock and bring to a simmer. Season generously with salt and pepper.

3. Warm the oil for the meatballs in a large skillet over medium heat and fry, turning, for 8–10 minutes, until deep golden and crisp all over, and juicy inside (you may need to fry in batches). Check that the meatballs are cooked through by cutting one in half if you're unsure. Divide the meatballs between 4 serving bowls.

4. Stir the herbs and lettuce through the broth, simmer for a minute or so until the lettuce wilts. Ladle the broth equally over the meatballs and top with a little extra Parmesan to serve.

When it comes to The Fiber Formula, rather than restricting foods in our diet, we need to make the foods we do eat work harder. For snacks that means choosing ingredients that balance fiber, protein, and healthy fats to support steady energy, better blood-sugar control, and long-term gut health. And it's perfectly possible! Think popcorn—light, crunchy, and full of whole-grain goodness; baked crisp vegetable bhajis; homemade crackers with vegetable-packed dips; prune and date crumble bars; and cookies made with rye. These are small, smart upgrades that make a big difference.

Sweet and savory snacks

Popcorn (3 ways)

Popcorn is a wonderfully high-fiber snack, providing around 15g of fiber per 100g (8–10 cups). Experiment with seasonings to rack up the plant points.

1. Pour the oil into a large, heavy-based pan over medium-high heat. Once hot, add the corn and shake gently to coat the kernels and distribute them in a single layer.

2. Cover the pan with a lid and leave it over the heat, shaking the pan gently every 30 seconds. The popcorn is ready when the pops slow down and are about 2–3 seconds apart—it should take about 3 minutes altogether. Pour the popcorn into a large bowl ready for coating.

 **Makes** 5½ oz (150g)    **Prep** 5 min    **Cook** 3–8 min (depending on coating)

For a Marmite coating

3 tbsp canola or sunflower oil

4¼ oz (120g) popping corn

1¾ oz (50g) butter or mild olive oil

4 tsp Marmite

1. Preheat the oven to 300°F (150°C). Cover a baking sheet with parchment paper. Melt the butter in a small pan over low heat (or heat the oil) and stir in the Marmite until you have a smooth, glossy liquid. Pour the Marmite mixture over the popcorn and stir to coat thoroughly.

2. Spread the popcorn over the lined baking sheet and bake for 3–4 minutes to crisp up a little (skip this step if you don't mind Marmite fingers).

For a spicy cheese coating

3 tbsp canola or sunflower oil

4¼ oz (120g) popping corn

4 tbsp nutritional yeast

1½ tsp smoked paprika

1½ tsp garlic powder

½–¾ tsp chili powder (depending on desired heat level)

1 tsp sea salt

A little butter, melted (optional), for drizzling

1. Place the ingredients in a clean spice grinder and blend until you have a fine powder, then toss the mixture through the hot popcorn. Add a drizzle of hot butter, if you like.

For a cinnamon sugar coating

3 tbsp canola or sunflower oil

4¼ oz (120g) popping corn

2 tbsp dark brown soft sugar

1 tsp ground cinnamon

½ tsp sea salt

A little butter, melted (optional), for drizzling

1. Place the ingredients in a clean spice grinder and blend until you have a fine powder, then toss the mixture through the hot popcorn. Add a drizzle of hot butter, if you like.

Nutritional info per serving

Fiber 4.8g
Protein 6.9g
Plant Point 1

Nutritional info per serving

Fiber 7.7g
Protein 9g
Plant Points 1.75

Nutritional info per serving

Fiber 5.1g
Protein 3g
Plant Points 1.25

Broccoli, carrot & celery root bhaji with cilantro chutney

 **Makes** 12
Serves 4

 **Prep** 15 min

 **Cook** 30 min

8 tsp olive, canola, or coconut oil

3½ oz (100g) broccoli, including the peeled stalk, roughly chopped

1 red onion, finely sliced, slices separated

3½ oz (100g) carrot, scrubbed and coarsely grated

2¾ oz (80g) celery root, peeled and coarsely grated

1¼ cups/5½ oz (150g) chickpea or yellow split pea flour

½ tsp baking soda

2 tsp black mustard seeds

½ tsp ground turmeric

½ tsp ground coriander

¾ tsp sea salt, plus extra

2 tbsp lemon or lime juice

For the cilantro chutney

2½ oz (75g) cilantro leaves

1¾ oz (50g) dried, shredded coconut, or raw cashews or peanuts

Juice of 1 large lemon or 2 limes

½–1 small green chili (depending on heat), seeded

1 garlic clove

½ tsp ground cumin

½ tsp sea salt

My love of Indian food inspired this colorful, veggie-packed bhaji snack featuring broccoli, carrot, and celery root for plant points and fiber. A fresh cilantro chutney adds the perfect finishing touch.

1. Preheat the oven to 400°F (200°C). Prepare a 12-hole muffin pan by adding ½ teaspoon of oil to each hole.

2. In a large bowl, combine the vegetables so they're nicely mixed, then sprinkle in the flour, baking soda, spices, and salt. Toss with your hands to combine, then stir in the remaining 2 teaspoons of oil and the citrus juice. Add 3–4 tablespoons of cold water (you want just enough moisture to help the flour stick to the vegetables).

3. Divide the mixture between the holes in the pan, trying not to compress them too much—you want them nice and crinkly on top. Bake for 25–30 minutes, turning them gently after 15 minutes, until dark golden and crisp.

4. While the bhajis are in the oven, place all the chutney ingredients in a blender and blend until smooth. You may need to add a few tablespoons of water to get it going. Transfer to a small bowl and adjust the seasoning to taste.

5. Remove the tray of cooked bhajis from the oven and leave them to cool for a moment (just until they are a little firmed up and cool enough to touch). Then, remove them from the muffin pan and serve immediately with the chutney.

Za'atar chickpea crackers

 **Makes** About 30    **Prep** 5 min    **Cook** 30 min

1¼ cups/4½ oz (125g) chickpea or yellow split-pea flour

½ oz (15g) sesame seeds

¼ oz (10g) chia seeds

1 oz (30g) sunflower seeds

¾ oz (20g) ground flaxseeds

½ tsp sea salt

2 tbsp nutritional yeast

1½ tsp nigella (black cumin/kalonji) seeds

2 tsp za'atar

2 tbsp olive oil

Za'atar is a fragrant Middle Eastern spice blend made with herbs, sesame seeds, and sumac, giving a nutty, citrusy flavor to these chickpea-based crackers. If you can't find it, though, you can experiment with other flavors to make the crackers your own: cumin, fennel, paprika, rosemary, turmeric, or even miso would all work well. Serve them with any veggie dip you fancy (see page 186 for ideas).

1. Preheat the oven to 350°F (180°C) and line a large baking sheet with parchment paper.

2. Combine all the ingredients in a mixing bowl with ½ cup/4 fl oz (120 ml) of water and mix well—you should have a thick paste.

3. Spread the paste onto the lined baking sheet. Use a spatula to evenly smooth it out into a rectangle measuring approximately 12 × 11¼ in (30 × 28 cm). Score the rectangle into rough squares with a knife (without cutting all the way through). You're aiming for 30 individual crackers altogether. Then, bake for 25–30 minutes until the single, scored piece is golden and firm to the touch. Remove the baking sheet from the oven and leave the cracker to cool at room temperature (it will harden as it cools).

4. Break the cracker along the score lines, then store in an airtight container for up to 2 weeks.

Dips (3 ways)

Making your own dips is a quick way to add more fiber, flavor, and plant points to your diet. Pair these with the crackers on page 185, or crunchy vegetable sticks.

Bean, miso & tahini dip

1 tbsp white miso paste

3 tbsp olive oil

2 onions, sliced into eighths

3 garlic cloves, skin on

½ tsp sea salt, plus extra to taste

1 × 14 oz (400g) can pinto, cranberry, or navy beans

1½ tbsp cider vinegar

1 tbsp tahini

Freshly ground black pepper

Snipped chives, to serve

1. Preheat the oven to 375°F (180°C). Mix half the miso with 1 tsp water. Stir in 2 tbsp oil and toss with the onions. Bake on a lined baking sheet, with the garlic, for 25–30 minutes. Peel the garlic and blend with the onions. Add the other ingredients and 5 tbsp/ 2¼ fl oz (75 ml) water. Season, purée, and sprinkle with chives to serve. Store for up to 5 days.

Green whipped tofu & butterbean dip

10½ oz (300g) silken tofu, drained

1 × 14 oz (400g) can lima or navy beans, drained and rinsed

2¼ oz (60g) spinach leaves

½ garlic clove, finely chopped

Big handful of dill, plus extra to serve

Big handful of parsley

Big handful of chives

1–2 tsp white wine or cider vinegar

2½ oz (75g) olive oil, plus extra to serve

Zest and juice of 1 lemon

1 tsp sea salt

Freshly ground black pepper

1. Blend everything together in a blender until completely smooth. Check the seasoning, and adjust with more vinegar or lemon juice until the dip is bright and perky. Transfer to a bowl and drizzle with oil before serving. Store for up to 5 days.

Muhammara

4½ oz (125g) walnuts

1 tsp cumin seeds

1 small garlic clove, finely chopped

9½ oz (275g; drained weight) roasted red bell peppers from a jar, rinsed

2 tsp Turkish chili flakes or ¼ tsp dried red pepper flakes

½ tsp smoked paprika

1 tbsp pomegranate molasses; or 1 date and 1 tsp red wine vinegar

1 tsp sea salt, plus extra to taste

5 tbsp/2½ fl oz (75 ml) olive oil

½ tbsp ground psyllium (optional)

Freshly ground black pepper

1. Toast the walnuts in a dry pan on medium-low heat for 5–7 minutes. Set aside. Toast the cumin for 30 seconds. Add the cumin, walnuts, and all the other ingredients to a processor. Pulse for texture or blend until smooth. Season, then store for up to 7 days.

Nutritional info per 100g

Fiber 3.9g
Protein 5g
Plant Points 3.75

Nutritional info per 100g

Fiber 3.1g
Protein 4.1g
Plant Points 5.25

Nutritional info per 100g

Fiber 4.1g
Protein 4.4g
Plant Points 4.25

Roast split peas with peanuts, coconut & crispy kale chaat

Fiber 7.8g
Protein 9.6g
Plant Points 6

 **Makes** about 275g

 **Prep** 10 min + overnight soaking

 **Cook** 20 min

5½ oz (150g) yellow split peas, soaked for at least 8 hours, ideally overnight

3 tbsp melted coconut oil

½ tsp sea salt

2½ oz (75g) kale, stem removed, chopped

2¼ oz (60g) roasted peanuts or cashews

1 oz (30g) coconut flakes

1½ tbsp chaat masala powder

Chaat masala powder

½ tsp ground coriander seeds

½ tsp ground fennel seeds

½ tsp ground cardamom

½ tsp ground ginger

1 tsp ground cinnamon

½ tsp amchur (sour mango powder)

Pinch of asafoetida

Pinch of chili powder

Chaat is a traditional Indian street food known for its bold, tangy, and spicy flavors. This version brings that same lively balance with roasted split peas, crunchy peanuts, toasted coconut, and crisp kale. If you don't have time to soak the split peas overnight, simply rinse and boil them first for 6–7 minutes until tender but still holding their shape. You can cook the kale in an air fryer at 375°F (190°C) for 4–5 minutes, turning once, to make sure it's completely dry for maximum crispiness.

1. Combine all the chaat masala ingredients in a bowl and set aside.

2. Preheat the oven to 400°F (200°C). You'll need two baking sheets—one lined with parchment paper, the other with a rack set above it.

3. Drain the split peas, pour them into a clean dish towel and pat them dry. The more dry they are, the more crispy they'll get.

4. In a mixing bowl, toss the dried split peas with 2 tablespoons of the melted coconut oil and the salt and spread them out over the lined baking sheet, making sure they have plenty of space. Roast for 10 minutes.

5. While the split peas are in the oven, toss the kale with the remaining tablespoon of oil, massaging it gently into the leaves so each leaf is lightly coated. Spread these out over the wire rack, making sure each piece has plenty of space (do this in batches, if necessary).

6. After 10 minutes, the split peas should be pale golden (don't let them get too dark as they get very crunchy). Stir them, and place the rack with the kale on the shelf beneath the split peas. Continue roasting for 10 minutes.

7. Sprinkle the peanuts and coconut flakes on top of the split peas and roast for a final 5 minutes until everything is golden and the kale is crisp.

8. Allow the split peas, peanuts, and coconut to cool slightly, then transfer to a bowl and toss with the chaat. Taste for salt, adjusting as necessary. Scatter over the kale, then gently toss everything together and eat immediately. The kale may not stay crispy for more than a day or two, but the rest of the mixture will last up to 2 weeks.

Prune & date crumble bars

 **Makes** 9    **Prep** 15 min    **Cook** 35 min

2 tbsp ground flaxseed

7 oz (200g) rolled oats

scant ½ cup/1¾ oz (50g) whole-wheat flour or whole-wheat spelt flour

2½ oz (75g) mixed seeds (such as 2¼ oz/65g pumpkin and sunflower and the remaining flaxseed and sesame)

1½ tsp ground ginger

½ tsp sea salt

3 tbsp maple syrup or honey or 6½ tbsp/2½ oz (75g) light brown soft sugar

6½ tbsp melted coconut or olive oil

3 tbsp smooth or crunchy peanut butter

1¾ oz (50g) mixed nuts (such as almonds, walnuts, hazelnuts, macadamias, or pecans), chopped

For the filling

3½ oz (100g) dates, pitted

3½ oz (100g) prunes, pitted

Zest and juice of 1 orange

I'm the self-proclaimed biggest crumble-lover in the world—it's my all-time favorite dessert, and now I can eat it on the go! These bars combine the digestive-friendly goodness of prunes with naturally sweet dates for perfect chewy-meets-crunchy texture. Medjool dates add extra stickiness. This is the most delicious, fiber-packed crumble-posing-as-bar you'll ever make.

1. First, mix the ground flaxseed with 6 tablespoons of water and leave to soak for 10 minutes (this is your flax "egg"). Set aside.

2. Preheat the oven to 350°F (180°C). Line an 8 in (20 cm) square brownie pan with parchment paper.

3. In a bowl, combine the oats, flour, seeds, ginger, and salt. In a separate bowl, whisk together the honey, maple syrup or sugar, prepared flax "egg," oil, and peanut butter. Pour the wet ingredients over the dry ingredients and use your hands to mix them together until fully combined.

4. Transfer two-thirds of the mixture to the prepared pan and push it down firmly with the back of a spoon until you have an even layer. Put it in the oven for 15 minutes until golden on the edges.

5. Meanwhile, make the filling. Place the dried fruit and orange zest and juice in a small pan and bring the mixture to a simmer. Simmer for 2–3 minutes to soften, then transfer the mixture to a blender or small food processor and blend until smooth-ish (a few chunks are fine). Add a few splashes of water if it needs help to blend properly.

6. Spoon the filling mixture over the baked base and smooth it out into an even layer. Combine the chopped nuts with the remaining mixture, then scatter this over the filling. Press down firmly again.

7. Return the pan to the oven for 15–18 minutes until the topping is golden. Leave the tray to cool completely, then lift out the parchment and cut into 9 equal squares (for smaller treats, you can cut into 12, but note the fiber and protein will be slightly less per square). The bars will store in an airtight container for 5 days.

Dark chocolate, date & rye cookies

 **Makes** 12

 **Prep** 15 min
+ resting

 **Cook** 15 min

7 oz (200g) 75%–85% dark (semisweet) chocolate, broken into pieces

1 oz (25g) unsalted butter or coconut oil, softened

2¼ oz (60g) pitted dates

⅓ cup/1½ oz (45g) rye flour

½ tsp baking powder

¼ tsp sea salt

2 eggs

½ cup (100g) dark brown soft or muscovado sugar

½ tsp vanilla extract (optional)

Rye flour not only gives these cookies an extra fiber boost but also a subtle nuttiness, making them both wholesome and craveable. They're quick to whip up and guaranteed to please. Top tip: if your dates are on the dry side, soak them in boiling water for 10 minutes to soften before blending.

1. Place the chocolate and butter or oil in a heatproof bowl set over a pan of barely simmering water and stir until melted and combined. Alternatively, heat in a microwave on the lowest setting in 30-second blasts, stirring between each, until just melted. Set aside to cool for 10 minutes.

2. Using a blender, blend the dates to a purée, then stir them into the melted chocolate.

3. Combine the flour, baking powder, and salt in a bowl and set aside.

4. In a mixing bowl, use an electric whisk to mix the eggs and sugar for 2–3 minutes until lighter in color and increased in volume. Fold in the melted chocolate mixture and the vanilla, followed by the flour mixture. Cover the bowl and refrigerate for at least 30 minutes.

5. Preheat the oven to 350°F (180°C) and line 2 large baking sheets with parchment paper. Divide the mixture into 12 spoonfuls and roll each one into a ball. Arrange the 12 balls on the baking sheet, leaving plenty of space between each one. Sprinkle with a little salt, then place in the oven for 12–15 minutes until firm on the edges and a little crinkly on top.

6. Leave the cookies to cool on the tray for 15–20 minutes, then transfer them to a wire rack to cool completely. Store in an airtight container for 1 week.

Quinoa & dark chocolate bark with cranberry & fig

 **Makes** 12–14 pieces

 **Prep** 15 min

 **Cook** 25 min + chilling

3½ oz (100g) mixed nuts such as pecans, walnuts, hazelnuts, almonds, pistachios, or peanuts, roughly chopped

1 oz (30g) pumpkin seeds

1½ oz (40g) sunflower seeds

1 tbsp chia seeds

3 tbsp ground flaxseed

3½ oz (100g) white, red, or black quinoa, rinsed

3½ tbsp (75g) maple syrup or honey

2 tbsp melted coconut oil

¼ tsp sea salt

7 oz (200g) 70% dark (semisweet) chocolate, broken into pieces

For the bark toppings

1½ oz (40g) dried cranberry or sour cherries, chopped

1½ oz (40g) dried figs, sliced

1 oz (30g) any nut (see above), chopped

Using dark chocolate for this bark not only gives it an intense flavor but also increases the fiber content. Decorate it however you like—it's a really impressive, "healthier" treat for the whole family.

1. Preheat the oven to 350°F (180°C) and line a large baking sheet with parchment paper.

2. In a mixing bowl, combine the nuts, seeds, flaxseed, quinoa, maple syrup, 1 tablespoon of the melted coconut oil and the salt in a bowl. Spread the mixture onto the lined baking sheet, then use the back of a spoon to smooth it to ½–⅝ in (1–1.5 cm) thick. Bake for 20–25 minutes until golden and firm to the touch. Allow to cool.

3. Add the chocolate and remaining coconut oil to a heatproof bowl set over a pan of barely simmering water. Heat until just melted, stirring to combine. Alternatively, heat in a microwave on the lowest setting in 30-second blasts, stirring between each until just melted. If you have a cooking thermometer, the chocolate is ready when the thermometer reading is 113–122°F (45–50°C).

4. Using a spatula, spread the chocolate over the bark to create a smooth surface. Scatter over your choice of toppings, then transfer the bark to a fridge or freezer for at least 20 minutes, until firm.

5. Break the bark into pieces to serve. Store it in the fridge or freezer.

Frozen peanut butter & banana-stuffed dates

 **Makes** 12

 **Prep** 5 min
+ freezing

12 Medjool dates

6 tbsp natural peanut butter, ideally crunchy

1 banana, cut into 12 slices

½ oz (15g) 70% dark (semisweet) chocolate, finely chopped

Pinch of sea-salt flakes

These are an absolute treat—like a homemade version of a popular peanut and caramel chocolate bar (you know the one). They are indulgent, but they are also packed with fiber, healthy fats, and plant points—and that makes them nourishing too!

1. Slice each date down one side and remove the stone, making a pocket and keeping the date intact.

2. Spoon ½ tablespoon of peanut butter into each date pocket and sit a piece of banana in the peanut butter.

3. Sprinkle each stuffed date with a little chocolate and salt, then place the dates on a tray in the freezer for at least 1 hour or until frozen solid. They are best eaten straight out of the freezer.

In this chapter, indulgence and nourishment sit side by side—a host of tempting desserts that quietly boost your fiber and improve the plant diversity of your diet too. You'll find warming puddings alongside others that are fresh and fruity. Best of all, they are easy to make. The mango and coconut chia pudding, so naturally creamy and refreshing, takes minutes from fridge to table; a new take on rice pudding—with brown rice, salted pear compôte, and dark chocolate—is far simpler to rustle up than its decadent name suggests; soft and flavorful vegan bread-and-butter pudding takes just 15 minutes to prepare, then the oven does the work. And then there's a sticky toffee pudding, because no dessert chapter, no matter how fiber-fueled, would be complete without it.

Desserts

Chickpea blondies with tahini, dark chocolate & raspberries

 **Makes** 12    **Prep** 5 min    **Cook** 25 min

1 × 14 oz (400g) can chickpeas, drained and thoroughly dried

4½ oz (125g) tahini, peanut, or almond butter, plus 1 tbsp to drizzle

55g (scant ½ cup/2 oz) oat flour

150g (scant ½ cup/5½ oz) maple syrup

¼ tsp baking soda

¼ tsp baking powder

½ tsp sea salt

2 tsp vanilla extract

3½ oz (100g) 70% dark (semisweet) chocolate, cut into small chunks

2½ oz (75g) fresh or frozen raspberries

I may be a nutritionist, but I'm also a firm believer in everything in moderation—and a gooey blondie-style treat can't be compromised. Made with chickpeas, tahini, and dark chocolate, these are high in fiber and protein yet taste every bit as indulgent as you would expect from a blondie. At the photoshoot for the book, everyone in the studio couldn't get enough of them.

1. Preheat the oven to 350°F (180°C) and line an 8 in (20 cm) square brownie pan with parchment paper.

2. Place everything except the tahini for drizzling, the chocolate, and the raspberries in a blender and blend until smooth. Stir through the chocolate, then pour the mixture into the pan and smooth the surface.

3. Evenly dot the raspberries over the top of the mixture, then drizzle with the tablespoon of tahini. Bake for 23–26 minutes until an inserted skewer comes out pretty clean. (A few crumbs are fine, you just don't want it to be sticky.)

4. Leave the blondies to cool completely in the pan, then cut them into 12 equal pieces. Store them in an airtight container in the fridge for up to 5 days.

Mango & coconut chia pudding

 **Serves** 4

 **Prep** 10 min
+ resting

2 ripe mangoes, pitted and peeled

Zest and juice of 1 lime

1 × 14 fl oz (400 ml) can full-fat coconut milk

Seeds from 3 cardamom pods, ground (optional)

2–3 tbsp maple syrup or honey, depending on the ripeness of your mangoes

1½ oz (40g) chia seeds

1½ oz (40g) flaked or dried, shredded coconut, toasted, to serve

I love chia seeds—their texture, consistency and versatility make them one of my favorite ingredients. They're a great source of fiber, protein, and omega-3 fats, all essential for long-term health. This mango and coconut chia pudding is creamy, refreshing, and naturally sweet. At home, my son adores adding pistachios on top for a lovely crunch and extra plant points.

1. Place the flesh of 1 mango in a blender along with the lime zest and juice and blend until smooth.

2. Add the coconut milk, cardamom, and maple syrup or honey, and blend again briefly. Transfer the mixture to a mixing bowl (or keep in the blender pitcher) and add the chia seeds. Stir well, then transfer the mixture to the fridge for 15 minutes for the seeds to hydrate.

3. Stir the hydrated mixture again to make sure the chia seeds are well distributed, then spoon it equally into 4 glasses or small bowls. Refrigerate for 30 minutes for the pudding to firm up.

4. Meanwhile, cut the remaining mango flesh into small chunks. Once the chia pudding is set, spoon over the chunks and top with some toasted coconut. Serve immediately.

Autumnal crumble with apples, pears & blackberries

 **Serves** 4    **Prep** 20 min    **Cook** 45 min

2 firm apples (such as Braeburn or Granny Smith), cored and chopped into ¾ in (2 cm) chunks

1 large not-too-ripe pear, cored and chopped into ¾ in (2 cm) chunks

5½ oz (150g) fresh or frozen blackberries or raspberries

3 tbsp maple syrup or honey

½ tsp ground cinnamon

1 tsp cornstarch

Skyr, or Greek or coconut yogurt, crème fraîche, or oat cream, to serve

For the topping

generous ½ cup/2½ oz (70g) whole-wheat flour or whole-wheat spelt flour

1 oz (30g) rolled oats

1 oz (30g) barley oats, or more rolled oats

1 tsp ground psyllium husk (optional)

2 tbsp (25g) light brown soft sugar

2½ oz (70g) mix of pumpkin, sunflower, and sesame seeds

1½ tsp white miso (optional)

2½ oz (75g) coconut oil or cold butter

Sea salt

Autumnal crumble reminds me so much of childhood. This version is all about maximizing fiber while keeping that homey, nostalgic feel. The miso adds a gorgeous salted-caramel note to the fruit—if you don't have it, nuts or shredded coconut make a lovely alternative. You can also play around with warming spices, like cardamom, nutmeg, and ginger if you like. If you're using frozen berries, allow a little longer (40–50 minutes) for everything to bake beautifully.

1. Preheat the oven to 350°F (180°C).

2. Combine the fruit, maple syrup, cinnamon, cornstarch, and 2 tablespoons of water in a small baking dish (about 8 in/20 cm) square.

3. In a mixing bowl, for the topping, combine the flour, oats, psyllium husk (if using), sugar, and seeds with a pinch of salt. Separately stir the miso into the coconut oil, then add the mixture to the dry ingredients. Rub them together briefly with your fingertips until the mix resembles breadcrumbs.

4. Sprinkle the topping over the fruit and bake for 35–45 minutes (a little longer if you're using frozen berries) until the fruit is bubbling and tender and the topping is dark golden—check halfway through the cooking time and cover with parchment paper or foil if the top is getting dark too quickly or before the fruit is cooked through.

5. Serve with yogurt, crème fraîche, or oat cream.

Vegan bread & butter pudding

 **Serves** 4    **Prep** 15 min    **Cook** 45 min

4 tbsp ground flaxseed

8 oz (225g) stale whole-wheat bread (ideally sourdough), crusts removed, sliced into thick triangles

1½ oz (40g) dairy-free spread, melted if a firm "butter," plus extra to grease

2¼ oz (60g) raisins or golden raisins

2¼ oz (60g) dried pitted apricots, roughly chopped (or use more raisins)

1 lemon

⅓ cup/3½ oz (100g) maple syrup, or ½ cup/3½ oz (100g) light brown soft sugar

1 tsp ground cinnamon

1½ tsp vanilla extract

generous 2½ cups/21 fl oz (600 ml) dairy-free milk (ideally oat milk)

generous 1 cup/9 fl oz (250 ml) whippable oat cream, plus optional extra to serve

¼ tsp grated nutmeg

Dairy-free yogurt, to serve (optional)

This vegan bread-and-butter pudding is a wonderful way to use up bread that's just past its best, and a simple way to boost your fiber intake. The result is rich, comforting, and full of flavor, proving that plant-based versions of traditional desserts can be every bit as delicious.

1. First, make the flax eggs. Pour the flaxseed into a bowl and cover with a generous ½ cup/4 fl oz (125 ml) of water. Leave to soak for at least 10 minutes.

2. Preheat the oven to 350°F (180°C). Lightly grease a 2¾-pint (1.5-liter) ovenproof dish (preferably ceramic or glass). Spread one side of each of the bread slices with the dairy-free spread and arrange the slices around the base of the dish.

3. Place the raisins or golden raisins and the apricots in a small bowl. Zest the lemon into a mixing bowl or pitcher, then squeeze the lemon juice over the dried fruit, and top off with just-boiled water so they're just covered. Set aside for 10 minutes to plump up.

4. Combine the maple syrup or sugar, cinnamon, vanilla, milk, and oat cream with the lemon zest and stir in the fully hydrated flax eggs.

5. Drain the dried fruit and evenly scatter it over the buttered bread. Pour over the milk mixture, then sprinkle over the nutmeg. Place the pudding in the oven for 40–45 minutes until golden on top but with a light wobble in the middle (it will continue to set as it cools). Serve warm with more oat cream or with dairy-free yogurt.

Brown rice pudding, salted pear compôte & dark chocolate

 **Serves** 4    **Prep** 10 min    **Cook** 1 hour

¾ cup/5½ oz (150g) brown risotto or short-grain rice

3¼ cups/26 fl oz (750 ml) whole milk or oat milk, plus extra if needed

3 tbsp maple syrup, or 2½ oz (75g) light brown soft or coconut sugar

1 tsp vanilla extract

Seeds from 5 cardamom pods, ground

1 tbsp ground flaxseed

1½ oz (40g) 70% dark (semisweet) chocolate, chopped, to serve

For the compôte

12 oz (350g) pears, skin on, cored and diced

1½ tbsp mild olive or coconut oil

1½ tbsp maple syrup

¾ tsp sea salt

Pears are such an easy ingredient, and they work especially beautifully with dark chocolate. In this rice pudding, I've used pears to make a salted pear compôte that adds a touch of elegance—as well as extra fiber and plant points—to the whole dish. Soak the rice beforehand to help it cook faster. I've used brown risotto or short-grain rice, but if you have only long-grain rice in the cupboard, that's fine—just soak it for at least 2 hours before you begin.

1. Place the rice in a small pan and cover with plenty of water. Bring to the boil and cook for 10 minutes to soften the outside of the grains. Drain, then return the rice to the pan with the rest of the pudding ingredients, except the flaxseed and chocolate. Bring everything to a simmer and cook for another 1 hour, or until the rice has plumped up and is tender. Stir in the flaxseed, and simmer for another 5 minutes until the pudding is lovely and thick. Add more milk or water if you feel it's looking dry.

2. To make the compôte, combine all the ingredients in a medium pan over medium heat. Bring to the boil, then turn down the heat and simmer for 8–10 minutes until the pear is just tender and you have a delicious syrup. Put to one side for a moment.

3. To serve, spoon the rice pudding into bowls and top with the compôte. Sprinkle with the chopped chocolate to finish.

Baked pears with walnuts & bittersweet chocolate

 **Serves** 4    **Prep** 5 min    **Cook** 50 min

2 large, slightly underripe pears, halved

1¾ oz (50g) walnuts, coarsely chopped

1¾ oz (50g) 70% dark (bittersweet) chocolate, coarsely chopped

2 tbsp tahini

2 tbsp maple syrup or honey

½ tsp sea salt

1 tbsp olive oil or coconut oil

Skyr, or Greek or coconut yogurt, crème fraîche, or oat cream, to serve

This elegant dessert combines the natural sweetness of pears with the rich depth of dark, bitter chocolate. The contrast is divine, and the addition of walnuts brings a chewy crunch, along with omega-3s and extra plant points. It's a simple yet sophisticated dessert that feels really special.

1. Preheat the oven to 350°F (180°C). Place the pear halves, cut-side up, in a baking dish and use a teaspoon to scoop out the cores, making a generous, deep hole in each.

2. Combine the walnuts, chocolate, tahini, half the maple syrup or honey, and the salt in a small bowl. Stuff the mixture into the pear holes, piling it high until it's all used up.

3. Combine the remaining maple syrup or honey and the oil and use a pastry brush to generously brush over the cut side of the pears. Cover the baking dish with foil and bake for 30 minutes, then remove the foil and bake for a further 15–20 minutes until the pears are tender, lightly colored at the edges, and you can easily insert a sharp knife into the flesh.

4. Serve warm with yogurt or oat cream.

Almond & berry cake

 **Serves** 4–6    **Prep** 20 min    **Cook** 40 min

14 oz (400g) frozen berries, such as raspberries, blueberries, strawberries, or blackcurrants

4 pitted dates, finely chopped

3 tbsp maple syrup or honey

2 tsp cornstarch

2 tbsp chia seeds

Juice of ½ lemon (optional)

For the sponge

2½ oz (75g) room temperature unsalted butter or coconut oil

6½ tbsp/2½ oz (75g) light brown soft or coconut sugar

2 eggs

2½ oz (75g) smooth almond or peanut butter

1 tsp vanilla extract

generous ½ cup/2½ oz (75g) whole-wheat flour or whole-wheat spelt flour

1½ tsp baking powder

½ tsp sea salt

1½ oz (45g) sliced almonds, salted peanuts, or seeds, to sprinkle

Skyr, or Greek or coconut yogurt, crème fraîche, or oat cream, to serve

I'm obsessed with the texture of this soft, gorgeous dessert. If you've chosen tart-flavored berries, like blackcurrants, you can skip the lemon, if you prefer; and feel free to use slices of peach, apple, or pear for a little variety. Make it vegan by swapping out the eggs for flax eggs.

1. Preheat the oven to 350°F (180°C) and grease an 8 in (20 cm) square or 7 × 10 in (18 × 25 cm) baking dish.

2. Place the berries, dates, maple syrup or honey, and 2 tablespoons of water in a small pan and simmer for 8–10 minutes, stirring occasionally, until slightly reduced and the berries are beginning to soften. Remove a large tablespoon of the syrup into small bowl, stir in the cornstarch to make a slurry, then return the mixture to the pan. Stir in the chia seeds and the lemon, if using. Pour the mixture into the baking dish and set aside while you prepare the sponge.

3. In a mixing bowl, whisk the butter or oil and sugar and with an electric whisk for 2–3 minutes until pale and fluffy, then, one at a time, beat in the eggs until fully incorporated. Beat in the almond butter and vanilla.

4. In a separate bowl, combine the flour, baking powder, and salt, then fold the dry ingredients through the wet, being careful not to overmix.

5. Spoon the sponge on top of the fruit, spreading it out with a spatula until smooth. Sprinkle with the almonds, gently pushing them into the batter so they stick.

6. Bake the pudding for 25–30 minutes until the sponge and almonds are golden—check halfway through and cover with parchment paper or foil if the almonds are burning, then test with a skewer before removing from the oven (it should come out clean) and give the pudding a little longer if necessary. Cool for 5 minutes and serve warm with yogurt, crème fraîche, or oat cream.

Sticky date pudding with figs

 **Serves** 6    **Prep** 10 min    **Cook** 35 min

5½ oz (150g) pitted dates, quartered

3½ oz (100g) dried figs, quartered

1 large orange

3½ tbsp canola, mild olive, or coconut oil or melted butter

4 tbsp (80g) maple syrup or honey

2 flax eggs (2 tbsp ground flax mixed with 6 tbsp water, and soaked for 10 minutes) or 2 eggs

¾ cup/3½ oz (100g) whole-wheat flour or whole-wheat spelt flour

1½ tsp baking powder

1 tsp baking soda

1¾ oz (50g) ground almonds

1 tsp ground cinnamon

½ tsp ground ginger

¼ tsp ground nutmeg

1¾ oz (50g) oat bran or oats, blended to a flour

¼ tsp sea salt

Skyr, or Greek or coconut yogurt, crème fraîche, or oat cream, to serve

For the sauce

1¼ tbsp cornstarch

scant 1 cup/7 fl oz (200 ml) oat, almond, or whole milk

½ cup + 2 tbsp/5 fl oz (150 ml) maple or date syrup

1 tsp vanilla extract

¼ tsp sea salt

1 tbsp melted coconut oil or butter

I've avoided putting a sticky toffee pudding in my books for years, but it's my husband's absolute favorite, and I couldn't resist creating a version that's a little more nourishing while keeping every bit of that nostalgic charm. The figs add a lovely jammy texture and pair beautifully with the dark, toffee-like sauce. This dessert is simple to make, endlessly adaptable, and a wonderful reminder that even the most indulgent traditional desserts can be given a wholesome twist.

1. Place the dates and figs in a bowl. Zest in the orange and squeeze in the orange juice, then pour over scant 1 cup/7 fl oz (200 ml) of boiling water. Leave for 10 minutes to soften.

2. Preheat the oven to 350°F (180°C) and grease an 8 in (20 cm) square baking dish or pan with a little extra oil or butter.

3. Using a hand-hand blender, blend the soaked fruit and its soaking liquid to a smooth purée. In a bowl, whisk the oil and maple syrup or honey into the eggs, then stir this mixture into the fruit purée.

4. In a mixing bowl, combine all the dry ingredients, then stir in the wet mixture. Pour the lot into the prepared baking dish or pan and bake for 30–35 minutes until golden on top.

5. While the pudding is in the oven, make the sauce. Stir the cornstarch into 3 tablespoons of the milk to make a slurry, then combine everything except the coconut oil in a saucepan over medium-low heat. Stir constantly and bring to a rolling boil—you should see the sauce thicken slightly. Turn the heat down a little, add the coconut oil and keep gently simmering until the pudding is ready.

6. Use a skewer to make a few holes in the pudding. Pour the sauce over the top and leave it for a few minutes to sink in.

7. Scoop the pudding into bowls and serve with yogurt, crème fraîche, or oat cream.

Baked banana split with berries & toasted seeds

Nutritional info per serving

Fiber 9.2g
Protein 10g
Plant Points 10.25

 **Serves** 4    **Prep** 5 min    **Cook** 25 min

For the bananas

4 ripe bananas

½ tsp ground cinnamon

1 tbsp maple syrup or honey

5½ oz (150g) raspberries, blackberries, and/or blueberries

For the toasted seeds

2 tbsp pumpkin seeds

2 tbsp sunflower seeds

2 tbsp sesame seeds

1 tbsp poppy seeds

2 tbsp dried, shredded coconut

1 tbsp psyllium husks (optional)

1 tbsp maple syrup

1 tbsp coconut oil or butter

generous ½ cup/5½–7 oz (150–200g) skyr, or Greek or coconut yogurt, to serve

Sea salt

This is a playful, fiber-rich update on a nostalgic classic. If you don't have any fresh berries to hand, the bananas are delicious topped with a quick berry chia jam instead; or use frozen, quickly defrosted in the microwave.

1. Preheat the oven to 400°F (200°C) and line a baking sheet with parchment paper.

2. Lay out a large piece of foil, then place a large piece of parchment paper on top. Hinge open the bananas by splitting them lengthwise in half (in the skins). Sit them in the middle of the parchment paper, sprinkle with cinnamon and maple syrup, then seal the parcels tightly by folding over the edge of the paper, then crimping the edge of the foil to trap in the steam. Place on a tray and put into the oven to bake for 25 minutes.

3. Meanwhile, in a small bowl, combine all the ingredients for the toasted seeds, add a pinch of salt and pour out the mixture onto the lined baking sheet. Spread out the seeds in an even layer, then bake for 10 minutes, stirring once, until golden brown. Remove from the oven and leave to cool.

4. Remove the bananas from their packages and transfer them to serving plates. Spoon some yogurt along the middle, top with a big spoonful of berries, and sprinkle generously with the toasted seeds. Eat immediately, drizzled with the syrup from the baked bananas, if you like.

Index

kefir 28, 29
ketogenic diets 72
kimchi 28, 29
    kimchi fried spelt with sesame fried
        eggs 145
kiwi fruit 26
kombucha 28, 29

L
labels 23, 70–71
legumes 60, 62, 63, 80–81
lentils 33, 47
    Persian herb & grain stewed lentils 151
    pork, lentil & ricotta meatballs in
        tomato sauce 162
    super high-fiber seeded nut & raisin
        loaf 108
    Turkish lentil & carrot soup 118
lettuce: beet Waldorf grain salad 117
    green goddess avocado sandwich 133
lima beans 33
    caldo verde soup with smoky lima
        beans 121
    green lima bean mac & fiber cheese
        137
    green whipped tofu & lima-bean dip
        186
long-chain fatty acids (LCFAs) 11

M
mango: blueberry & mango frozen
        smoothie bowl 93
    mango & coconut chia pudding 202
    vegetable summer rolls 113
marketing 72
Marmite popcorn 181
matcha tea 68
meat 64, 66
meatballs: chicken & quinoa meatballs
        with white bean broth 177
    pork, lentil & ricotta meatballs in
        tomato sauce 162
Mediterranean diet 46
medium-chain fatty acids (MCFAs) 11
men, fiber intake 21
menopause 32, 46–47
mental health 10, 13, 24, 37
microplastics 52
Milanese, whole-wheat baked eggplant
        173
milks, plant-based 68
    vegan bread & butter pudding 206
mindful eating 57
mint: mint yogurt 141
    potato farls with smashed avocado,
        feta & mint 104
    Turkish lentil & carrot soup 118
miso: bean, miso & tahini dip 186
muffins 78
    prune & walnut banana muffins 94

muhammara 186
muscles 30, 31, 32, 40, 44, 46
mushrooms: adaptogenic 75
    mushroom & bean stroganoff 174
    pearl spelt & mushroom "risotto" 169
myths 74–75

N
nutritional yeast: spicy cheese popcorn 181
nuts 43, 47
    30:30:30 fiber formula 59, 61, 62, 63,
        73, 80–81
    nutty barley, cinnamon & dried fig
        granola 88
    prune & date crumble bars 190
    quinoa & dark chocolate bark 194
    super high-fiber seeded nut & raisin
        loaf 108

O
oat milk 68
oatmeal 75
    barley oatmeal with blackberry, apple
        & bay leaf compôte 97
oats 13, 33, 39, 43, 47
    barley oatmeal with blackberry, apple
        & bay leaf compôte 97
    grape & fennel seed baked oats 90
    IBS-friendly diets 34, 35
    nutty barley, cinnamon & dried fig
        granola 88
    oat beta-glucan 59, 65
    prune & date crumble bars 190
    super high-fiber seeded nut & raisin
        loaf 108
olives: creamy artichoke, green olive &
        parsley pasta 142
onions: caramelized onions 151
    chickpea pancakes with onion,
        tomatoes, cilantro & coconut
        sambol 103
    roast cauliflower & chickpeas with
        green tahini & pink onions 114

P
pancakes 78
    carrot pancakes 99
    chickpea pancakes 103
pancreas 42, 50
pasta 12, 13, 66
    creamy artichoke, green olive &
        parsley pasta 142
    gigli with red pesto & tofu sauce 147
    green lima bean mac & fiber cheese
        137
    pasta e fagioli with squash 160
    whole-wheat baked eggplant
        Milanese 173
peanut butter: blueberry & mango frozen
        smoothie bowl 93

frozen peanut butter & banana-stuffed
        dates 197
    prune & walnut banana muffins 94
peanuts 30
    roast split peas with peanuts, coconut
        & crispy kale chaat 189
pears 43
    autumnal crumble 205
    baked pears with walnuts &
        bittersweet chocolate 211
    salted pear compôte 209
pectin 28, 43, 53, 65
peppers: chickpea ratatouille 166
    muhammara 186
Persian herb & grain stewed lentils 151
Persian-style chicken 159
pesto: gigli with red pesto & tofu sauce 147
    arugula & sunflower seed pesto 148
phytates 73, 77
phytochemicals 12, 13
phytoestrogens 46, 47
pickled onion 114
pie, creamy white bean fish 157
plant-based milks 68
plant foods: eating 30 per week 56, 62–65
    energy-dense 40
    how plant-based nutrition boosts fiber
        11–12
    plant points 62, 75
    weekly plant tracker 80–81
plastics, dietary 52–53
polyphenols 12, 24, 48
pomegranate, Persian-style chicken
        with walnut & 159
popcorn (3 ways) 181
pork, lentil & ricotta meatballs in tomato
        sauce 162
portion sizes 21
posture 59
potatoes 12, 13, 67
    caldo verde soup 121
    creamy white bean fish pie 157
    potato farls with smashed avocado,
        feta & mint 104
    stuffed potato skins with cashew
        sauce 154
prebiotics 12, 13, 24, 28–29, 37, 47, 77
    and diabetes 51
    psyllium husk 26
    side effects of 73
probiotics 28–29
processed food 15, 16, 17, 22, 23, 41
protein 30–33, 40, 41
prunes: prune & date crumble bars 190
    prune & walnut banana muffins 94
psyllium husk 26, 27, 34, 35, 38, 65

Resources and bibliography

Books

The Science of Nutrition by Rhiannon Lambert

The Science of Plant-Based Nutrition by Rhiannon Lambert

The Unprocessed Plate by Rhiannon Lambert

Podcasts

The Wellness Scoop with Ella Mills and Rhiannon Lambert

Food for Thought with Rhiannon Lambert

ZOE Science and Nutrition with Jonathan Wolf

Reports

Romanello, Marina et al. (2025). Countdown on health and climate change: climate change action offers a lifeline. *The Lancet*

The Food Foundation (2025). The Broken Plate 2025

Find all scientific references for the information provided in this book here:

www.dk.com/en-us/blogs/ resources/the-fibre-formula- bibliography

The publisher would like to thank the following for their kind permission to reproduce their data:

(a) above; (b) below/bottom; (c) center; (l) left; (r) right; (t) top

27 (r) Copyright Clearance Center – Rightslink: Illustration based on Fig. 1 Bristol Stool Scale from the *Scandinavian Journal of Gastroenterology*, "Stool Form Scale as a Useful Guide to Intestinal Transit Time" (1966; Lewis, S. J., Heaton, K. W.) reprinted by permission of Informa UK Limited, trading as Taylor & Francis Group, www.tandfonline.com, https://www. tandfonline.com/loi/igas20. **37 (br) Elsevier:** © 2022 The Authors. Published by Elsevier Inc. / Graph based on Konstantinos Prokopidis, Panagiotis Giannos, Theocharis Ispoglou, Oliver C. Witard, Masoud Isanejad, "Dietary Fiber Intake is Associated with Cognitive Function in Older Adults: Data from the National Health and Nutrition Examination Survey", *The American Journal of Medicine*, Volume 135, Issue 8 (pp.e257-e262), 2022, ISSN 0002-9343; https://doi. org/10.1016/j.amjmed.2022.03.022.; (https://www. sciencedirect.com/science/article/pii/ S00029343220025583) CC BY 4.0-https://creativecommons. org/licenses/by/4.0/. **38 (b)** © 2025 Pressbooks: Allison Calabrese / CC BY 4.0 / Illustration based on image by Allison Calabrese / CC BY 4.0- https://creativecommons.org/ licenses/by/4.0/ from "Digestion and Absorption of Lipids", Copyright © by Langara College-https://pressbooks. bccampus.ca/nutr1100/chapter/digestion-and-absorption-of- lipids/

About the Author

Rhiannon Lambert is celebrated as one of the UK's leading practitioners in the complex field of nutritional science. In 2016, she founded **Rhitrition**, her private clinic on London's Harley Street. Rooted in scientific evidence, the clinic stands in sharp contrast to the sea of pseudoscience often promoted by fad diets. She has worked with both individuals and globally recognized brands—including Deliveroo, Wagamama, Samsung, Alpro, Yeo Valley, and Tesco—helping them transform how they think about and approach nutrition.

Registered with the Association for Nutrition, Rhiannon obtained a first-class degree in Nutrition and Health and a Master's degree in Obesity, Risks, and Prevention. She holds additional diplomas in sports nutrition and pre- and post-natal nutrition. She is a Master Practitioner in Eating Disorders, accredited by The British Psychological Society, and a Level 3 Personal Trainer. A prolific author, Rhiannon has penned five books, two of which—*The Science of Plant-Based Nutrition* (2024) and *The Science of Nutrition* (2021)—achieved Sunday Times Bestseller status.

In 2018, Rhiannon launched her highly acclaimed podcast, *Food for Thought*, which has had over 10 million downloads since its inception. Since 2025 Rhiannon has also co-hosted the podcast *The Wellness Scoop* with Deliciously Ella founder Ella Mills. Expanding her mission, Rhiannon relaunched **Rhitrition+** in 2023, a web-based supplement brand designed to cut through the misinformation in the supplement industry.

Rhiannon also cherishes her life as a wife and as a mother to two young boys, Zachary and Theodore—and her cat Aurora. She remains dedicated to creating a brighter, healthier future for both people and the planet.

Acknowledgments

Without the exceptional team at DK, this book wouldn't be possible. Izzy, Cara, Judy, Georgia, Rosie, Clare, Tania, Holly, Lu, Eden, Charlie, Issy P., Silvia, and everyone working behind the scenes, thank you for your unwavering support in bringing this mission to life. We managed to create a helpful and inspiring resource for everyone and should be very proud. Your dedication to your work is truly inspiring. I am deeply grateful.

Thank you to Pam Lyddon for her incredible enthusiasm and unwavering support; to the brilliant Victoria Simmonds, the most amazing stylist, for guiding us through the shoot days for this book; and to my wonderful MUA, Melissa Oldridge, for somehow making me look awake even on no sleep. And a special thank you to Claire P. and Claire L. for the glow up—you helped me feel my best and navigate the huge feat of book-writing throughout highs and lows of life.

My deepest thanks go to my brilliant team: Aoibhinn Connolly and Kitty Costelloe; and, above all, Abi Robertson, who has supported me at all hours to help bring this book to life. I simply could not have completed it without her tireless hard work, dedication and calm presence, no matter what time of day. My team is the backbone of everything Rhitrition stands for—transparency, trust, and a genuine mission to help others—and they consistently go above and beyond to make that mission a reality.

As a mother and a working professional, I can't ignore the state of nutrition, in this country or across the world, nor the direction in which things are heading. My hope is that this book, in its own small way, can be a force for change: for better health, for greater understanding, and for good that lasts. My family are my constant inspiration and the reason I keep going every single day. To Billy, to my boys Zachary and Theodore, and even to our cat, Aurora, you are all my why. And to my dad, thank you for stepping in with childcare at the drop of a hat so that I can chase these dreams and do my best to make a difference.

Publisher's acknowledgments

DK would like to thank Georgia Levy for the recipe development,
Katie Hardwicke for proofreading, and Vanessa Bird for indexing.
DK would also like to thank Judy Barratt and the team at Studio
Noel for all their work on this project.

Editorial Director Cara Armstrong
Project Editor Izzy Holton
US Editors Lori Cates Hand, Kayla Dugger
Senior Designer Tania Gomes
Editorial Assistant Abi Reeves
Sales and Jackets Coordinator Serena Sclocco
Senior Production Editor Becky Fallowfield
Senior Production Controller Stephanie McConnell
Art Director Maxine Pedliham
Publisher Stephanie Jackson

Editori Judy Barratt
Designer Studio Noel
Photographer Clare Winfield
Recipe Developer Georgia Levy
Food Stylist Holly Cowgill
Prop Stylist Charlie Phillips
Food Stylist Assistants Lu Cottle, Eden Owen-Jones & Katie Smith

First American Edition, 2026
Published in the United States by DK Publishing,
a division of Penguin Random House LLC
1745 Broadway, 20th Floor, New York, NY 10019

Text copyright © Rhitrition Limited 2026
Rhiannon Lambert has asserted her right to be identified
as the author of this work.

Disclaimer

Neither the publisher nor the author is engaged in rendering
professional advice or services to the individual reader. The
ideas, procedures, and suggestions contained in this book are
not intended as a substitute for consulting with your doctor or a
professional. All matters regarding your health require supervision.
Neither the author nor the publisher shall be liable or responsible
for any loss or damage allegedly arising from any information or
suggestion in this book.

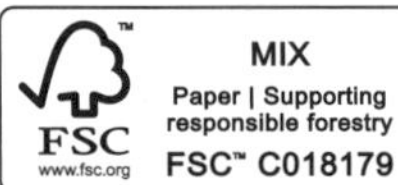

This book was made with Forest
Stewardship Council™ certified
paper – one small step in DK's
commitment to a sustainable future.
**Learn more at www.dk.com/uk/
information/sustainability**